The Politics of Youth
in Greek Tragedy

Also published by Bloomsbury

Becoming Female: The Male Body in Greek Tragedy, Katrina Cawthorn
Greek Tragedy: Themes and Contexts, Laura Swift
The Lost Plays of Greek Tragedy (Volume 1), Matthew Wright
Surviving Greek Tragedy, Robert Garland

The Politics of Youth in Greek Tragedy

Gangs of Athens

Matthew Shipton

BLOOMSBURY ACADEMIC
LONDON • NEW YORK • OXFORD • NEW DELHI • SYDNEY

BLOOMSBURY ACADEMIC
Bloomsbury Publishing Plc
50 Bedford Square, London, WC1B 3DP, UK
1385 Broadway, New York, NY 10018, USA

BLOOMSBURY, BLOOMSBURY ACADEMIC and the Diana logo
are trademarks of Bloomsbury Publishing Plc

First published 2018
Paperback edition first published 2019

Cover design: Terry Woodley
Cover image © CribbVisuals (shadow) and De Agostini / Archivio J. Lange, Getty

A catalogue record for this book is available from the British Library.

Library of Congress Cataloging-in-Publication Data
Names: Shipton, Matthew, author.
Title: The politics of youth in Greek tragedy : gangs of Athens / Matthew Shipton.
Description: London : Bloomsbury Academic, 2018. |
Includes bibliographical references and index.
Identifiers: LCCN 2017041473| ISBN 9781474295079 (hb) |
ISBN 9781474295093 (epdf)
Subjects: LCSH: Greek drama (Tragedy)–History and criticism. |
Youth in literature. | Politics in literature. | Euripides–Criticism and interpretation. |
Sophocles–Criticism and interpretation. | Aeschylus–Criticism and interpretation.
Classification: LCC PA3136 .S55 2018 | DDC 882/.0109–dc23
LC record available at https://lccn.loc.gov/2017041473.

ISBN: HB: 978-1-4742-9507-9
PB: 978-1-3501-2496-7
ePDF: 978-1-4742-9509-3
ePub: 978-1-4742-9508-6

Typeset by RefineCatch Limited, Bungay, Suffolk

To find out more about our authors and books visit
www.bloomsbury.com and sign up for our newsletters.

Contents

Acknowledgements

This book is about the relationships between generations, how these are expressed in literature and what that might reveal about society. But the process of writing can also be considered a partial narration of one's own generational background. The choice of subject matter, theoretical and methodological approach, writing style and argument are all intimately responsive to one's individual, social and familial circumstances. As I hope to show, these choices and their contexts are not fixed but can change over time. It is yet unknown how a future self might look back at a book that emerged from doctoral study and from a period in which I began a family of my own. What will remain steadfast is a feeling of gratitude for all those who have helped bring this work to publication. With the usual acknowledgement of personal liability for any inaccuracies I must express particular thanks to the following people for various forms of help: Richard Alston, Sarah Butler, Donald Campbell, Timo Hebditch, Justine McConnell, Sheila Munton, James Robson, Henry Stead, Phiroze Vasunia, Alice Wright, staff at the Archive of Performances of Greek and Roman Drama at the University of Oxford and an unnamed editor at *The London Review of Books*. I give separate, specific and boundless thanks to Edith Hall, who supervised my PhD thesis and to whom I owe my full education. The number of my own genealogy to whom I am most grateful for their unfailing practical and emotional support are my mother, Geraldine Shipton and my wife, Lenka Shipton. But quite rightly this book is dedicated to the next generation, in the form of my children: Hugo and Lyra.

Matthew Shipton

Introduction

The most cursory survey of the plays of Aeschylus, Sophocles and Euripides offers the reader a dizzying variety of themes and plotlines relating to youth: the townsfolk condemning a young brother and sister to death, the murder of a mother by her son (and vice versa), a grandfather abused by his crazed grandson or a young woman either actually subjected to, or only just saved from, calculated execution by her father. So dominantly has conflict between generations featured in Greek tragedy that hardly a play exists that does not include the strained relationships between young and old. From the Persian Queen's condemnation of Xerxes' immaturity in Aeschylus' *Persae* of 472 through to Oedipus' final denunciation of his son, Polynices, in *Oedipus at Colonus* of 401, the relative positioning – the polarization – of young and old as opposites extended throughout the golden age of Greek tragic theatre. This opposition breaks out into unequivocal violence in plays such as *Prometheus* or *Bacchae,* and even in those dramas, such as *Helen,* that are generally regarded as less negatively charged, the opposition between generations appears as an important theme. And yet, this opposition is not always straightforward. Characters such as Antigone, Haemon and Neoptolemus all face manipulation or downright hostility from older men and their responses can be considered in a positive light, regardless of what other flaws may have been authored into their dramatic presentation.

So what underlying influences in this 'golden age' of tragedy helped shape such a startling diversity of characterizations? This book argues that the influences were in part political and sets out to examine the extent and the precise nature by which youth and intergenerational relationships in Greek tragedy were shaped by social constructions of these concepts. In some ways, this is not virgin territory. Indeed, almost all major work on Greek tragedy, or on any particular play, will include at least passing reference to the tragedians' use of the theme of intergenerational conflict. Clusters of research have developed from the study of generational relations – from the structuralist to the psychoanalytic – of the *Oresteia* and *Oedipus Tyrannus* in particular.[1] And the tragedies of the fifth century have been used to support socio-historical theories on the realities of generational relations of the period, sometimes without due respect for the way that 'reality' is aesthetically mediated by the playwright's craft.[2] As we shall see, the unusual circumstance has evolved where 'intergenerational conflict' is often used to explain character interactions in Greek tragedy without the basis for the term's application having been subject to extensive investigation exclusively within the genre of tragedy.[3] Just as worryingly, phrases such as 'generation gap'[4] have often been wrenched from their twentieth-century semantic moorings and applied to a wide range of historical and literary settings without the benefit of a full interrogation of the associations implicit in such terms. As a consequence, conflict as a broad category has been taken for granted as something of a normative state between generations. The evidence used in such scholarly contexts has tended to focus on literary presentations of troublesome young people written by adults and viewed from the perspective of an adult audience. This position has led to an unreflective use of the label 'intergenerational conflict' and synonymous terms in ways that mask the factors that underpin literary presentations of conflict between generations. Scholars make the assumption that a state of opposition exists without questioning why it is that themes to do with youth and conflict are so widely deployed in tragedy. To be clear, I do not suggest the theme of intergenerational conflict should be examined in isolation from the historical reality of the fifth century BCE: far from it. Important non-tragic evidence exists for relationships between age groups in the society and historical period that produced the tragedies, and, as a counterpoint where relevant, analysis of the literature of the preceding, 'archaic' period is highly instructive. This does not mean that detailed, one-to-one pieces of evidence for specific historical events will be sought from the tragedies of the period. Rather, occurrences of themes relating to youth and conflict in the plays will be considered as part of the contemporary Athenian imaginative tradition, a general process that encompassed a whole range of political discussion in the broadest sense including but not confined to the question: How should society operate in the polis?[5] This question obviously had some basis in the lived experience of the citizen audience, and they will have related it to issues in their empirically discernible reality of life in Greece's pre-eminent polis. Thus this investigation focuses on sources from, and society in, Athens, and does so unapologetically.

Such a specific geo-cultural focus is justified because the high point of ancient Greek culture, the fifth century BCE, offered an astonishingly direct cultural transmission of the tensions within society, via the dramatic medium of tragedy, to a large-scale audience. For its time, this process was comparable to modern popular media in supporting a dynamic link between society and culture, and so offered evidence for the popular social constructions of the period. Quite simply, until the emergence of early modern theatre in sixteenth-century England, no art-form ever again emerged in such perfect synergy with its method of production and transmission that would allow social and political consciousness to be created, framed and communicated via drama to a large part of the community (in Western European culture at least).[6] Just as importantly, the direct democracy of the period I have chosen to explore, and the various revolutions and counter-revolutions of the last decade of the fifth century, would have meant that the audience of productions of Greek tragedy, accustomed to witnessing overtly political performances in a public arena, would have their own lives discernibly impacted by the real-world equivalent of the issues explored in theatre. What this would have meant is that the ancient audience would have been well equipped to compare political content in Greek tragedy with their contemporary context, all the while being aware of the consequences of political decision-making.

'Youth' as a category of historical study, and as a thematic focus in various classical works, is fairly well embedded as part of the history of classical scholarship. Where such works fail to deepen our understanding, and where this book intends to focus, is in exploring the sheer diversity of representations of 'youth' in tragedy, over time and alongside known political factors. The widest range of political and social settings is available for discussion, as provided by the diversity of actions and scenarios dramatized in the fifth-century Attic tragic plays, as well as an incredibly varied political backdrop. This allows the assessment of a variety of presentations (through drama or other literature) of young people whilst acknowledging the changing nature of tragedy within its historical-cultural context, thus unlocking concomitant reflections on the relationships between generic, political and social constructions of youth identity. My hope is to initiate a shift in perspective within classical scholarship that will transform the study of the category of 'youth'. Ideally, youth studies can be established as an independent sub-category in its own right in the Classics in the same way as the study of women in ancient society in general, and tragedy in particular, has become intensely more sophisticated through the absorption of elements of gender studies by classical scholars (or ethnic 'otherness', as a result of the now largely mainstream acceptance of anthropological theories in the discipline).[7] I hope to show that the plays of Aeschylus, Sophocles and Euripides incorporate in some way the dominant attitudes of the society that shared the playwrights' historical context. In short, that there was a relationship between culture and cultural artefact. This approach, too, has been used before but I intend to add the category of 'age' to David Konstan's argument that, 'where society is riven by tensions and inequalities of class, gender and status, its ideology will be complex and unstable, and literary texts will betray signs of the strain involved in forging such refractory materials into a unified composition.'[8]

At this very early point, the thorny issue of definition of terms must be addressed, particularly in relation to the English word 'youth'. This word seems to be politically charged in contemporary society with solely negative associations (the terms 'teenagers', 'young people' or 'adolescents' don't seem to share this burden), but these modern negative associations are useful when using the term to refer to themes within tragedy, because these plays almost always have an antagonistic dimension. Just as importantly, the term encompasses the full spectrum of both those who may be almost part of adult society, but are not yet enfranchised, as well as those who are younger but intellectually mature enough to have begun to embrace a recognizable group identity, one which is separate from those associated with adults or children. This corresponds well with the use of the term in sociological contexts for a group that can include a range from very young teenagers to those who are in their twenties, but have not reached a point of separation from the group identity of their (younger) peers. More technically, the term 'youth' in sociology is also one that is considered to encompass a society's web of references of attitudes towards a group in transition – that is, as occupying some sort of liminal conceptual space rather than as a group defined in biological or developmental terms.[9] Granville Stanley Hall, a pioneering early twentieth-century psychologist, linked the ancient and modern conceptions of this transitional phase: 'It is an age of natural inebriation without the need of intoxicants, which made Plato define youth as spiritual drunkenness . . . We see here the instability and fluctuations now so characteristic.'[10] And, as has been noted by at least one scholar, 'the notion was very strong that young men, although they have reached full physical manhood, were still not quite up to the standards of adults'.[11]

In classical Greek, too, there are a large number of terms – such as *hēbē, pais, teknon*, or *neos* – that can be used to refer to different (young) age groups, and this has caused difficulties in finding correspondence between specific words, both in Greek and between Greek and English.[12] But, I suggest, the technical categorization by biological or developmental phases is not necessarily useful. The identification of 'youth' as a social category defined by transition is a concept not easily definable in a single term other than 'youth' in English and a whole raft of other words in Greek.[13] The psychologist Steven Pinker refers to Steiner's (1984) analysis of *Antigone* as a play that retains a contemporary relevance through the encoding of the constant of conflict and confrontation between, amongst others, youth and age.[14] With this view in mind, that youth is a social category, figures such as Orestes (in his name play), Pentheus (in *Bacchae*) or Zeus (in *Prometheus*) will be discussed within the context of the social construction of their literary characters and thematic settings without a primary emphasis on the specific Greek words used within these plays. That is not to say that philological concerns will be completely abandoned, but rather that no direct attempts will be made to link *neos*, for example, with a specific English word that covers its usage and meaning in all instances, since such a task would be unlikely to throw adequate light on the presentation of youth in the plays. Indeed, subsequent discussion of the use of *hēbē* and its cognates in Euripides' *Heraclidae* demonstrates the great extent to which not just the semantic but also the ritual context influences meaning. And for simplicity, I use 'youth' in a highly flexible way, largely when referring to groups of young people but also the characteristics attributed to this group.

There are other lexical complications too. I have already referred to (inter-) generations, opposition and conflict (sometimes in combined form) and these also require explanation. 'Intergenerational conflict' is a term used extensively by scholars in the secondary Classics bibliography to signal a broad explanatory framework for antagonistic interactions between younger and older members of society (or more precisely in the context of classical Greece, younger and older citizens), and this meaning will be retained.[15] 'Generational opposition' is a somewhat softer term that I shall use as shorthand for what will be shown to be a 'value gap' between the attitudes, identity and codes of youth and those of the generation before them, and incorporates a sense that the nature of the relationship between generations is defined both by the youth group and society outside this group. This is nowhere clearer than in Euripides' *Orestes*, when the titular character gives clear primacy to *hetairous* (friends of the same age) over kin. Similarly, the term 'generation' has so far been deployed without comment and some qualification is also necessary here.

The Hungarian sociologist Karl Mannheim's essay on *The Problem of Generations*, first published in 1923, is still considered by some as a seminal sociological treatment of generations.[16] The 'problem' in question was the failure of various intellectual traditions within the social sciences, namely Positivist and Romantic-historical, to adequately explain how states of generational actuality emerge. In response, Mannheim proposed a radical new view, defining generational groups not just by their age, but by 'geographical and cultural location; by their actual as opposed to potential participation in the social and intellectual currents of their time and place; and by their differing responses to a particular situation'.[17] This stratification of a biological generation results in the formation of generational units defined by class and the group's 'participation in the same social and historical circumstances'.[18] Thus, in Mannheim's view, political, social and cultural factors are primary in defining a group's identity, rather than mere biological category. It must be kept clearly in mind that the young men in tragedy are always from the same elite social group. In the Mannheimian lexicon, they form a part of a common generational unit with a shared experience of their generational actuality and this demarcation demonstrates a clear and highly regrettable limit to what can safely be said about *all* young people. The question could be asked: why discuss only conflict and not cooperation, too, between generations? Simply, as we shall see, conflict or opposition is the point around which group identity began to coalesce during the height of tragedy's first productions.

The case for the existence of the concept of 'intergenerational conflict' in the ancient world has already been made: such as in Barry Strauss' brilliant *Fathers and Sons in Athens* (1993); Vidal-Naquet's *The Black Hunter* (1986a),[19] containing detailed speculation on the role and provenance of the *ephēbia*; and Froma Zeitlin's journal article entitled 'The Dynamics of Misogyny: Myth and Mythmaking in the "Oresteia"' (1978), in which she reveals the demonstrably structuralizing tendency of Greek tragedy in relation to enforcing gender roles in the context of intergenerational conflict. And as early as 1968, W.G. Forrest introduced the term 'generation gap' into the discussion of youth in classical Athens.[20] This lively intervention took the Oligarchic revolution of 411 as a point from which broad conclusions were drawn about the motivations of the coup's main protagonists, mainly that the young group of upper-class citizens saw this as an opportunity for adventure and a way of asserting their youthful aristocratic ideals in opposition to an older, more democratic and *arriviste* section of society. This suggestion by Forrest is problematic not least due to the modern-day associations of the 'generation gap' with a very specific temporal context. The 'baby boomer' generation, roughly those born in the two decades after the end of the Second World War, appear to be those who first self-consciously considered themselves as discretely different from previous generations, creating their own cohort identity.[21] In this way, the term does represent the opening up of difference, but, in popular use, masks the various drivers that caused social change in the mid-twentieth century. Most critically, talk of 'generations' suggests a homogeneity that might not be present and downplays the likely differences in identification by class, culture or social grouping, rather than generation. I would agree that at times the differences between generations gain greater clarity, often when allied to political, demographical or more latterly technological advances, but the term appears to me to be too bound to the twentieth century to be used without extreme caution.

Mannheim's view of generational units ties different generational units to different sets of socio-historical experiences, which are articulated by temporal-specific language, and the lexicon of the 1960s appears a good example of this intimate link between language and generation. Around the same time as Forrest's use of the term 'generation gap', other classicists were beginning to include contemporary lexica in their work. Stephen Bertman's *The Conflict of Generations in Ancient Greece and Rome*, published in 1976, contained four chapters with the phrase 'generation gap' in their titles, none of which properly questioned how the term's twentieth-century construction would shape the discussion.[22] There followed something of a hiatus in interest in the subject before a resurgence of work on youth emerged in the 1990s.[23] Within a few short years, classical scholarship benefited from a number of major works on youth, most notably Golden's (1990) *Children and Childhood in Classical Athens*, Garland's (1990) *The Greek Way of Life: From Conception to Old Age*, Kleijwegt's (1991) *Ancient Youth*, as well as Strauss' (1993) *Fathers and Sons in Athens*, and Euben's (1997) *Corrupting the Youth*.[24] And in 1996 Alan Sommerstein presented a paper that was subsequently published under the title: 'Problem Kids: Young Males and Society from *Electra* to *Bacchae*'.[25] A decade later, Davidson's important chapter on age-class in Goldhill and Osborne's (2006a) *Rethinking Revolutions through Ancient Greece*, included very important identification of age groups, albeit largely using evidence from the fourth century or later. More recently, the field has been improved further by sociologically minded works on childhood in the classical world, which do include some discussion on generational relations as well as life stages and processes, such as Beaumont's (2012) *Childhood in Ancient Athens* and the volume edited by Evans Grubb and Parkin (2014) *The Oxford Handbook of Childhood and Education in the Classical World*.

But to my mind, the opportunity to examine closely how tragedy reflects and confuses the material realities of youth in Greek society has yet to be exploited fully. While commenting on Menander and Comedy, Lape's view of drama's 'tendency both to reproduce and to rebel against existing Athenian political and cultural arrangements' could equally be applied to tragedy, especially if seen through the lens of residual, dominant and emergent cultural drivers, such as those formulated by Raymond Williams.[26] At the heart of the matter is the fact that political changes in the late sixth century, introduced by Cleisthenes, had weakened vertical relationships in the family and strengthened horizontal ones between age groups, increasing greatly the sense of opposition between generational units, rather than between individual family members. The result of this change culminated in the factionalization of Athenian politics by 413, in the period after Nicias and Alcibiades had presented political arguments explicitly framed by age.

This is a critical point in the history of age-related politics at Athens. In the *Ekklesia*, older citizens had once been given priority to speak (Aeschines,

Against Timarchus, 23; *Against Ctesiphon*, 2–4). The minimum age for most offices, outside membership of the *Ekklesia*, appears to have been thirty.[27] For the *Areopagus*, the minimum was thirty-one, '... and with a median age of about fifty-five; and the arbitrators for private suits were chosen from citizens in their last year of liability for conscription, when they were fifty-nine'.[28] This apparent gerontocratic tendency is comparable to that reflected in the average age of current British legislative and judiciary members: the average age of Members of Parliament is fifty, of Members of the House of Lords is sixty-nine, and of magistrates it is fifty-seven.[29] Even if the *Ekklesia* admitted citizens from the age of eighteen, it would seem likely that then, as now, active politicians (roughly corresponding to the small group who would frequently put forward proposals or make speeches) would be significantly older, whether by protocol or as a consequence of the experience older citizens could gain by membership of other offices. The problem remains that the nature of relationships between generations, thus manifested in political conflict, is still primarily considered by scholars in terms of interactions between individuals within families whereas the real tensions between generational groups in society receive less attention. Put differently, the unmet challenge is in producing a unified view on how young people were considered both individually and collectively.

Thus I set out to address this absence from current scholarship by way of a systematic interrogation of the theme of youth in tragedy, one that challenges the terms of reference such as 'generation gap' or 'intergenerational conflict' and evaluates rigorously the political nature of such themes against the backdrop of considerable political upheaval. In summary, I attempt a synthesis that both builds on some of the work that has gone before and does not make assumptions about, paradoxically, both the universality and specificity of youth in classical Greece. To do this, use must be made of modern sociological, anthropological and psychoanalytic theory on the subject to help calibrate our analytical apparatus. This is not to privilege theory that will be anachronistically applied to readings of Greek tragedy, but to reveal the inherent contradictions that persist in social constructions of youth which, I shall argue, appear in all presentations of youth in democratic societies. Or more broadly, those societies that allow some plurality in cultural views.

Chapter 1 offers evidence for much more rigid views on youth in pre- or non-democratic systems. With terms such as 'generation gap' included in almost all of the classical works on youth in the ancient world, it appears that contemporary notions of the place that youth occupies in the popular consciousness have repeatedly seeped into scholarly discussion. Unsurprisingly, the first use by classical scholars of such terms followed the explosive emergence of what can be broadly classed as '. . . the conflict and change associated with the 1960s'.[30] There are many who trace the rise of today's understanding of youth identities to 1950s America and indeed some, such as Jonathon Green writing in the 1960s, do point to the pre-1950s as a markedly different period. But it was in the 1960s when the beginnings of mass communications, in particular television, allowed the image of 'youth' to be refracted back into the gaze of youth themselves, allowing a degree of response and control of their public image. Of course, 1968 was a critical point of this decade when youth and politics combined explosively and provided the modern archetype for youthful militancy.[31]

In contrast to work by classicists, the systematic study of groups of youths by sociologists predates this watershed moment in the mid-twentieth century, negating the notion that the post-war generation pioneered the identification of cohesive youth identities. In particular, there was not only Granville Stanley Hall writing in 1904, but other seminal works of great contemporary relevance, such as Frederic Thrasher's ground-breaking sociological study *The Gang*, first published in 1927, that provide a point from which we can trace today's perspectives on youth within the framework of criminality.[32] It is on the subject of the 'youth gang' that I draw much inspiration, since for almost a century it has been this concept that has proved the primary vehicle for negative popular social constructions of youth, conceptions that I shall argue were similarly articulated in Greek tragedy of the fifth century. The importance of some of these works and how they relate to the Classics is central to the investigation of how youth is presented in tragedy, and offers some reasons why some scholars have sometimes been unable to grasp fully the dynamic nature of presentations in tragedy. That is not to say that I set out to recover evidence for gangs in the ancient world (though undoubtedly they existed – and through discussion of *Philoctetes* and *Orestes* I suggest one form they may have taken). Instead the concept of 'gangs', as a highly visible contemporary example of the social articulation of often paradoxical views about young people, is used as shorthand for the manifestation of the socially constructed world, of which tragedy was and remains a part.

In recent times, the view that the youth of today do not respect their elders (and therefore betters) is a commonplace, reinforced by the willingness of society to view stories of an out-of-control younger generation as directly reflective of societal trends towards the breakdown of social restraint. Research shows that few of these perceptions are supported by evidence of actual changes in society. Moreover, those that are, such as the perception of an increase in antisocial behaviour by young people, can be at least partly explained by political conceptualization of such categories, which are in turn transmuted into criminal definitions (such as the UK's Anti-Social Behaviour Orders [ASBOs], introduced in 1998).[33] Instead, such stories appear to demonstrate a kind of modern mythmaking, the modification or distortion of limited or minor events that enhance and enlarge an underlying tendency toward suspicion of those on the verge of adulthood. The current proliferation of sociological works on youth, gangs and crime is just the most recent indication of a sustained concern with how youth are integrated into society and reflect a specific political context.[34] However, this recent research does provide a voice for the young that is missing in the ancient sources. What emerges is a sense that opposition to adult values, thus the values of society at large, forms a part of the construction of group identity of young people. Correspondingly, adult definitions of youth as excluded and dangerous, regardless of their real social character, help reinforce youth's own oppositional identity.[35] While the very existence of a gang may be a fantastical construction of a group by society, one that the adult world has helped create as an expression of their own anxiety about young people, the construction also helps to conceptualize the oppositional place these young people find themselves occupying in relation to the society from which they have yet to win adult acceptance. In this way unified political discourse is formed.[36] In this exchange, the social reality of the gang is subordinate to a broad social and political conceptualization of the in-group, in literature and the media, that helps articulate society's anxiety about relationships between younger and older generations. In the texts of classical Athens, we do not find the voice of youth, but rather the characterization assigned to them by an older generation.

In psychoanalytic theory, this view of a tacitly accepted opposition between young and old is most brilliantly drawn out by Donald Winnicott. Winnicott's view on youth is well summed up in a very short chapter in his work *Deprivation and Delinquency*, prefaced by an excellent quote from Shakespeare's *A Winter's Tale*, which demonstrates a generalized, trans-historical and negative view of youth:

> I would there were no age between sixteen
> and twenty three or that youth would sleep out the
> rest; for there is nothing in between but
> getting wenches with child, wronging the ancientry,
> stealing, fighting.[37]

Winnicott sees these activities as having some positive elements in allowing those in a liminal stage of personal development to act out impulses that they will then go on to master, eventually allowing them to identify with a society that attempts to hold and contain young people's antisocial behaviour (although one doubts this generous view would be held by the 'wenches'). In the words of a commentator on Winnicott: 'the point is for there to be a healthy and if necessary conflictual engagement, in which the strong feelings on both sides are expressed and perhaps acted out, but which can then often lead to some resolution through the renegotiation of relationships.'[38] Where there are negative portrayals of youth, apparently far more frequent in the ancient world than positive ones, Winnicott suggests that these are generated because: 'Infinite potential is youth's precious and fleeting possession. This generates envy in the adult who is discovering in his own living the limitations of the actual.'[39] As a social scientist, Winnicott would not ascribe a universality to this social analysis of youth. But the paradoxical view of youth expressed by adults that both envies and condemns youthful exuberance echoes across the centuries and certainly appears consistent with presentations in tragedy. It could well be that this paradoxical view is one that allows the relationship between generations to remain oppositional without negating the ability of the younger generation to eventually integrate socially and politically with wider society. And contained within this paradox are very well-known ancient views on youth that express admiration of their physicality whilst criticizing their psychology, as we shall see.

Frederic Thrasher, writing in the 1920s, was the first to undertake a large-scale and rigorous survey of youth gangs and what can be loosely termed 'gang culture'. Claiming the study of 1,313 gangs in Chicago, Thrasher framed his investigations by in-groups and liminality, both in geographical terms and in relation to the in-between spaces between social institutions, families and friendship groups.[40] Remarkably sympathetic to groups of youths, and the circumstances in which they form '. . . a rudimentary society with a constructive tendency',[41] rather than a purely criminal or delinquent enterprise, Thrasher shared the same view of more recent sociologists, even criminologists, that the perceived formation of gangs is largely in response to a society that has '. . . failed to provide organized and supervised activities adequate to absorb his interests and exhaust his energies'.[42] This view is not too dissimilar to Forrest's perception of the motivations behind the oligarchic tendencies of Alcibiades and others. Interestingly, this definition of causal factors omits mention of social status other than an implicit sense of social exclusion that is not qualified by economic class. In a strikingly similar passage, Bertman discusses the concept of intergenerational conflict in the ancient world, and states: 'In the first half of the fourth century BCE their [youth's] scorn for their elders took the form of rejecting integration into the political and social institutions of their elders. Instead the energies of the educated and affluent youth were channelled into degenerate practices: dissipation of all sorts, debauchery, drinking, squandering wealth and general idleness.'[43] This sounds positively Shakespearean, such descriptions could well be applied to 'gangs' at all times in history and Bertman offers other examples of descriptions of youth and what could be considered youth gangs that have contemporary resonance: Aristotle describes the short-sighted, honour-obsessed nature of youth,[44] and Isocrates offers a damning speech on youth's role in the decline of democracy (the political) and morality (the social), albeit caused by an indulgent older generation.[45] Such judgements leave the overriding impression of youth negatively cast by those who have the economic, social, political and cultural power in society, that is, the adult elites. But it must be remembered that it is also the offspring of the elite who appear to be castigated, as discussed above, in relation to the term 'generation'. Thrasher's 'gangs' were also engaged in adventurous activities that have a fertile myth-generating capacity. There is a remarkable correspondence between the types of experience Thrasher finds in gang life and the kinds of stories we find in mythology. It is worth quoting Thrasher more fully on his view of what a gang is in terms of experience:

> Here are comedy and tragedy ... here is melodrama which excels the recurrent thrillers at the downtown theatres. Here are unvarnished emotions. Here also is a primitive democracy that cuts through all the conventional social and racial discriminations. The gang, in short, is life, often rough and untamed, yet rich in elemental processes significant to the structure of society and human nature.[46]

Using broad definitions, Thrasher sets out what he sees as the typical gang experiences, including: quests for new experiences, entertainment through cultural pursuits, romantic mythmaking about the group, construction and defence of group territory, economic endeavours, wanderlust, gang warfare, the establishment of identity through gang membership and initiation, and sexual intrigues. These types correspond well with the plotlines of myth.

It is not my intention to map gang experiences onto the development of stories in society but it is noteworthy that gangs appear to be used both by the viewer and the participant as a way of creating a mythology, as a social construction that reinforces identities via storytelling. I aim to show that formation of such ideas about youth gangs is not new, that in fact Greek tragedy offers multiple examples of the construction of identities that correspond with Thrasher's experiences of youth gangs. The key is not to follow, what I believe to be, the mistakes of recent sociology in concentrating on gang composition, structure and criminal activities but to consider conceptualized gang experiences as a way to penetrate through the fabric out of which youth gangs are socially constructed.[47] In contrast to Thrasher, and the Chicago School of which he was a part,[48] the recent rise of criminology has set a firm focus on investigation of the factors that lead to supposed deviancy in youth gangs, and their subsequent impact on society, rather than the descriptive form of social ecology of the earlier period. The overwhelming majority of discussion is on what the social or economic factors are that have created the gangs of young (mainly ethnic minority) men who pose a threat to themselves and society at large. Fortunately, dissenting voices can be heard and the critical survey by Katz and Jackson-Jacobs[49] reveals the extent to which political or cultural trends had distorted the assumptions made by some academics when designing their research. As Jackson-Jacobs neatly summarizes the problem, a supposedly objective frame can be misleading: 'windows can be dangerous tools, hiding what is on the other side by fascinating the viewer with nothing more than a reflection of the gazing perspective'.[50] The viewer of Greek tragedy needs similarly to be warned to step back from attempting to form opinions about youth in ancient society, and to look instead at what formulations of a potentially mythical generational unit have been created by the tragedian.

All the similarities in attitudes to youth introduced so far, transcending temporalities and cultures, appear to form a consistent backdrop of anxiety about the period of transition from child to adult. The extensive work already carried out in both Sociology/Anthropology and Classics has already demonstrated how such anxieties are clearly evident in classical Greek literature. The universality of anxiety about youth is beyond doubt. Instead, it is the specific presentation of themes of youth, their treatment and modification in fifth-century Greek tragedy that will form the focus of this book – that is, the literary expression of the social construction of the period of transition as presented in tragedy. No apology will be given for what may be considered the blatant Athenocentrism of my focus. I believe that a special case can be made for Athens of the period, not least on the basis of the rich evidence available in the three great Attic tragedians, for which there is no parallel from other Greek cities at the same moment in history; and that tragedy of this period was written, produced, acted and viewed (largely) by a single culture – the Athenian.

With the role of youth and anxiety about this group in mind, we can now turn to the plays of the fifth century for a brief review of the potential for investigating social constructions of youth. Of Aeschylus' extant plays there are significant aspects of intergenerational conflict in all. In *Persae*, the ghost of Darius blames his people's defeat by the Greeks on the youthful folly of Xerxes (780–5). In *Seven against Thebes*, Oedipus' intergenerational transgressions loom over the action (741–55), along with Eteocles' and Polynices' stubborn determination to kill each other in violation of their father's wishes (874–80). *Suppliants* involves the conflict of two authorities, the older Greek Danaus and Pelasgus and the younger foreign sons of Aegyptus (176–8). And of course, the *Oresteia* abounds in examples of intergenerational conflict, from Orestes' murder of Clytemnestra to the conflict over authority between the younger Olympian Athena and the older chthonic generation of the Erinyes. Relations between parents and children are also shown to be problematic in many of Sophocles' and Euripides' works. Of Sophocles' extant plays, the tragedies set in Thebes most obviously contain the intergenerational conflict theme and the tension between authority and independence is predominant in *Philoctetes* and *Electra*. Even though we have inherited a larger proportion of Euripides' works, the theme still appears consistently as part of the plot, most clearly in *Medea, Heraclidae, Hippolytus, Electra, Phoenician Women, Orestes* and *Bacchae*. However, in one play in particular, the Aeschylean *Prometheus*,[51] the conflict between generations provides not only the mythic backdrop of the drama but also the core around which all interactions take shape; and the theme permeates almost all speech. And ultimately, if we consider the possible resolutions to what seems to have been a trilogy about Prometheus, it must have involved yet more confrontation between youth and the preceding generation. The central relationship of the Aeschylean play, between Zeus and Prometheus, is placed within a wider set of relationships between the gods, the titans and mortals whose intergenerational transactions are brought to the fore. The play offers the opportunity to look closely at the real and metaphorical struggles that the author presents to his audience. Thus, *Prometheus* will provide a first attempt to understand generational opposition in tragedy.

To make explicit this volume's structure, in each chapter a play will be examined in the attempt to identify the tensions within society related to youth as articulated through social constructions. While no direct links will be attempted between themes and the precise details of real events, a careful assessment will take place of whether the general shift through the century from relative political stability to war, revolution and counter-revolution in some way affected the nature of the social construction of youth. So for example, in the chapter on *Prometheus*, reference will be made to the well-known historical cases of tyranny. And both *Orestes* and *Bacchae* will receive dedicated chapters in which I question whether the turmoil of the oligarchic revolution of 411, and subsequent stasis in Athens, affected Euripides' presentation of youth. Analysis of *Heraclidae, Philoctetes* and *Antigone* will also aim to demonstrate the variety and flexibility of social constructions. I hope the result will be a comprehensive view of how youth is presented in tragedy, the ways in which these presentations might give insight into the complex view of youth in classical Greece and how this might have changed from the earliest surviving full tragedies of Aeschylus' first plays to the final productions of Euripides and Sophocles as the great democracy of Athens finally unravelled.

Youth in Tragedy's Literary Forebears and Contemporaries

We have nobody younger than you, Antilochus . . . why not race out and see if you can bring a Trojan down.

Homer, *Iliad*, 15.569–70

When a man is drunk he is led along, stumbling, by a beardless boy

Heraclitus, fragment, 117

Greek tragedy did not emerge fully formed independently of other cultural influences. Indeed in the case of its performance, its place within religious festivals and its use of mythic material, it was shaped by a great many prior literary genres, sacred rituals, folk song and dance. But it wasn't just in form that tragedy drew on a great legacy, it was also in the concepts and ideas, themes and tropes that tragedy reached back, however obliquely, to the archaic period preceding the dawn of the classical fifth century. It is of little surprise, then, that important themes such as the place of young people in society can be found in many works outside of tragedy. But this dramatic genre would become the most sophisticated form of cultural expression of political issues to the polis in fifth-century Athenian society. No other art form engaged such a wide and diverse audience – historical and philosophical texts were not available for any but small groups of specialists. Nor could epic or lyric poetry, more widely accessible, render adequately into a demotic form contemporary political concerns, at least not in a way that was as responsive to the political climate as could tragedy. Indeed, Aristotle remarked that everything one could find in epic one could find in tragedy, but not everything in tragedy can be found in epic.[1] The only other art form that could lay a similar claim to the one that I make of tragedy was the other pre-eminent type of drama, Old Comedy, which was also played out in front of large crowds in the theatre. Comedy does offer many examples of what are, apparently, normative, even clichéd views of youth in Athenian society presented (albeit in a typically extreme and comical Aristophanic way) either directly or inversely. But this is in acute contrast to tragedy's more complex reflection, refraction, mediation and confusion of political ideas.[2]

To make clear this sophistication and responsiveness to political and cultural milieux, I pause to review briefly sources other than tragedy, both prior and contemporaneous. I hope to demonstrate the changing nature of attitudes towards young people through time as well as the differences in the presentation between tragedy and other (largely textual) sources. While tragedy became the dominant cultural form in the fifth century, the popularity of archaic literature also remained strong. Although the works of Homer and Hesiod predate even the earliest tragedy by at least a clear two centuries and were composed within a very different political context, they were known intimately by all Greeks – the Homeric epics were performed as a regular feature at the important annual festival, the Athenian Panathenaia – and feature many of the characters and plotlines that the tragedians would later use in their works. The complex relationship between tragedy and archaic literature is outside the scope of this volume but a brief review of the handling of youth in Homer and Hesiod is highly illustrative of the traditional picture of youth that the Greek tragedians inherited and from which, I suggest, tragedy was later to depart.

Homer was the most important, or at least most widely known, archaic literary source in classical Athens. His first work, the *Iliad,* would have been a story familiar to almost all Greeks and the characters he presents would later feature heavily in tragedy. In this dramatic imagining of the last year of the siege of Troy, the army seems to be mainly comprised of young men. This impression is continuously reiterated, those involved in the prayers to Apollo specifically referred to as *kouroi* – youths (1.473), the same term used later by Poseidon (13.95). Whilst narrating Hector's battlefield ascendency he is described as decimating the young (*neōn*) phalanx (11.503). With the exception of Diomedes, who acknowledges his youth and therefore inferior status (14.111), the voice of the dominant Greeks is the voice of the older commanders: Agamemnon, Odysseus, Menelaus and Nestor.

The most superficial reading of the epic also reveals obsessive reiterations of personal genealogies. Almost all characters are introduced via their parentage. While this seems to demonstrate the importance of an individual's place within a family's generational context, it is also used to reflect on the honour (or in some cases dishonour) of a character in relation to their forebears. The clearest example of this is demonstrated by Aeneas' speech in Book 20 (20.200–59), regaling Achilles with an account of his lineage. This type of speech adds a degree of instant characterization in a narrative where individuals come and go at an accelerated pace. The high value placed on family, as these speeches demonstrate and as is woven poetically into the fabric of the *Iliad*, such as in the story of Agamemnon's sceptre (2.100–8), is seemingly at odds, however, with the reality of the Greek army's circumstances. As Agamemnon points out, 'nine of great Zeus' years have now passed . . . our wives and little children sit at home and wait for us' (2.1313). Or not such little children as the case may be, startlingly so in that of Telemachus in the *Odyssey* or Orestes (of whom more later). To be more precise, the importance of family is more accurately described as the importance of an individual's place within the male generations – but even this appears subordinate to the pursuit of *kleos* or glory. Hector relates his reasons for leading the battle lines to Andromache: not just to win and save Troy, but to win glory for himself, and for his father (6.438). Hector also sets out his aspirations for his son Astyanax: to win greater honour than he has done (6.480). The link between the honour of fathers and sons is shown in reverse by Agamemnon's taunt of Peisander and Hippolochus before he strikes them down: 'You shall now pay for your father's disgraceful insult' (11.141). The speeches of the older characters appear to support the primacy of honour over the survival of their young kin. Nestor, in particular, as the voice of the older Greek generation at Troy, consistently exhorts the young warriors to battle. Strengthening an impression of long-held paternalistic autocracy is the reference to age and authority that tends to feature in Nestor's speeches. At 1.249–51, Nestor's intervention in the argument between Agamemnon and Achilles fails to achieve reconciliation between them, but his paternalism is immediately established ('He had already seen two generations of men born . . . He had their interests at heart')[3] and he quickly moves to assert his generational status: 'Now listen to me. You are both my juniors' (1.260). 'Godlike' Achilles, responding to Nestor's entreaties in hardly a godlike way, complains: 'a pathetic little nonentity I shall be called' (1.293), leaving the impression of a debate between a self-indulgent younger man and a calm and rational elder.[4] Indeed, throughout, Nestor is presented as the voice of age and reason, intervening between Diomedes and Agamemnon, and in Book 9, asserting that, as an older man, he can 'take the whole situation into consideration' (9.60), implying the rashness and lack of foresight of the young and the ability to give good counsel that comes with age.

These exchanges, however, do not actually involve conflict between generations but reflect a theme of entrenchment of societal status of different age groups and the importance of deferment to older men. Agamemnon, after hearing fairly sharp criticism of his actions by Nestor, concedes his 'lamentable impulse and ... blind folly' (9.119). That is not to say that all of the older generation are allowed authority over the young, since Phoenix fails to persuade Achilles to fight for the Greeks. But this failure can also be attributed to Achilles' absolute implacability and the fact that Phoenix is just a symbolic surrogate for generational authority. Achilles, once the humiliation of his loss of Briseis is complete, provides further negative reinforcement of the characterization of youth, bursting into tears and demanding that Thetis, his mother, should help him get revenge (1.353–413). Specific criticism of characteristics of youth is presented elsewhere. Menelaus, in Book 3, proclaims that: '... the youngest men *(hoploterōs)* are never dependable ...' (3.108), and asks that Priam swear an oath in place of Paris, in whom he has little trust. This judgement of youth goes uncontested and appears to be presented as a matter of fact. The precedence of age is asserted on the divine plane, too, as Hera argues '... I take precedence in two respects – (firstly) because I am the eldest by birth ...' (4.60), and Zeus often iterates his authority as 'senior by birth' (15.181, 15.198). 'The privilege of age' (4.324), as Nestor later calls it, is unassailable. This is the privilege of directing the actions, and in some cases deciding the fates, of other, younger men. This privilege is quickly and brutally demonstrated when the youthfulness of one of the first to die, Simoisius, is set out in the description of the first clashes between Greek and Trojans (4.472–89). Later, in Book 7 (7.122–60), it is again Nestor who urges the Greeks to nominate a champion to take on Hector and it is Nestor who reminds Patroclus of his father Menoetius' advice to enter negotiations as while, 'Achilles is of nobler birth than you ... you are older than he is' (11.788). Odysseus also invokes age and authority over Achilles when he says that, '... my judgment is much sounder than yours' (19.219), and Menelaus also uses age as a condition for subordination when he says, 'we have nobody younger (*neōteros*) than you, Antilochus ... why not race out and see if you can bring a Trojan down' (15.569–70).

Although one must be mindful of due military protocol – after all, the poem is about an army at war – these passages do seem to reiterate two key attitudes towards youth, first that they should be subordinate to their elders, and second, that it is their place to face death, their rash nature being naturally suited to this role. The younger appear to share this view of the rightful allocation of authority, Diomedes apologizing for disagreeing with Agamemnon's views, requesting that he does not 'resent the fact that I am the youngest man among you' (14.111). The gods' honour and age shape individual actions as much as mortals. Poseidon, challenging Apollo, says, 'You are my junior, and with my greater age and experience, it would not be honourable for me to start' (21.440). The young mortal warriors appear respectfully subordinate to the older generation, the senior members of the military community who encourage them to compete for honour when sending them into battle. A high value is placed on personal relationships, such as between fathers and sons, but not so high as the *kleos* gained from death in battle. Characteristics that appear to be associated with youth are both negative (mental immaturity, emotional instability) and positive (physical prowess). The overall impression is of a society in which the young and the old have well embedded positions of power in relation to each other. Tensions in these relationships are both revealed and resolved through competition for honour.

If the *Iliad* offers an insight into the anxieties and pressures of men, both young and old, at war, the *Odyssey* offers a view into the lives of those left behind awaiting their fathers' return. Part travelogue, part imagined reality of a world without a ruling-age male population, this later epic provides – in some lengthy sections – a domestic counterpoint to the *Iliad*'s narrative of Greek overseas exploits. From the beginning of Book 1, one is introduced to a gang of suitors for Penelope's hand who threaten Odysseus' legacy, and that of his son, Telemachus. That these suitors are young men is made clear in Book 2 when the elderly Aegyptius asks: 'who has summoned us now? Was it one of the young men (*neōn andrōn*) or one of the older generation (*progenesteroi*)?'

(2.28–9). Ithaca is a land without a middle-range adult male population, that is: women aside, there are just the old, the young men and the children. The resultant society appears to be one in which social control of the young has broken down. 'There is no one like Odysseus in charge' (2.59) to stop the young men exploiting Telemachus' lack of political power – and thus ability to check the potential violence on those who would be Penelope's new husband. The term *kouroi* is used to refer to the suitors, making clear their ages relative to Odysseus (16.248, 17.174). In line with the general view of youth as described in the *Iliad*, the characteristics of these young suitors are locatable on a spectrum of youth misbehaviours, from insolence and arrogance (2.324–32) to hubristic. Telemachus' status as an extremely young man appears negatively reflected in others' perceptions of him, too: Antinous admonishes him for his 'bold and haughty way of talking', although such an evaluation could equally be applied to Antinous (1.385).[5] While the suitors' youth is presented in a negative light, the general view of youth offered does not do the younger generation much credit either. Athena proclaims: 'Few sons are like their fathers. Generally they are worse' (2.276). In a curious passage, in Book 10, Odysseus repeats the story of Elpenor, the youngest of his party, who dies an unnecessary death due, it seems, to pure absent-mindedness. However, the reference to his young age, made twice in two lines (10.551–2), suggests that his lack of judgement is a result of youthful intellectual immaturity. While Telemachus does, on the whole, display the characteristics of how other characters think a young man should behave, such as deference towards the old (3.22), his youth means he is vulnerable to the nefarious influence of older men and he is liable to be incited to violence (2.189).

Competition for honour between fathers and sons, as in the *Iliad*, also features in the *Odyssey*. Close to the end of the poem, Laertes expresses delight, saying, 'what a day this is to warm the heart. My son and grandson competing in valour' (24.512–13). But this intergenerational competition for honour can reach unedifying extremes, such as when Telemachus proposes to string Odysseus' bow and so win the hand of his own mother (21.112). Telemachus even moves beyond contemplation; it is only his father's intervention that thwarts his proto-Oedipal intentions (21.130). This appears to be the closest to true conflict between mortal generations that is evident in any of Homer. Even though it is true that the suitors are young men, there are reasons why the

Odyssey cannot be considered to reflect themes of true intergenerational conflict between groups. There appear to be no men of Odysseus' age range on Ithaca, owing to the Trojan War and the disastrous journey home. As such, any conflict can only be between the single Odysseus and the ranks of Telemachus' generation. The suitors also appear to have been encouraged by older members of their families to encroach on Odysseus' property and authority, so respect for the authority of an older generation does exist. And critically, at the end of the poem, all three generations of the family stride out to face off an angry crowd. At the heart of the drama is a personal battle, not a societal one, reflecting the personal-power structures of the kingship society over the partial socializing of power of an incipient movement in the local islands towards democracy.

The overall treatment of youth in the *Odyssey* would appear similar to that in the *Iliad*: the young are generally prone to rash behaviour; each generation tends towards a lower standard of heroism; and the authority of an older generation is a necessary requirement for enforcing justice. And yet, in the references to Orestes and Telemachus' decision to attempt to string his father's bow, the embryonic strains of direct challenge between young and older men do seem to begin to emerge. This developing theme could reflect the beginnings of real political change in Greece. Griffin points to the differences between political content in the *Iliad* and the *Odyssey*.[6] In particular, he argues that a more realistic political organization is on display in the *Odyssey*, and suggests that the threat to Odysseus' power comes from an emerging aristocracy, reflecting material reality. Much has been written about age in Homer, and particularly about Telemachus and his embodiment of 'youth'. Belmont's *Telemachus and Nausicaa: A Study of Youth* and Austin's *Telemachos Polymechanos* both contain the argument that Telemachus achieves adulthood through his journeying around the Peloponnese, and that he develops the wily nature of his father by the end of the epic. Both writers suggest it is only by following in his father's footsteps that Telemachus can reach maturity.[7] This is not a model of youthful rebellion, rather the start of a planned succession of kingship. Using a socio-psychological model, Felson argues that Telemachus only reaches maturity by rejecting the female parent and internalizing the idealized father. Felson's view of women in the *Odyssey* is peculiar, particularly when she says, of Telemachus' slaughter of the maids, at Book 23: 'this act of vengeance cleanses him of his animosity towards women and rescues him from the misogyny of an Agamemnon' (in psychoanalytic terms Telemachus evacuates from his mind any love for a woman, thus cleansing him).[8] This statement seems to demonstrate the caution required in applying modern psychoanalytic theory to ancient literature as it can lead to speculation on the meaning of ancient literature that may not have been recognizable to the original audience.

There is a huge corpus of ancient Greek lyric from which evidence can also be drawn, especially from the extensive fragments of Stesichorus or from Pindar. Space and the fragmentary and lacunose nature of most of these texts allow only a brief review of the sources. Lyric was intended for performance and often dealt with the contemporary and prosaic – desire, envy, ambition, achievements and misfortunes etc. – depending on which of the myriad forms of lyric was used. The lyric poets drew on the everyday world for their material and as a result the material reality of society can be found in many lyric texts. Along with other notably prominent themes, such as love and politics, youth features strongly as both a theme and constituent of character and this appears relatively stable across the four centuries from which we still have lyric texts (eighth to fifth centuries BCE). In Callinus and Tyrtaeus, both seventh-century poets, we have poetry to match the hexameter of the *Iliad* for exhorting young men to battle valiantly. Indeed Tyrtaeus was recited to young Spartan men before battle and favourable parallels could be drawn with Homer for locating society's expectations of young men in war in his poetry, where a young man in battle, 'felled in the front line, he is lovely yet' (fragment 10).[9] This loveliness of youth is deployed in different forms, with Mimnermus lamenting the short blooming of life's most beautiful flower (fragment 2), or an anonymous writer comparing youth with accursed age (Theognidea fragment 271–8).[10] The type of negative views of youth's intellectual or moral fabric that we see here can also be found elsewhere, such as in a late sixth-century elegiac poem by Simonides, where he says: 'A mortal, while he has the lovely bloom of youth, has many empty-headed, vain ideas' (el. 20) and similarly in anonymous Theognidea, the line: 'The prime of youth and vigour goes with empty brains; it oft emboldens men to go astray' (629–30). And amongst all these fragments of varying degrees of authenticity and completeness we have an extended description attributed to Solon by a first-century Christian writer, Philo. This text is very valuable indeed, offering a rare systematic description of the characteristics one should expect of a man during and after sets of seven years of life, such as the casting off of youthful recklessness after 35 and one's intellectual apex reached between 42 and 56.[11] If this was the work of Solon it represents a type of demarcation by age of expectations of a citizen in relation to political and societal participation (prime age for martial service, for marriage, fatherhood, political debate, retirement from deliberations, etc.) that fits well within a Solonian framework of constitutional reforms based on an individual's changing state of means or being. But as one finds in other archaic textual sources, there is a basic view in plain sight that young men's physical prowess and older men's deliberative abilities are the desired and natural attributes by age category.

In the poetry of Hesiod (thought to have been composed relatively close to when Homer created his works), the poet mythologizes the power relationships between the gods, that is, the political structure of the divine. As immortal beings, violent action by successive generations is the only way in which power can transfer from group to group: it would be questionable divinity that negotiated a transfer of their power. The central succession myth (the Ouranos – Kronos – Zeus conflict) can thus be explained in part by cosmological expediency. Still, there are other factors at work that qualify this process of intergenerational power shift – such as the negative way in which the soon-to-be-defeated fathers are described.[12] Ouranos is described as evil and cruel and is defined by his wicked behaviour towards his children (*Theogony*, 161–91). Kronos is described in a similar fashion when he carries out a comparable imprisonment of his offspring (462–96). In both cases, the mothers of the oppressed children enlist the support of other gods to begin a process that will lead to the overthrow of their spouses' generation and the passing of power to the cohort of gods to which their children belong. Critically, Hesiod frames these passages as the naturally just passing of power from generation to generation. The natural justice of Zeus' eventual reign, reflected in his union with Themis, the personification of justice and law (901), demonstrates the correct order of things in the shifts of power between generations. But even this ordered cosmos, presented through a teleological retelling of the central Greek succession myth of the gods,[13] cannot resist the inevitable rupture that will be brought about by the next generation. The open-endedness of the succession cycle is summed up in the story of Zeus' swallowing of Metis – allowing for a future revolution within the world of the gods when the prophesized overthrowing of Zeus will occur (897).

Hesiod's didactic poem, *Works and Days* is in some ways a mortal counterpart to the *Theogony*'s guide to the gods, and provides a commentary on two aspects of gradual deterioration in the esteem in which generations can be held. At an epochal level, in the famous 'Ages of Man' passage, Hesiod recounts the present age's failings in comparisons to earlier ages (*Works and Days*, 110–200). Within this age of 'toil and misery … constant distress … [and] harsh troubles' (175i) there are, to Hesiod, further signs of continued deterioration. Hesiod says of children, 'soon they will cease to respect their ageing parents, and will rail at them with harsh words, the ruffians, in ignorance of the gods' punishment …' (180), an interesting prolepsis of the kinds of themes later to be found in comedy and tragedy. In Hesiod's view, things are getting worse and this decline is both reflected in the behaviour of children and propagated via their eventual seizure of power from an earlier generation. In these primary archaic sources, young men need to be carefully controlled as even when such management is carried out successfully there is a cosmic propensity towards declining moral standards. Any conflict between generations appears in a personal, context-specific way, rather than as a wider conflict in society. This, perhaps, is understandable given the political and social milieux from which archaic literature emerged, where the political structures of society were differently configured than those in the fifth century: power relations in the king-ruled *polis* were not open to realistic debate on potential for change.

The presentation of epic and tragedy as representative of two discrete textual epochs does not quite give the whole picture: there was some literary continuity between the seventh- and fifth-century intellectual and literary cultures. The earliest of those texts that we categorize as belonging to the pre-Socratics comes from the period pre-dating democracy. While the sophists and their surviving work are culturally and historically much closer to Greek tragedy, to the extent that stereotyped sophistries can be traced in the plays,[14] strands of thinking that begin in the pre-Socratics are also evident in these texts and such continuities allow the early sophists, such as Gorgias or Protagoras, to be considered as part of the same tradition as the pre-Socratics.

Taken as a relatively coherent group of texts we have a useful vantage point from which to triangulate the shifting attitudes towards young men in a changing political society. A brief consideration follows of attitudes to youth that are present in the philosophical sources up to Antiphon.[15]

Not all writers who are classed under the heading of pre-Socratic can be productively mined for information on attitudes towards youth. The earliest recognizable philosophers, those associated with the city of Miletus, lived and thought between the seventh and sixth centuries BCE. Thales, Anaximander, Anaximenes and Diogenes of Apollonia (resident of a Milesian colony) are mainly concerned with natural sciences, rather than social philosophy, and it is unlikely that any of their abstractions on cosmology or ontology can help our understanding of youth, however valuable the study of early philosophical thought. The later peripatetic Xenophanes offers interesting thoughts on man's relationship with the divine, in terms of the literary presentations of Hesiod and Homer that attribute negative characteristics to the gods,[16] and he writes about the tendency for humans to create pictures of the gods in their own images,[17] but it is difficult to see how this can affect intergenerational relationships. The various positions on the 'singular versus the plural universal' model argued for by Parmenides and Zeno of Magna Graecia, and Melissus of Samos' proto-atomism, do little to help reveal attitudes to youth either. More helpful comments are found in Heraclitus (died 475 BCE), who says, 'a man is thought as foolish by a supernatural being as a child (*pais*) is by a man',[18] and he likens drunkenness to immaturity, 'when a man is drunk he is led along, stumbling, by a beardless boy'[19] – a comparison that would become well-worn, echoes of which are found later in Plato's *Laws*.[20] More generally, he also introduces the explicit concept of strife and necessity: he sees ongoing conflict in the world is the natural order of things.[21] More directly useful material can be found in the work of Pythagoras, Anaxagoras, Empedocles and the Atomists in the early fifth century. In an interesting passage in Isocrates' *Busiris*[22] the fourth-century commentator claims that Pythagoras became so famous that all the young men wished to join his community, a desire welcomed by the older men. According to Isocrates, the mystic-mathematician's followers '... are more impressive in their silence than those for the greatest reputation for eloquence.' Held against Isocrates' famous criticism of young men's tendency towards degeneracy and outspokenness,[23] this comment suggests Pythagoras encouraging a cultic discipline amongst his followers that would be beneficial to youth in a society.

This view is in stark contrast to the vast majority of later views on philosophers' influence on youth, in particular that of the sophists and in old comedy, holding that to equip young men with the intellectual abilities to out-perform their elders was a very dangerous thing indeed. It could be that Isocrates admired Pythagoras' disciplined way of life, including silence, rather than his role as a teacher, although Isocrates' own biases are clearly projected here too. Active some sixty years after Pythagoras, Anaxagoras (510–428 BCE) belonged to a much different political and cultural context, as a contemporary and political ally of Pericles. His philosophy of pluralities within pluralities would seem like a useful fit with an emergent democracy – one that saw the whole democratic community as distinct from other political systems, and with separate entities (*deme*s, age groups, social classes, etc.) constituting it.[24] Anaxagoras' view was that, while there is order within the diversity of pluralities, there is a tendency for like to attract like. Logically, conflict between like and unlike is a naturally resultant state.[25] Furthermore, the view that nothing is generated or destroyed could be applied to relational systems of plural groups, in terms of the generational flow of political power (fitting well with the Hesiodic view of intergenerational divine power).[26] Empedocles, like Anaxagoras, believed in a materialism of things, that there cannot be nothing.[27] Conflict seems to have played a larger part in his world view too, with love and strife having generative and degenerative powers.[28] He shared the poetic approach of Heraclitus, using verse to articulate his perspective, and, in one passage, Empedocles suggests that love and strife alternately shape the human experience and also the universe in totality, in a natural cycle consisting of combination and dispersal (as similarly theorized by Anaxagoras).[29] Other fifth-century thinkers, such as Democritus and Leucippus (who are conventionally referred to together as the early Atomists), make a leap of imagination from the earlier materialist view to a more sophisticated theoretical standpoint on the fabric of the world: the atomic structure. It is difficult to see how this might affect more general thinking about societal relations, but the fragments of Democritus containing ethical judgements are perhaps more useful. These relatively numerous fragments seem to reflect a conventional conservatism, particularly relating to moderation and balance,[30] that form a picture of the idealized citizen, one who is mature in age and outlook. And, in the midst of a lengthy passage from Theophrastus, it is claimed that Democritus believed people are atomically different depending on their age or physical state.[31] In combination, these views offer a very hostile morality for young people, considering them as being inherently incapable of right-mindedness. The young are thus ineligible for full political office until they are at an age where their atomic composition would allow them the balanced minds they would need to participate in governance.

The sophists, all fifth century or later, have been treated by ancient and more modern writers in a less than sympathetic manner, perhaps influenced by the comedy of Aristophanes and the writings of Aristotle and Plato. Looking beyond some of these criticisms, there is much in the sources relating to the views of sophists on a range of social, political and cultural issues that is relevant. Indeed it could be argued that youth is central to all that has been associated with the sophists. Although not the case for all who have been categorized as sophists, adolescents of the citizen elite appear to be an important audience for sophistic ideas – tuition fees seemed to have been high enough to exclude students from all but the wealthiest families.[32] There are some traces of the kind of natural science and philosophy of the pre-Socratics, such as in Gorgias' discussion of nothing and being,[33] but primarily the sophists are associated with ethics and a kind of early sociological and political theory. Protagoras (490–420 BCE) is the key source for this period, not just because he was closely associated with the Periclean circle at Athens, and so the dominant political ideology, but also because his views set out a clear manifesto to equip youth with the skills to gain political influence.[34] This is astonishing. At a time when those below thirty years of age could not hold full political office, and there were age restrictions on inheritance and property ownership, the aim of empowerment of those constrained by law was revolutionary. Moreover, both the supporters and detractors of Protagoras hold up antithetical argument pairings as typically Protagorean and this reflects a perspective that has conflict, of *logoi* in this case, at the heart of the intellectual system.[35] It is not improbable to suppose that, in classical Athens at least, the link was made, quite easily, between the inherent conflict perceivable in Protagorean arguments and the potential for this to encourage physical violence, a will to power, of those who had studied under him. The representation of Socrates in Aristophanes' *Clouds* is one example of such a possible popular conception.

That said, we cannot make claims of sophists as an undifferentiated group. Gorgias' rhetorical teachings, for example, were not so explicitly tailored to the young, in fact his oratorical training would have been of greater use for those already giving speeches in the courts and council,[36] and he shows adherence to traditional values, such as respecting one's parents, that is not in sympathy with Protagoras' relativist view of ethics.[37] Likewise, Prodicus is perhaps best known for the '*choice of Heracles*' story in which a moral choice is presented to Heracles who is '... on the cusp between childhood and manhood, at the age when the young become independent and show whether they are going to approach life by the path of goodness or the path of wickedness'.[38] Hippias is also presented as respecting traditional values, by Xenophon, when he describes an exchange with Socrates that has the sophist agree that it is custom everywhere to honour your parents.[39] In combination, these figures seem hardly representative of teachers corrupting young minds into subverting adult political power. The importance of education and discipline for the young is found in Antiphon, too,[40] although the surviving collection of aphorisms suggests a more pronounced interest in ethics than Prodicus, Gorgias and Hippias (but not to the extent of Protagoras). The fragment from Oxyrhynchus that we have for Antiphon tantalizingly shows the beginnings of an assessment of the ethics presented by the poet and how this might impact on the young.[41] But drawing any sort of conclusion from this, other than that Antiphon was interested in the effects of education, is a step too far towards speculation. In contrast, Thrasymachus of Chalcedon offers the most specific challenge to the old by the young in a fragment that deserves full quotation: 'I wish I had been alive in the old days, when the younger generation could happily remain silent, since matters did not force them to make speeches and their elders were looking after the city in an appropriate manner'.[42] If this is an accurate report of Thrasymachus' speech, this is an extraordinary attack on the power structures and traditional organization of Athenian society. It is true that Thrasymachus' overall view of society was one that relied deeply on an idealized 'ancestral constitution', but in this passage all respect for older members of society seems to have been lost. Conflict between the generations, in this sophist's eyes, is a necessary step towards re-establishing an idealized former political state of affairs. The sophists seem to bring to the fore the issue of competing value systems for youth and some, such as Protagoras and Thrasymachus, seem to set out a specific policy of equipping young men with the political skills to compete against older citizens. This is in contrast to the pre-Socratics who seem to have much less of an interest in society, other than to support traditional values or warn against the general poverty of existence and the universality of strife. In short, the earlier writers offer a view of unified cosmologies, with conflict as a natural force; and the later writers, a stratified society with conflict as a social force. It is difficult not to point to the historical events of the Peloponnesian War as playing a large part in fuelling the potential for this kind of conflict. The increasing ratio of young men to older men in Athens, and mounting pressure on Athenian social structures, must have impacted on all parts of the city's social and cultural outlook. The democratic institutions of the time, those that would have reinforced group identities, including age-groups, must have provided the opportunity for sophists to find their market and formed part of the combative intellectual milieu from which the philosophically minded could draw inspiration.

But other intellectual endeavours were being undertaken simultaneously outside the philosophical schools. Herodotus' *Histories* provides a wider regional perspective on the workings of societies and contain an impressive number of stories, anecdotes and alleged historical accounts that offer a wealth of sociological and anthropological material. Much of Herodotus' writing is more concerned with the 'Barbarian', rather than the Greek, but a careful approach can help to reveal the writer's view of what a normative state is in relation to society and traditional roles within it.[43] In relation to youth, this is demonstrated effectively, in Book 2, when Herodotus likens the respect that Egyptian young men have for their elders to the attitudes in Sparta, the famously non-democratic Greek city-state (2.80–1). Like earlier writers and thinkers, Herodotus too shows an interest in succession and conflict and immediately in Book 1 we are introduced to the tyranny of Pisistratus (1.59–64) and the conflict between grandfather and grandson, Astyages and Cyrus (1.123–31). Further brief digressions on tyrants and their rise to power appear fairly frequently, such as those regarding Hippias or Periander. The anthropological approach that Herodotus takes results in many stories regarding strange and, to the Ionian Greek author, foreign rituals. In a passage in the lengthy description of Egypt, Herodotus retells the story he claims to have heard from the priests at Papremis of the origins and features of a ritual involved in the festival of Ares (2.63–4). The ritual, it seems, involved a staged gang fight of sorts for entry to the shrine and is associated with the young adulthood of Ares (who by some mythological sources shares as siblings Hebe, the goddess of youth, and Eileithyia, goddess of childbirth).

Other passages also include reports of various rituals that are associated with young men passing into adulthood, such as the Nasamonians' adventures in the Libyan Desert that runs like a rites of passage story (2.32–3). Many of the observations are made in a subjective and personal way that's typical of Herodotus' historiography, but when speech is reported, more familiar tropes on youth emerge. In Book 3, Croesus advises Cambyses not to, 'act on the passionate impulse of youth', although this is from a Lydian to a Persian (3.36.1). The intercultural view of impulsive youth appears again in the story of the Macedonian Amyntas' futile attempts to stop the rash and violent actions of his son, Alexander (5.19). In, perhaps, the most explicit passage on youth in the work, Xerxes explains his flip-flopping over whether to take up his deceased father's campaign against the Greeks as due to his *neōtēs*, youth-like, state of being that also led him to lose his temper and insult a man older than himself (7.13).[44] In these few lines, Herodotus presents the centuries-old and region-wide tableau of youth: intellectually incapable, disrespectful to elders and prone to violent eruptions of temper. But, by some accounts, Xerxes was probably in his mid-thirties, certainly older than Darius when he came to power, and most likely older than both Cyrus and Cambyses when they began their reigns.[45] We read here not just a normative representation of previous societal views on young people, but one that has the nascent qualities of suggesting the fragmentation of the concept of youth. That is, we can see how certain defining characteristics of youth (biological or psychological) begin to be understood as discrete elements within the conceptual whole. As has been pointed out extensively in scholarship on Herodotus, he presents a picture of the barbarian that helps define what it means to be Greek.[46] The normative view of youth in Persian society, though, doesn't appear to be much different from that of the Greek. In Xerxes' speech, however, Herodotus shows the different political view of youth, the ridiculousness, to the Greek, of a youthful ruler, a political circumstance that can only exist within a monarchic society.

The case of a naturally deteriorating morality in the line of kings or relations is shown consistently in Persian society, according to Herodotus, who reports the popular saying that: 'Darius was a tradesman, Cambyses a tyrant, and Cyrus a father' (3.89), the effect being to see the more recent generations to be concerned only with money and power, respectively.[47] Herodotus' own view on the theme of deterioration is more flexible, and he says: 'for people who were brave once might easily have deteriorated today, just as people who in old times were nothing to speak of might by now have improved' (9.27). Other stories about young people are almost always horrific in detail and seemingly designed to display the barbarity of some communities, such as the sacrifice of the eldest sons at Thessian Halos (7.197) and the horrific revenge story of Xerxes' chief eunuch, Hermotimus, where the father is forced to castrate his own sons before he suffers the same fate at their hands (8.105–6).[48] Hermotimus' father/victim is shown to have acted under compulsion, unlike the story of a Thracian chieftain who, in revenge for disobedience, gouged out the eyes of his six sons freely (8.117). *The Histories* contains the same casually negative portrayals of the psychological states and actions associated with youth as the previous works discussed above. What *is* striking, though, is the omission of reference to youth in the extended descriptions of war, when considering the generally positive descriptions of young men in terms of physicality, in other contemporary and earlier texts, and when compared to the extensive description of young warriors in the *Iliad*.

We come now to the primary source for a comparative treatment of tragedy: Thucydides. Although contemporaneous, *The History of the Peloponnesian War* composed towards the end of the fifth century is very different from Herodotus' partial account of Athenian military history. Primarily, Thucydides is a political writer, attempting to shape an understanding of how war begins and strategy emerges in response to factors to which any *polis* at war is subject, i.e. social and demographic upheaval, political unity or factionalism and the economic impact of warfare. In this context the role of young people or relations between generations can be considered highly political in that societal concerns shaped and were then subject to political decision-making. Whereas Herodotus gives an interesting anthropological perspective on how youth fits into the idea of Greek/Barbarian polarity, Thucydides maps the points at which fault lines might appear in a society under immense stress between different classes, ethnicities, genders or ages. The emphasis on differences between Greeks – or rather Athenians and their opponents – facilitates a narrowing of focus from regional to national that allows a closer view of culture-specific attitudes to society. That is not to say that commonalities between *poleis* are not to be found in Thucydides: in speeches attributed to both the Corinthians and Athenians, representatives speak of the importance of the young learning from the old before making decisions on whether to break treaties, form alliances, or declare war.[49] What the young should learn, Thucydides seems to suggest, is not to be too eager for battle. Athens, at the outbreak of war had, 'great numbers of young men (*neotēs*) who had never been in a war and were consequently far from unwilling to join in this one', (2.8) and this impulse should be restrained. The Spartan general at the onset of war, Archidamus, is reported to have had similar expectation, basing his initial strategy on luring out the young and inexperienced soldiers by laying waste the surrounding land (220–1).

As in much earlier work by Homer, power remains with older men, even at times of extreme ruptures in society. During the civil war in Corcyra, fathers belonging to the Democratic Party were reported to have killed their sons, but no reports of patricide are given (3.81). Stasis and bloody revenge, according to Thucydides, go hand in hand and at these times, 'family relations were a weaker tie than party membership' (3.82). Intergenerational conflict and political revolution, at least in the account of civil war in democratic Corcyra, would seem naturally to coexist. Tyrannies also feature prominently here, but the narrative is less personal and more political than in Herodotus, as befitting Thucydides' stated historiographical method (1.20 and 5.53–9 make explicit the perceived failings of other historical writers, often taken to be directed at Herodotus directly). At 1.13, the political progression from hereditary monarchy to tyranny, as a precursor to oligarchy or democracy, is explicitly stated. There appears an important paradox here: whilst the natural progression towards democracy from monarchy is considered positive, there is a pervasive schema of degeneration, particularly amongst political leaders, over time. This could simply be anti-democratic sentiment but it also demonstrates that these incompatible views are not necessarily works of logic, more like general impressions.[50] As in Homer, the exhortation to battle in honour of the glorious deeds of one's forebears is a common ploy in swinging popular opinion round to an aggressive view on how to proceed. Pericles' peroration in his speech to the Athenian assembly before the outbreak of war, 'we must live up to the standard they [the previous generation] set' (1.144), sets a generational precedent and challenge that prove impossible to ignore. And comparison to the achievements of the previous generation is encouraged in Pericles' famous funeral oration (2.36). Understandably, the martial abilities of the citizen hoplite class are, in part, stratified by age. In Book 2.13, the eldest and the youngest in the army are tasked with the defence of Athens, presumably a less physically strenuous activity than combat in the field and, crucially, one requiring less combat experience, such as the formation of a phalanx.[51] That is not to say that the young are shielded from the worst of war: far from it. Brasidas tasks the youngest of his soldiers with dangerous harrying of an advancing enemy as he led a retreat in Thrace (4.125), and Thucydides states, 'the flower of Thespian youth had fallen', during fighting in Boeotia (4.133).

More than anything else, Thucydides is important as he writes extensively about the figure of Alcibiades, the ancient embodiment of the brilliant but reckless aristocratic youth.[52] That Alcibiades is defined by his age is undisputable: at his introduction, his relative age is immediately stated (5.43),[53] and his keenness for renewed war with Sparta is attributed, in part, to the fact that he felt politically marginalized because of his relatively young age.[54] Nicias, in his opposition to the Sicilian expedition, is explicit in his use of Alcibiades' youth as a criticism of his ability to make rational choices, saying: 'he is still too young for his post' and that such an important decision should not be made, 'by a young man in a hurry' (6.12). It is not an overstatement to suggest that this speech by Nicias is one of the most important in Greek literature for evidence of a fracturing of society in late fifth-century Athens between different age groups. Of course, Thucydides does tend to present speeches, opinions and evidence in binary pairings, but when Nicias, at 6.13, makes clear that party lines have formed around the young and the old, the difference of opinion based on experience, as set out in Book 2, has mutated into political age-factionalism.[55] Alcibiades doesn't let the accusation of youthful incompetence pass, retorting: 'so, in my youth and with this folly of mine which is supposed to be so prodigious, I found the right arguments for dealing with the power of the Peloponnesians' (6.17). Even more persuasively, he goes on to ask that the young/old distinctions be broken down, that, 'neither youth nor age can do anything one without the other' (6.18). This is an astute political move, and clinches the argument but, as Thucydides goes on to show, there are real undercurrents of intergenerational opposition ready to erupt into outright conflict. By the end of Book 6, Alcibiades is under suspicion for his involvement in the mutilation of the *Hermae*, and there is a general feeling of resentment towards young men who appear to have grown in number in the city and are thought to be involved in sacrilegious activities (6.26–8). The imminent Sicilian expedition would have offered a very timely release and redirection of aggression in Athens.[56] These speeches are mirrored by those taking place in Syracuse where age is again identified as a factor that shapes the political landscape. Athenagoras, comparable as a demagogue to Athens' Cleon, makes the case against youth clear, claiming that the young are not fit for office and have oligarchic tendencies (6.38–9). By the time news of the total annihilation of the Greek expeditionary force at Sicily reaches Athens, the political system in the city is on the brink of collapse.

The Athenian's first response is to appoint an advisory group, one that excludes young men, to oversee decision-making (8.1). This *Proboulē* had a minimum age requirement of 40,[57] emphasizing the shift of power away from the political factions of young men. The point is clear: the errors of the expedition, initiated by the fiery and youthful Alcibiades must be put right by the older, wiser generation. Experiencing unbearable external pressures, the survival of democracy at Athens becomes untenable and an oligarchy is established. A new 'council' of four hundred is self-appointed with the support of a group of so-called 'Hellenic youth' (*Hellenes neaniskoi*), which Thucydides presents as some sort of militia (8.69).[58] At this most crucial point in the history of Athens, an old form of generational relations reappears as the old in society use the young to inflict violence and bolster their political authority. Youth becomes a political instrument rather than a coalescence of political affiliation. Famously, Thucydides' work ends mid-sentence, unfinished, and Western literature misses out on a great historian's presentation of Athens' final defeat. However, an overall trajectory can still be traced for society's, or at least Thucydides', views of youth as the political crisis at Athens deepened. For much of the work, views of youth resemble those found in much archaic literature: the young are shown to be generally reckless but also encouraged to take part in dangerous military activities to prove their physical prowess. Youth's lack of experience results in the need to balance out their more rash tendencies with the sage advice of the older generation. Before the Sicilian expedition, something seems to change – in part, it seems, due to demographic changes in the city. The natural polarity between young and old has morphed into a formal political opposition with Alcibiades and Nicias representing generational units around which well-defined sets of attitudes have coalesced. Following the Sicilian expedition, and once Athens itself is under threat, youth come to be considered with greater suspicion, particularly for their perceived sympathies for oligarchy (the lack of textual sources for youth in oligarchic societies in the late fifth century is to be much regretted, but the nature of political systems means that it is only really in democracies that a full range of views on social factors has the potential to be heard. Oligarchies, like monarchies, do not tolerate open expression of dissent and as this often comes from young people it is not surprising that only the dominant voice is heard in these societies). And when there is full-blown stasis and political trauma, youth are presented as either belonging to secretive 'clubs' or roaming the city ready for trouble. Youth, from the perspective of Thucydides, is a key political factor in the war history of Athens. With the final years of the war corresponding with the decline in the production of new tragedy – and, I shall argue, the intensification of political presentations of young people by Euripides – a view can be formed of the empirical reality that tragedy reflected a society in which an art form, a political form and a set of constructions of the perceptions of youth combined in a final amplified set of plays.

And so to the other mass cultural forum of the period, old comedy, and exclusively that of Aristophanes as, apart from fragments, the works of all other ancient comic writers from the period have been lost. Aristophanes produced plays contemporaneously with many of the works of Sophocles and Euripides and they contain extremely fertile material for the analysis of themes relating to youth and politics. There are eleven surviving plays by the playwright, the majority of which were produced and performed during the latter third of the fifth century. Indeed, Comedy occupied the same dramatic space, being performed at the City Dionysia and Lenaea, as was tragedy. Moreover, Aristophanes incorporated much of the tragic genre into his work through parody, paratragedy and straightforward reuse of material.[59] And convincing arguments can be made for the genre's responsiveness to social and political factors.[60] Indeed, a detailed investigation of old comedy and Aristophanes' handling of youth would be of great value in triangulating societal views on youth in later fifth-century Athens. But with an unfortunate scholarly lacuna in this respect a necessarily superficial review of youth in Aristophanes appears to show well-worn negative characterizations of young people, particularly in their relationships with older generations. But such presentations go beyond those commonly found in archaic literature to show young men openly antagonistic towards their fathers, such as in *Birds* (1347–70) when the character Patraloias (literally father-killer) desires to strangle his father in order to inherit his wealth. This type of comedy-facilitating hyper-characterization is found throughout Aristophanes and no more so than in his drawing of youth. In *Clouds*, the working-class father Strepsiades both denounces the sympotic activities of the elite, to which his son aspires, whilst demanding that he be taught by a sophist in order to become rich (in the play's parodic stichomythia, Aristophanes also draws on tragic conventions and the role of sophists for comic effect). And towards the play's end we again see acts of violence, in this case realized, on the father by the son (1321–44). Thus, relationships between young and old in Aristophanes appear to be defined by conflict, and yet comedy was well known to amplify to ironic extremes normative views, making the use of Aristophanes in determining social conditions and attitudes very problematic. One can only hope that future research on youth in classical literature includes a rigorous analysis on Aristophanes' work.

Apart from the philosophical, historical and fictive sources, a great deal of evidence of views on youth in society can be found in other textual and extra-textual material, particularly oratory, biography and epigraphy. However, there are some limitations to the use of such sources, most obviously the lack of temporal proximity to tragedy. With the exceptions of Antiphon, Andocides and Lysias, almost all the orators for which we have extant sources (Isaeus, Demosthenes, Hyperides, Aeschines, etc.) were working rather later than the tragedians, in the fourth century. The earliest surviving biographies, by Isocrates and Xenophon, are also fourth-century works. As is the *Constitution of Athens* attributed to Aristotle. Rather than analyse these texts in detail, I simply refer to them in the course of the argument when data they preserve are relevant. Many of these sources are excellently summarized in

Dover's ground-breaking (1974) *Greek Popular Morality*, which covers roughly the 420s BCE to the 320s. Dover dedicates a whole section to the various attitudes of ancient sources to age, but he suggests an uninterrupted continuity of attitudes towards young men unaltered by political influence on social constructions, whereas I suggest that popular conceptions were much less stable as the fifth century progressed.[61] In the case of epigraphical records, I cannot assay an analysis of all remaining fifth-century Athenian inscriptions in *Inscriptiones Graecae*, however worthwhile a study of the language used about age groups in this medium would be (very). But the sort of social and familial history which both oratory and epigraphy so usefully document has, fortunately, been scrutinized in several works which paint revealing prosopographical pictures of key aspects of life in the Athenian polis, which are very useful for understanding the background to the tragedians' presentation of social relationships. The two most important here are Davies's (1971) *Athenian Propertied Families* and Whitehead's (1986) *The Demes of Attica*. Davies's work on the 'liturgical class' is massively useful on a number of counts. First, the overall picture offered of Athenian society is one in which powerful families can retain huge economic and political power over many generations. The families of key fifth-century figures, such as Callias, Demosthenes, Pericles and Critias appear to maintain huge, sometimes astronomical, amounts of wealth over hundreds of years and the evidence suggests that this economic power was, as a matter of routine, converted into political power by the requirement that these families provide a trireme or fund a dithyramb or theatrical performance, all activities that would give some form of political advantage over those who could not afford ostentatious public displays. What is especially interesting is that, even with the institution of ostracism, many of these families kept hold of their power and influence in fluctuating political times: the *Realpolitik* of democracy or oligarchy appears to have had limited impact on the politico-economic power of amassed and inherited wealth. But the generational flow of wealth does sometimes come to an end, with death, misfortune, war or sometimes plain ineptitude. In this respect, one wayward young man could jeopardize the entire family legacy. Cumulatively, a generation of young men from the established families, unwilling to accept the old ways, could endanger the entire edifice of interconnected power and influence. But they would also present a stark and constant reminder of the real power that lay behind the machinery of democracy. Then, as now, class was intergenerational. The political responses to family identity and influence are discussed extensively in Whitehead in relation to the *deme*.

It is clear that the reforms by Cleisthenes at the end of the sixth century – the restructuring of political organization – contributed towards the weakening of political power of wealthy families, but only to a point at first. Discussing Cimon, Whitehead concedes that, in the mid-fifth century at least, political authority via local kinship power was still achievable.[62] Later in the century, personal political skill, rather than economic power, appears to have been a more important factor in election to important political office.[63] In relation to political power and youth, the shifting of influence away from hierarchical family lines to lateral community cohorts is reminiscent of Mannheim's theory of generational units (see the Introductory chapter). The breakdown of the hierarchical-familial political primacy of family in favour of locality-based politics would suggest that influence would first of all be sought amongst peer groups, rather than kin groups. Naturally, this would lead to stratified political groups defined by common features, of which age is an evident category in Thucydides. With this sort of political revolution (or *neōterizein*) in mind, discussion now turns to the plays themselves, beginning with the Aeschylean *Prometheus*.

Intergenerational Conflict in the Aeschylean *Prometheus*

Prometheus is a play that has long provided a challenge to those who struggle to reconcile its characters' actions with Aeschylus' supposed piety, and indeed its allegedly 'anomalous' theology is one of the main arguments deployed by those who doubt that Aeschylus wrote it.[1] Regardless, it is a fascinating play, one which contains many semantic clusters of terms associated with justice, authority and *stasis* in its 1,100 or so lines. The overall impression is of a play that is a product of the general Athenian imaginative and political milieu of the mid-fifth century, and profoundly political.[2] Such terms are directly reflective of the play's themes, most clearly in the discussion of Zeus' so-called tyranny. It could quite easily be concluded that if a single subject of the play needed to be identified it would be the discussion of the political nature of Zeus' rule; and yet there is another major theme in the play: intergenerational conflict. While this concept has been widely discussed by scholars in their commentaries, it has most often been in relation to the Ouranos/Kronos/Zeus generational succession that forms part of the Hesiodic cosmology from which the play draws its inspiration. The political presentation of tyranny as a dramatic theme has not yet been fully explored within a wider social framework of relations between young and established members of ancient Greek society. By discussing the political theme in the play in a vacuum, isolating it from its social contexts, previous scholars' analyses of the speeches of the characters have found it difficult to achieve consistency of interpretation. This chapter will attempt to begin to re-address these problems by demonstrating how the political in the play, i.e. the concept of tyranny, is intimately related to the movement of power *between* generations, evident through the play's use of language associated with youth, a major source of tension between generations in contemporary Greek society.

To understand properly how generational factors influence the descriptions of Zeus in the play, it's crucial that we gain familiarity with the mythology of how he came to rule, as well as how he is judged to wield that power. The 'newness' of Zeus' regime, signified by the use of *neos* and its cognates (such as at 149–50) enhances his tyrannical appearance as the violent conflict of the mythologically proximate Titanomachy of Hesiod echoes through the play's speeches. But *neos* can also be translated as 'young', fixing the play in generational as well as mythic sequential terms.[3] And the characterization of Prometheus can be interpreted as intrinsically oppositional to that of Zeus, as he becomes increasingly associated with, if not loyal to, the defeated generation of Titans, reinforcing the tyrannical nature of Zeus' new rule. There are other features of the play that enhance the sense of intergenerational difference. The links between new technologies (especially Zeus' thunderbolt), for example, cause further reflection on 'newness' as a feature of tyranny, conflict and the passing of power between generations.[4]

The play builds from a reworking of a myth that – as far as the textual record shows, since oral tradition on the subject predating Hesiod's eighth-century work has not survived – was first systematically recorded in Hesiod's *Theogony*. This is the rise to power of Zeus, his overthrowing of the Titans and his anger at Prometheus for his trickery and deceit. Throughout the *Theogony* the predominant theme is inter-familial strife: between father Kronos and son Zeus, between older Titans and younger Olympians and between the authority of Zeus and the insubordination of his older cousin Prometheus. The 'Succession Myth'[5] and aspects of the Prometheus/Zeus relationship are subsequently redefined by a changed genealogical background of Prometheus in the play. In Hesiod, Prometheus is the son of Iapetos, a first-generation Titan, and the Oceanid Clymene, of the second generation (*Theogony*, 507–12). The family history is rewritten in *Prometheus* and the protagonist claims direct descent from Themis who, he states, is the same divinity as Gaia.[6] Assuming he bears the same paternity as in Hesiod, this places him much more centrally in the Titan genealogy by virtue of birth to a primordial mother and first-generation Titan father.[7] This change also places Prometheus centrally within the play's account of the Titanomachy, the battle between Olympians and Titans, as a major protagonist and traitor against his brotherly combatants, and heightens the intergenerational aspect of his relationship with Zeus. More broadly, the modified presentation of the conflict between Olympians and Titans frames Prometheus' account of his role within the Titanomachy in *Prometheus* as an illustration of '... the vicissitudes, the changing circumstances, of cosmic politics'.[8] The effect on the presentation of Prometheus is to show him as being defined by political events that are inextricably linked to power relations between generations, and in particular his place in a sequence of 'tyrannical' episodes of divine power transfer. Some other features of the Hesiodic story of Prometheus are retained by Aeschylus who innovates a more expansive rendering of the Titanomachy than found in Hesiod. Much greater prominence is given to the aspects of Prometheus' actions that relate to mortals, including speeches on the implications of Zeus' revenge for humans, and the tragedian brings to the fore Prometheus' motivations for assisting humankind. However, where Hesiod frames his language with positive evaluative terms when including Zeus,[9] the much more negative presentation of the god in *Prometheus* continues to provoke much scholarly debate.

One argument, that 'newness' is the primary defining factor in perceptions of Zeus' character and his rule, clearly supports the view that intergenerational conflict is a primary political theme.[10] Likewise, it has been argued that while Zeus' actions may be unpalatable they are at least understandable within the context of political struggle. Yet this is a rare example of the analysis of political or social context rather than pure literary context when interpreting Prometheus' speeches.[11] Both views show how a more nuanced evaluation of Zeus can be developed that fixes the characterization within a wider material context – that is, a producing culture that had complex views on intergenerational relations and political power. Complicating this argument is the fact that many Athenians would have considered 'innovation' to be an important part of their self-definition and that there would have been an unusual tolerance for the new at Athens of the period. D'Angour correctly contrasts the use of *neos* in *Prometheus* with that in Sophocles' *Antigone* to demonstrate the various dramatic presentations of new regimes. But neither play offers an uncomplicated view of new rulers and both problematize popular conceptualizations of the ideal form of generational relationships, perhaps refracting the various tensions associated with youth and politics evident in contemporary Athens.[12]

For all the debate on issues of presentation and authorship, intergenerational conflict *is* embedded within the personal mythology of Zeus' rise to power. The opening lines of the prologue, delivered by Kratos (literally 'power'), offer an immediate view of Zeus as a political power, one holding authority and issuing orders for punishment in revenge for insubordination:

> We have come to a remote region of the world, to the land of Skythia, uninhabited, a desert. Hephaistos, you must follow the instructions given you by father Zeus, to bolt this criminal to a lofty cliff with bonds hard as adamant that cannot be broken. For it was your glory, fire's blaze, basis of every craft, that he stole and gave to mortals; For such a crime he must pay a penalty to the gods, So that he may be taught to love Zeus's Tyranny, and stop his human loving ways (1–11).[13]

This is an oddly negative description of Zeus as tyrant and belies a number of underlying complications in relation to the transfer of power from one generation to another. As the mute figure of Bia (violence) stands by menacingly, Kratos threatens that Prometheus will be taught to love Zeus' tyranny (10–11). While some consider this an 'oxymoron, if not a contradiction'[14] we must be careful not to foreground our modern understanding of tyranny, thereby diminishing our appreciation of the semantic nuance the term would have had for Aeschylus' original audience. The various angles at which interpretation of the initial understanding of Zeus' character could be approached are indicative of multiple interpretations of the play's language.[15] While the potential for different interpretations is already clear, the repeated use of the term 'tyranny' and its cognates, which occur a total of thirteen times during the play, is significant. All but one refer directly to Zeus[16] and clearly frame the opening speeches within a political, rather than personal, context, particularly as the term tyranny is applied by a member of the new regime.[17] In some ways, the attempts to assign primacy to the centrality of Aeschylus' play to either the context of the experience of a new regime or a personal, almost familial feud misses the point. These two views can be combined if instead we consider the new regime as a new generation, effectively an extended family defined by their genealogical proximity to Zeus. Tyranny, in this setting, is something experienced as a process in the shift of power, in this case from an established generation to a newer one.

At this point it is valuable to widen the discussion of the concept of tyranny from *Prometheus* to its more general ancient context, as the term is used extensively in the play and is open to a variety of interpretations. The modern semantic range for tyranny is much narrower than that of the fifth century BCE, and even then, the meaning had only just begun to change from purely descriptive to primarily pejorative.[18] When considering the use of 'tyranny' by Herodotus and other later ancient scholars (such as the author or authors of the problematic '*Suda*') a convincing backdrop is produced for a growing association between Medism and tyranny that would eventually lead to the glossing of tyranny as a kind of orientalized despotism.[19] Unfortunately, the realities of everyday usage of the term in mid-fifth-century Greece cannot satisfactorily be recovered, and it is uncertain as to how the ancient audience would have interpreted the meaning as in Aeschylus' plays. But Athens had experienced tyranny in her recent history and the rule of the Peisistratos' family – relatively benign rule established by force of character until a collapse into paranoia – must have resonated as a strong cultural memory well into the following century. And Aeschylus is known to have produced tragedies for Hieron I, 'tyrant' of Syracuse, when invited to Sicily in the 470s, providing a close personal encounter with this type of political system. Quite possibly the term was not yet anchored semantically to a negative set of stereotypes, although perhaps it was increasingly suggestive of a non-democratic, foreign-influenced intervention.[20] However, some scholars have gone so far as to suggest that tyranny, in the sense of a form of government rather than a general experience, could have been considered a positive intervention when the new regime replaced a decaying or corrupt monarchy or aristocracy.[21] Tyranny has also been considered as a justifiable response to a form of gang behaviour, the mafia-like rule of eighth- and seventh-century BCE ruling clans necessitating a violent overthrow,[22] and this would reinforce the potential for cycles of tyrannical shifts in power between generations. The point that emerges, albeit qualified by an ongoing refinement of the concept, is that in some way the use of violence to overthrow a regime and to replace it with another may not always have been tyrannical in the modern sense for the *poleis*' inhabitants and may have been at times the only way in which power could have been seized by one section of society from another.[23] But such transitions would undoubtedly be traumatic, the familiarity of one system replaced by the uncertainty of an as yet untested new form of political rule. Likewise, as each new generation emerges there is uncertainty as to what characteristics will define them.

The use of the term *neos* in *Prometheus* has a clear duality of purpose, to signify the tensions bound up in the emergence of new political factions and young generational cohorts. Tyranny has thus been abundantly discussed in relation to the concept's broad political application, but as we have already seen there is an experiential aspect to the concept. Tyranny can be viewed as partly political, as rule that is un- or extra- constitutional[24] and partly the result of a pathological aggressive aspiration to rule.[25] In this light, tyranny is both a psychological state and a political classification, neither of which is inherently negative except when compared with competing political systems, or idealized psychologies. This bipartite form, part psycho-sociological, part political, fuses via cultural forms, in this case the form of tragedy, into a concept with an extraordinarily wide associative field. But the psychological characteristics that have been associated with tyranny appear to match those frequently associated with a younger generation. As we have seen in the archaic sources, as well as those relatively contemporary to fifth-century tragedy, intolerance and a desire for conflict are traits associated with young men, and eagerness for conflict is well attested in Thucydides (especially 2.8, 2.11 and 6.12).[26] Literary and historical representations of characters such as Alcibiades present, perhaps, a paradigm of the young would-be tyrant. In tragedy the pairing of tyrannical rule and youthful psychological tendencies has also been identified, most clearly in the case of Pentheus in *Bacchae*.[27] The psychological conditions that act as enablers to tyranny within a tragic character appear to be linked to both youth and the opposition to older or fading authority, aspects that are clearly present in *Prometheus* but have hitherto been considered in terms of 'newness' rather than 'youth'.

In *Prometheus*, the characterization of Zeus fits this overall picture of tyranny well. Zeus' new regime is achieved through singular ambition to power (the pathological), is presented by some characters as reckless in the violence used to suppress opposition to his authority (the youth-like psychological) and results in extra-constitutional rule of heaven and earth (the political). In this light, Zeus is not so much the remorseless autocrat as the unpredictable, vengeful and intemperate young overlord. Aeschylus gives us not just the 'shock of the new' but the 'tyranny of the young'. Such is the centrality of tyranny to Athens' own mythology and political history that when language related to tyranny is deployed in *Prometheus*, it would be possible to consider the term to have a transformative impact on all related themes and concepts in the play, transmuting the social issue of intergenerational conflict into political form. From the prologue onwards the political tyranny of Zeus' actions is closely linked with the rise of an unstoppable new regime. But there is a dissenting voice within the Olympian camp, that of Hephaistos. It is through this character's speeches that the issue of generational loyalty is first raised. In contrast to the unqualified hostility evinced towards Prometheus by Kratos, the figure of Hephaistos appears much more sympathetic to Prometheus' plight. Whilst undertaking his task of binding Prometheus to the rock he commiserates with his charge, saying, 'But I can't bring myself to bind by force a god, my kinsman, to this stormy chasm' (14–5). This passage is curious as an open display of discontent with Zeus' actions by one of his own, particularly in light of the presence of the enforcers, Bia and Kratos. Even stranger, the genealogical address of Prometheus that Hephaestus then makes (18) explicitly places him amongst the Titans as son of Themis, and not of an Olympian (Themis, as has already been discussed, is later aligned with Gaia by Prometheus himself). The notion of kinsman, *syggenē*, cannot mean genealogical affiliation, and some have suggested that instead the term is used in reference to the two characters' similar technical background in myth and the corollary of their cultic associations in religious ritual activity.[28]

That Hephaistos recognizes the painful humiliation resultant from Zeus' wrath should be of no surprise. Homeric reworking of Olympian mythology also shows the god similarly experiencing exile and torment as a result of insubordination.[29] Hephaistos is also an outcast amongst the gods, his physical imperfections marking him as inferior to his divine peers.[30] Such similarities then may go some way in explaining the use of the term 'kinsman' as one with a shared experience. The effect is to encourage reflection on what it means to have allegiance to another, should it be along the lines of personal sympathy or familial (or, more broadly, genealogical) bonds, or indeed by generation or some other form of relationship (indicated by Hephaistos' use of *homilia*, companionship or close association, at 49). The highlighting of Prometheus' exclusion from and by the generation in power by another former victim of the new regime (but one who was brought back into the fold) also refocuses our attention on Prometheus' former relationship with the Olympians, in that he was never truly one of them in the way it counts most, i.e. by birth.

Hephaistos' powerful speech, predicting the torments the Titan will suffer ('baked by the sun's bright flame, your skin's bloom will wither') (22–3) is reiterated in the passage's final lines, 'Many laments and useless moans you'll utter, for Zeus' heart cannot be swayed: for everyone fresh to power is harsh' (33–5). This final line echoes the speech's opening, where Kratos affirmed Zeus' reign as tyrannical in respect of its newness. Later commentators have used the remarks in Aristotle's *Rhetoric* that argue, 'the young and wealthy are given to insults; for they think that, in committing them, they are showing their superiority' (2.2.6) to suggest *hubris*, the subject of Aristotle's comments, as a character trait of youth.[31] Yet this is not entirely straightforward. There have been lengthy discussions as to the exact meaning of the term in classical Greece and, although precise usage appears tied to individual context, the term is generally seen to encapsulate a form of physical and/or verbal shame-causing self-assertion of superiority through dishonouring of a victim. However, *hubris* has also been widely associated by scholars with arrogance and rashness of character. Fisher surveys *hubris* in Aristotle's *Rhetoric*, which casts it as partly driven by excessive action, a state commonly ascribed to youth (as well, it could be said, as a facilitating action in the assertion of a new regime) before discussing the wider views on hubristic youth in Athenian society.[32] It would seem that once one reached full maturity, *hubris* had much more serious consequences, in that it was closely linked to reducing the status, political or otherwise, of the insulted. It appears likely, then, that there would have been an overlap between popular conceptualizations of youth and *hubris* (as these negative traits, arrogance and rashness, are often associated with youth), and that there is often an aim, conscious or otherwise, of achieving some sort of superiority over the target for insult that would also fit naturally with the actions of a new regime.

Kratos' response is to cajole Hephaistos into action, first by indirect threats ('. . . how can you turn a deaf ear to Father's word. Aren't you afraid of that?'; 40–1), before he adopts a more conciliatory tone, saying, 'everything's a burden – except lordship over the gods. Because no one is free except Zeus' (49–50). Swiftly, though, his menacing nature returns as he warns, 'Hurry, won't you, in putting chains around him. So father won't see you taking time off' (52–3). The warning is suggestive of a childlike tempestuousness as possessed by Zeus, a stubborn refusal of reason or empathy that Aristotle would comment on years later. The figures of Bia and Kratos are presented in a wholly negative light, as henchmen of Zeus and concerned with nothing but administering Zeus' brutal retribution. Such intimidating figures have appeared elsewhere in Aeschylean work, such as the Egyptian Herald in *Suppliants* (lines 881–4 in particular). The violent agencies of Bia and Kratos map closely on to the 'irresoluble antagonism'[33] that the herald of *Suppliants* is central in sustaining. In an aggressive, cruel manner Kratos prefaces Prometheus' opening monologue: 'Here, now, show insolence (hubris)! Plunder the gods' prerogatives!' (82–3), inviting Prometheus to attempt the impossible and break his adamantine chains. This vicious taunt fails to impose any moral superiority and is another example of the Aristotelian view of insult as an attempt to assert authority. There appears hypocrisy in the hubristic accusation of hubris by this supernatural being, a statement of irrationality and rhetorical illogicality reminiscent of the normative perception of spiteful insults of youth. More importantly, this hubristic utterance by Kratos can be considered reflective of the sentiment of most of the new regime and be considered directed towards the entire older generation of gods and Titans.[34] In this sense, the closing speech of Kratos is characteristic of the new divine order: aggressive, liable to insult and to physically intimidate.

The evolving presentation of Prometheus' character so far has been via third party speeches and through existing audience expectations; his muteness greatly increasing the dramatic impact of his opening speech. Prometheus is not just outcast politically (in terms of the loss of power and prestige after the Titanomachy) but also socially (by his exclusion from the society of gods) and his muteness can also be seen as expressive of the inability to articulate political dissent in the new regime: any articulation of opposition can only take place outside of the dominant discourse, shaped and represented on stage by the agents of the new power. Both the political and social fabric of the divine planes have been reformed and voices belonging to the older generation have been marginalized. 'Look on me, a god, how the gods make me suffer . . .' (92), implores the chained Prometheus: '. . . such disgraceful bondage the new ruler (*neos tagos*, this phrase could equally be translated as 'youthful ruler') of the blessed gods devised for me!' (96–7). Immediately, Prometheus introduces the moral quality (or lack of) of Zeus' authority and Aeschylus' precise use of language, using the term *aikeiaisin*, frames the speech within a legal lexicon.[35]

Not only are Zeus' moral actions measured against the moral judgements of Prometheus but also against those of the wider society of the divine. The chief arbiter of justice is thus labelled unjust. Prometheus' speech is full of regret for his circumstances, anger and defiance of Zeus' actions. His plaintive cries are sharply curtailed with a sudden realization of: 'Yet, what am I saying? I have clear and thorough knowledge of all that is to come; no unexpected misery will come to me' (101–3).

This section is notable for a number of reasons. Prometheus' *volte face* from weary dejection to rugged determination following the revelation of his prophetic powers has important implications. First, it suggests that Prometheus is no simple figure of stoic godly defiance. He is almost mortal-like in his intellectual and emotional inconsistency. Second, the very sudden recollection of his prophetic powers demonstrates the limited effectiveness of this skill.[36] Indeed, for the mythic material and dramatic action in the play to combine effectively, his prophecy must be faulty or at least limited in scope of temporal reach. The alternative suggestion is that Prometheus knew the full consequences of his actions and that he would be tormented by Zeus as a result of his indulgence of mankind. To trick Zeus and suffer the results, even with mankind benefiting, and to be conscious of the results would suggest a masochistic pathology that would be unlikely to appeal to an ancient Greek audience. It is more likely the case that Prometheus' fallibility as a prophet was redrawn by Aeschylus to present a highly sympathetic picture of a god not entirely in control of his own destiny. Indeed, we are presented with a character of defiant stubbornness, a trait, as we shall see, that would have been associated with the old when set in opposition to the flightiness of youth, such as in Aristophanes and particularly later in Menander. Furthermore, his prophetic abilities are also associated with older members of society. In tragedy the most obvious representation of the 'old seer' is Tiresias. In Euripides' *Bacchae*, for example, Tiresias is not just a typical old seer but his age and foresight are in direct opposition to youth and lack of perspicacity of the young Pentheus.[37] His durability in tragedy and fullness of characterization appear determined by the common association of prophecy with the old, and old men in particular (with the very obvious exception of oracles).

More characters then arrive on stage as the chorus come into view uttering soothing words and revealing themselves to be Ocean nymphs: 'Do not be

afraid: our loving band has raced to this rock with a rapid rush of wing'
(129–30). To emphasize the composition of the chorus Prometheus responds
'Aah! Children of Tethys who had many offspring and of your father Oceanus'
(136–8). Aeschylus' use of genealogy here not only places the chorus within the
mythic context of the play but also allies the chorus to a generation of gods
that pre-dates the Olympians.[38] Generationally aligned, the characters on stage
are free to voice their opinions of the new regime and this starts almost
immediately: '. . . new (*neoi*) steersmen hold power on Olympos and with laws
that are new (*neochmois*) Zeus wields power unlawfully' (149–50) claim the
Oceanids, reflecting the legal terms used in Prometheus' opening monologue
and deploying *neo*-stemmed words twice to signal newness and youthfulness.
The legitimacy of Zeus' rule is questioned in technical, moral and age-related
terms. The chorus' final line in the first antistrophe is telling: 'Those who had
strength before he is now annihilating' (151). Clearly referring to Kronos, the
Oceanids selectively omit to acknowledge that the same crime of which they
accuse Zeus was committed by Kronos against his own father Ouranos. Just as
Prometheus has damned the rule of Zeus as 'new or young', the chorus provide
a similar condemnation on the basis of 'newness or youthfulness'. Commentators
have supported the view of the chorus here by stating how Zeus can be nothing
more than a tyrant and questioning the god's 'legitimacy to issue binding
nomoi'.[39] In narrow legal and *mortal* terms this is a reasonable judgement but,
as discussed above, there is a divine tradition in myth of rule by force with no
other legitimate form of gaining power. The Oceanids support a former regime
that by their own terms would be equally as 'tyrannical' as Zeus'. This shows
their case, and so that of Prometheus, to be at least in part self-interested and
factional. Comparison can be made with the parodos in *Eumenides*, where
similar accusations are made by the Erinyes against the new generation of gods
which could be interpreted as carrying age-based accusations: 'These new gods
(*neōteroi theoi*), this is how they behave, their power exceeds the bounds of
justice' (162–3). In this instance, the chorus of Erinyes are depicted in a negative
way and yet their accusation is the same as that of the Oceanids. Prometheus
appears as a willing participant in this exchange, lamenting his fate in a
decidedly unheroic way: '. . . I am a pathetic plaything of the breezes . . .' (158).[40]
His suffering is clearly appreciated by the factional pre-Olympian chorus who
respond: 'What god could be so hard hearted as to enjoy this . . .' (160–1) as a

preamble to the lines that come next and which are startlingly oppositional to Zeus and directly confrontational:

> Zeus; with inflexible purpose he vengefully suppresses the race of Titans sprung from Ouranos, and will not stop until his heart is sated or someone uses a trick to snatch from him the empire so hard to capture (164–7).

Again, the chorus look back favourably on the Titans and this time leave no ambiguity as to their partial conception of tyranny. Ouranos is mentioned by name, the very deity first overthrown by his own son. The chorus' final words appear to exhort others to 'trick' Zeus' authority from him, a course of action surely tantamount to tyranny by the chorus' own definition of the importance of a quasi-legal basis to rule and authority. Podlecki points out that '*palame*', 'trick', means literally 'palm of the hand' – a phrase associated with violent actions – and that in Pindar the phrase appears meaning 'hand of the gods'.[41] While Podlecki sees this phrase thus to 'demonstrate negative testimony regarding Zeus from a neutral witness', quite plainly the chorus, genealogically bound to the older generation of Titans, including Prometheus, are far from neutral. The sum effect is to show the chorus' bias towards the former, older generation via opposition to the current one, a formula already played out cosmologically in Zeus' elevation to status of ruler and that of Kronos before him. Applying the chorus' logic to themselves, they can only object to the fact that Zeus rules, rather than the nature of his rise to power or execution of authority thereof. Regardless of the illogicality of the chorus' statement, their speech appears to simply reiterate that the transfer of power amongst the divine can only be accomplished through violent means. Perhaps encouraged by the chorus' support, Prometheus engages his prophetic skills to predict that Zeus will later need his assistance, help that will 'rob him [Zeus] of his sceptre and prerogatives' (171). The tone of Prometheus' speech then changes to reveal his wily and stubborn character, the reason for his punishment, as the insult of Zeus' actions bites: 'I know that he is harsh and keeps his own kind of justice. Still, I think his intent will someday be softened when he is smashed in the way I said' (186–9). Prometheus' fear has dissipated and he even takes up the language his enemies have used to insult him when he says that Zeus will be smashed.[42]

By contrast to his daughters, Oceanus, appearing after Prometheus' account of the Titanomachy (284–397), appears fearful of offending Zeus throughout his speech. While it is true that he too refers to Zeus as a tyrant who as 'a harsh monarch wields power, without controls' (324), Oceanus offers reconciliation with the new regime rather than commiseration or sympathy. But the Titan's arrival provokes Prometheus into reflection on the punishments of their fellow Titans, and in particular Atlas and Typhon (340–76). By expanding the scope of Zeus' vengefulness, Prometheus focuses on what has been lost by his siblings and the generational isolation in which Oceanus now finds himself. The view of Oceanus in this scene as a 'dull, foolish and ineffectual old man'[43] sums up the fate of those not yet outcast but on the margins of power following the destruction of their generational support.

The combination of Kratos' insults and Prometheus' stubborn victimhood provides a picture of youthful bullies menacing a wise (or wily) but weaker older person, a scenario played out repeatedly in Greek comedy. In particular, this popular view abounds in the comic plays of the fifth and fourth centuries and is articulated most clearly in the fully extant plays of Aristophanes and most likely in *Banqueters*, if the fragments are an adequate indication.[44] Later, plays by Menander offer similar representations of popular conceptions of intergenerational strife.[45] For all the ubiquity of such scenes of youthful rebellion, it must be remembered that such presentations are unswervingly damning of the inversion of ordinary power relations. Normal social structures are always reasserted at the play's close: men controlling women and the old controlling the young. The comedy in such scenes as the parricide's desire to strangle his father in Aristophanes' *Birds* is in the corruption of the *nomoi* of Athenian life, just as in the reality reversed political decision-making by women in *Lysistrata*, or the abolition of private property in *Ecclesiazusae*. Such scenes are comic because they acknowledge the very slim potential for change in society without actually reflecting real world societal shifts. Aristophanes seems especially concerned with youths of *ephebic* age rather than childhood and the use of characters that are young men on the verge of adult political enfranchisement allows the exploitation of many social anxieties towards youth and the inevitable drift of power from one generation to the next. As identified in the 1980s,[46] *ephebic* ritual appears to have at its core the exploration of values and behaviours in opposition to the adult world of which the ritual's initiates are about to become a part. Although caution must be applied to any theorizing that is underpinned by reference to the *ephēbia*, evidence for which is fragmentary at best and generally unreliable for the fifth century, conflict does appear to be embedded within the transitional phases through a person's ages. However, in Aeschylus' dramatic world, Prometheus and the gods do not have some absolute age but are compared to each in order of genesis.

At a poetic, mythical level, the very essence of being is laid out in generation-like segments in Hesiod's 'Ages of Man' in *Works and Days*.[47] This passage clearly outlines the inevitability of transitions from generation to generation until conflict between children and parents appears as the defining characteristic of life in the present, the Hesiodic Iron Age, the period of Aeschylus' authorship. The sense of a general deterioration over time appears to be applied metaphysically, socially and politically and so it is not surprising that the combination of themes of generational conflict and tyranny form a presentation of a youthful and new regime in a negative light. There is a sense, then, that tyranny is linked to youth and the tyrannical to youthful recklessness. Even the legendary 'tyrant killers' Harmodius and Aristogiton were judged by Thucydides to have acted recklessly, due in part to the dishonour that the young Harmodius' sister suffered, thus causing a truer and more frightening tyranny to be visited upon later sixth-century Athens.[48] Prometheus' role in bringing about an end to the tyranny of the Titans (i.e. Kronos' violent overthrowing of Ouranus), reflects this cycle of a tyranny replaced by another tyranny. Later, in Xenophon, the view is expressed that the concept of tyranny – that is, in its psychological form (i.e. the ruthless aspiration to power) – was a legitimate pedagogical discourse, and thus associated with those brought up under the tutoring of sophists. Xenophon's *Hiero*, for example, could have been used as useful instruction for young would-be tyrants. And in Xenophon's *Memorabilia* the ancient author makes the suggestion that Socrates' downfall was in part due to his teaching about tyranny.[49] Of course, Xenophon had his own axe to grind, given his exile from Athens, and cannot be considered to reflect typical Athenian thought. But his views reflect, at least, part of a recognizable Athenian discourse. Thus, the early exchanges in the play between Hephaistos, Kratos and Prometheus include the use of language that can be considered closely associated with normative descriptions of youth.

But it is at the end of the play, as we have it, that the most explicit use of language to define the actions of the generation of Olympians in terms of youth is found. Most starkly, the exchange between Hermes and Prometheus unfolds in a sequence of stichomythic insults reminiscent of the interplay between Strepsiades and Pheidippides in *Clouds*. From Hermes' opening address of the Titan, 'you there, sophist' (944), Prometheus replies, showing none of his earlier taciturnity when insulted by Kratos, 'Very elevated and full of fiery spirit your talk is as befits the gods' lackey. You are young, young in power' (953–5). The repetition of young (*neon, neoi*), also used in line 960 (*neous*) emphasizes Prometheus' seniority over Hermes and makes unfavourable comparison obvious between the Olympian's characteristics and normative ones associated with youth, such as the intemperance suggested in line 953. The insults continue and by 982 the youth-defined language is even more emphatic. Prometheus, like a world-weary old man, condescends to say, 'But time as it grows old teaches everything', provoking, amongst continuing insults, Hermes' accusation, 'why, you're mocking me as a child!' (986). The Titan's reply could not be clearer, or more categorical 'Well, aren't you a child, or even stupider than one?' (987). Hermes' barely suppressed rage shortly after erupts into exactly the kind of youthful hubris of which his generation of Olympians has been accused (1007–35).[50] The presentation of a new tyrannical regime acting like young tyrants could not be clearer.

A widespread scholarly view has been to consider Prometheus as a victim unjustly persecuted by Zeus, a hyper-authoritarian figure portrayed by Aeschylus in a deeply unsympathetic manner. The speeches of *Prometheus* at first sight appear to support this view. But the presentation of the god can be considered to show not a consistently stoic figure but a flawed character, whose mythological background is largely revealed only via the self-interested speeches of the protagonist himself or those aligned to him and his fellow Titans by generation or genealogy. The most obvious difference between Prometheus' retelling of the Titanomachy and that in *Theogony* is the very absence/presence of Prometheus. In Hesiod it is the Hecatoncheires who sway the battle in the Olympians' favour. There is absolutely no mention of Prometheus whatsoever, and at lines 697–731 Hesiod describes the hundred-handed daemons as hurling the defeated Titans to Tartaros. Second, in the *Theogony* there are multiple and consistent references to the benevolence of Zeus, not just to the honours he promises to bestow (although this is also included); and this justness of character appears to galvanize the other gods (such as at 655–60). The second part of Prometheus' speech is also a stark departure from the mythological textual record, regarding his relationship with mortals. Not in *Theogony*, not *Works and Days*, not in any Homeric works nor in Plato's *Protagoras* is found the striking claim that Prometheus next makes. Zeus, he claims, 'wanted to annihilate the entire race (of mortals)' but 'I prevented humans from being smashed to bits', resulting in Prometheus being 'mercilessly brought into line, a sight disgraceful to Zeus' (232–41). However, such a clear departure from the known mythology also suggests a characterization of Prometheus that communicates a tragic element of the protagonist: a once powerful and respected deity whose personal mistake, his refusal to defer to any leader, leads inevitably to catastrophe. Generationally, 'not fitting in' is tacit opposition to the values of the group of newly powerful Olympians and thus a challenge to the new hegemony. The speeches by Hephaistos, fearful yet damning of Zeus' actions, are oddly familial and yet the Olympian and the Titan are associated by occupation only. The reason for the closeness of the relationship may be found instead in Hephaistos' own earlier persecution by Zeus: he shares in a brotherhood of torment. Aeschylus' modification of the Hesiodic version of the Titanomachy, or at least the one that he has Prometheus deliver, is stark in the absolute centrality that Prometheus claims to have played in the Olympian's victory. The impression given is that Prometheus' actions and pitiful speech are designed to heighten the alleged injustice he has experienced and to distract from the generational betrayal of which he is guilty.

At many points his speeches verge on hubris, a fact many scholars seem to acknowledge but fail to include in their final summing up in moral favour of his victimhood, perhaps because the objects of his hubris, Zeus and his cohort, are presented in a consistently negative light. And yet Zeus, by proxy, does appear to behave in a vicious and disproportionate way towards Prometheus. His presentation by Aeschylus seems at odds with a typically Aeschylean characterization of the gods (which in turn has led to questions of authorship). This interpretation has been driven in part by the inclusion, in parts of Prometheus' and other characters' speeches, of the word 'tyrant' to describe Zeus. Although it is true that Kratos himself describes Zeus' rule as a 'tyranny', the uncritical glossing of this word by translators and scholarly commentators without acknowledging the semantic range covered by the term in Aeschylus' time contributed to the coalescence of the 'Zeus problem' in academic discussion of the play: the supposed incompatibility of the god's characterization when measured against the piety of the tragedian.[51] It surely appears to be the case that Prometheus' special relationship with mortals in text and visual art forms has encouraged later, favourable, responses to the literary character in the ancient Greek theatrical text. The acceptance of Prometheus' and the chorus' use of the term tyranny has resulted in a failure to tackle the question of how else Zeus would have come to power in the heavens other than by using violence or trickery. Prometheus and his cohort's bemoaning of Zeus' ruthless ambition is an empty piece of moralizing: violent succession appears to be the only form of celestial succession while the hypocritical moral rectitude put forward by those associated with the old order is all that's left for those stripped of political power by a young generation.

Meanwhile, much has been made of the consistent presentation of the theme of 'newness' in the play, with the equation of new regimes with tyranny. Again, the next logical step of examining why such regimes may be regarded as tyrannies has not been adequately explored. The 'newness' issue is most obviously linked to the generational aspect of the Olympians' rule, and here, at least, appears to be some consensus that the use of terms to define the Olympians and their behaviour as 'youthful' emphasizes that succession is defined by intergenerational conflict. However, amongst all these methodological questions of consistency, some themes do appear to emerge as consistent. These are themes of intergenerational conflict, revenge, honour, the violence of the gods and the inevitable rise of the young at the expense of the established authorities. The characters of Bia, Kratos (and later on the cynical and unpleasant Hermes) all demonstrate haughty and insulting behaviour in their intimidation of an older rival. Prometheus by turn exhibits characteristics of an older generation, such as the capacity for prophecy, and refers to the Olympian gods as childlike.

Of course, these are just some of the many themes that feature in *Prometheus*, which also include the gods' relationship with mortals or the endurance of exile and punishment. The absence of other plays in the original tetralogy is also inhibitive of a fuller understanding of the work. But plays by Aeschylus and other tragedians do offer examples of the use of intergenerational conflict as an enduring theme, over a long enough period and through a sufficient variety of contexts to demonstrate this concept as a popular commonplace of contemporary Athenian discourse. The power of *Prometheus* is to show that the violent revolutions of the gods, just like those of mortals, can result in the formation of perceptions of tyranny that are less to do with the reality than the emotional loss of a stable authority, however 'tyrannical' (Ouranos and Kronos would quite easily fit into this category). The anxiety about an aggressive younger generation, prone to violence and determined to take control, is a legitimate concern in the face of the relentless generational shift of the ages. Even the gods are shown to be subject to these forces.

The Politics of Age and Integration in Sophocles' *Antigone*

As we have seen in *Prometheus*, age and authority can have a complex relationship in tragedy, such as where the authority of the new generation of Olympians is questioned in clear age-related terms. There are other plays too, such as *Bacchae* or *Persae*, in which the authority of the young central character is questioned in relation to their age and psychological state. But most commonly, authority figures in tragedy are middle-age-range male citizens of their polis. The challenge to their authority, a recurrent theme in tragedy, often comes from some extra-communal source, whether this is from a foreign army (*Seven Against Thebes*), divinity (*Hippolytus*) or the threat of 'the other' (Aeschylus' *Suppliants* or Euripides' *Medea*). But the challenge to authority from *within* society appears most often in the form of threats from the younger generation, such as from Orestes in the *Oresteia*, Electra in her name plays by Sophocles and Euripides or Oedipus in *Oedipus Tyrannus*. But perhaps the most striking and direct example of the antagonism between young and old in tragedy can be found in Sophocles' *Antigone*. In this play, Sophocles reveals the tension between generations in relation to political authority, but can also be seen to dramatize a deeper concern about how to integrate different generations, and a diversity of moral viewpoints, into the life of the polis and its political decision-making.[1]

Antigone opens with the play's namesake damning a public proclamation made by the autocrat of Thebes, Creon. The city's ruler has forbidden burial rites for Polynices, Antigone's brother, a declaration presented by Antigone as, 'the evils of our enemies . . . coming upon our own people' (10).[2] So begins the struggle by the play's characters to establish the justice and injustice, righteousness and profanation of the treatment of Polynices' unburied body.

For all the strengths and weaknesses of the polar arguments put forward by Creon and Antigone – and supported, modified or distorted by the chorus, Ismene, Haemon or Tiresias – the play's antagonistic exchanges are as much about the psychological conditions necessary to rule justly and the importance of the ability to give and receive advice (*bouleuesthai*), as the destructive power of unreflective moral or religious certainty.[3] In some respects, *Antigone* is not unique, since those tragic plays that present the central character's political authority as a tyrannical force, such as *Prometheus*, can be plausibly expected to contain speeches that question the political legitimacy of autocratic rule. But in *Antigone*, this discussion takes on an extra resonance when the quality of political authority, in this case centred on the psychological ability to formulate effective policy, is said to be greatly influenced by the ability to receive and act on advice, which is highly interdependent on a sound '*dianoia*', or thought process, and control over one's emotions (*thumos*). I hope to demonstrate that Sophocles presents this ability as one inextricably associated with intellectual maturity. While the preceding chapter discussed how tyrannical political powers have been presented as 'youth-like' (*neanikos*),[4] this chapter will consider how each of a triad of characters – Creon, Antigone and Haemon – is also presented by Sophocles using language that relates their actions to their relative ages. In particular, discussion will closely examine the language that Sophocles uses during the characters' speeches about decision-making and political authority when age is invoked to weaken or strengthen an argument. Along the way, I shall take time to consider the historical circumstances in which such an unusual picture of youth, murderous and insubordinate and yet still sympathetic, could have emerged.

Before proceeding, the term '*thumos*' requires some consideration, having a complex semantic range over time that retains commonalities between its use in Homer and in the classical period, but also some marked differences in treatment by later philosophers.[5] In perhaps the most important work on *thumos* in recent years, *Plato and the Hero: Courage, Manliness and the Impersonal God*, Angela Hobbs sets out the philosophical conceptualizations of the term by Plato and Aristotle.[6] Synthesizing a picture of uncontrolled *thumos* as something causing one to respond disproportionately and erratically to perceived slights, Hobbs considers the human subject as having 'no internal checks, but requires the outside assistance of reason to calm it'.[7] It is interesting to note that the two literary characters that Hobbs deploys most readily to demonstrate cases of *thumos* unleashed are Alcibiades and Achilles, who both have large literary histories of *neanikos* behaviour of their own. The various sketches and definitions of *thumos* are still open to challenge, but I deploy the ambiguous nature of *thumos* that Hobbs points to: it is the seat of emotion or unconscious desires, but also a state of unmitigated emotion, often, specifically, anger. This closely follows the Homeric, poetic use of the term and thus part of the tradition from which tragedy emerged, rather than a more technical part of the Platonic construct of the tripartite *psychē* – less likely to be a direct expression of a widespread popular understanding at the time Sophocles was writing.[8] However, the more psychological conceptualization does also remain fundamental: *thumos* is what drives the 'impulse to strive after an ideal self-image,'[9] a dangerous process that I will argue is at the heart of the action in *Antigone*. In short, I will use the term *thumos* referentially as a psychological, rather than philosophical, concept. In relation to the tragic genre, successful arguments have been put forward[10] that many protagonists in tragedy can be seen to be conflicted between the desire to follow their heart (*thumos*), often badly affected by jealousy or desire for revenge, and their recognition of the importance of external capacity to deliberate (*to bouleutikon* as Aristotle called it in *Politics* [1260a]),[11] which creates a capacity for cognitive dissonance that is fundamental to their tragic status (or at least serious self-deception).[12]

To return to the play's action, from Antigone's perspective, Creon's combined psychology (his *dianoia* corrupted by an inflamed *thumos*) must be faulty as he has buried Eteocles in accordance with law and custom and yet failed to do the same for Polynices. When Creon enters, at 165, he provides irrefutable evidence for a deep-seated hypocrisy, if nothing else. His entrance, announced by the chorus as, 'here comes the king ... he has proposed this special conference of elders' (155–61), signals not his initiation of discussion, but the delivery of a fully formed and rigid pronouncement on the fate of Polynices. Unwittingly anticipating the action to come, Creon proclaims: 'It is impossible to gain full knowledge of any man's character, mentality and judgement (*psychēn te kai phronēma kai gnōmēn*, arguably the visible elements of his psychological interior), until he is tested in rule and law-giving' (175–7). By the play's end, Creon has allowed us full knowledge of this range of characteristics through his repeated failure to make judgements based on anything other than his own anger and fear of the weakening of his authority. Primarily, Thebes' ruler is shown to have failed to be properly in control of his thought processes because of his 'violent tongue' and lack of understanding (that is, Creon's inability to properly communicate with others and his failure to control his own *thumos*), demonstrated when Tiresias abandons Creon to 'vent his rage upon some younger man' (1084–5).[13] These perceived characteristics, haste and passion, anger and aggression, are also common criticisms of young men. The ability to provide or receive good counsel (*bouleuesthai*) was thought to be severely weakened by attacks of haste and passion (*tachos kai orgē*), and both Thucydides and Herodotus provide historical evidence for such views in relation to youth, most explicitly in the cases of Alcibiades, Cambyses and Xerxes.[14]

In perhaps the key scene for analysis of the psychological state of Creon, the arrival of Haemon and the *agon* that follows, concluding with the famously tempestuous stichomythia (626–780), the younger man's calm politeness and his father's extreme haughtiness are striking counter-examples of the socially constructed ideals of behaviour for those of a young and an older age group. At first, Haemon chooses his words carefully, so as not to further inflame his father's passion whilst Creon fails to rein in his anger in setting out his position, using harsh and sarcastic language (640–80).[15] Haemon continues to show remarkable restraint in avoiding a direct challenge to his father's faulty deliberation, suggesting that 'other words might also be good' (687), that counsel is necessary for reaching a sound decision. But in the final lines of this speech, Haemon does display naivety in his use of language as he draws attention to their relative ages, he as '*neōterou*', and in his suggestion that Creon is muddled by anger (719–24).[16] The chorus' apparent attempts at neutral diplomacy, 'there have been good words spoken on both sides', serve only to cause Creon to angrily retort: 'shall men of my age be taught wisdom by one of his?' (726–7). By this point, any pretence of civility collapses and Creon propels the exchange towards a psychologically catastrophic climax, leading Haemon eventually to falter in the calm and tact he has shown up until the final lines of the preceding speech. Replying to Creon, and initiating the stichomythic exchange, Haemon says: 'if I am young, you should consider my actions, not my age' (728–9). The point appears clear: Haemon's advice is justifiable by his intellectual maturity, demonstrated by his encouragement of Creon to consider a plurality of views on how to treat Antigone, to seek external moderation. The relative ages of the two characters are important but not as important as the ability to properly consider the options, take counsel, tame the emotional urges and master one's thought processes. Measured against the standard virtues that adult men would strive to demonstrate (wisdom, self-control, courage and justice), Creon is found wanting whilst Haemon demonstrates all four characteristics. The picture of 'youth' that begins to emerge is one of a psychological state rather than biological age. When Creon scoffs, 'shall the city tell me what orders to give?' Haemon replies: 'You see? You sounded all too young (*neos*), in saying that' (735). By modern standards, this is strong criticism from Haemon, and by ancient Greek standards it is outrageous. The suggestion that a father and son have somehow adopted reversed positions, in terms of the integrity of their *dianoia* and their ability to control their *thumos*, would have been a shattering insult to a Greek father, but it is all the more shocking for being manifestly true. Creon proves Haemon's point immediately when he launches into a barely coherent tirade about the outrage of his (perceived) concession of popular authority to women (740–66).[17]

The final, and most extreme, provocation of Haemon, Creon's threat to kill Antigone as well, 'in the presence of her bridegroom' (760–1), is an act of pure indulgence in haste and anger and is the point at which Haemon, too, exhibits youth-like behaviour, storming off with the threat of killing himself. The *agon* might have been won by Creon, Haemon's swift departure and failure to convince his father to change course is evidence for this victory, but 'his rhetorical and moral defeat is transparent'.[18] The moral victory belongs to his son, and Creon's defeat by a younger man can be taken as further proof of his psychic instability. But Haemon does not simply attempt to persuade his father, however tactfully, to take advice and so demonstrate how wrong he must be (if the correct course of action is obvious even to his son, that is). He also makes the case for the legitimacy of his own *dianoia*, regardless that he is still a *neos*. By approaching the *agon* with restraint and moral clarity, Haemon demonstrates his own maturity by way of *psychēn te kai phronēma kai gnōmēn* in the face of Creon's implacable, all-consuming rage, his *neanikos* indulgence of an uncontrolled *thumos*. However, Creon's extreme provocation has had the effect of making the youthful *thumos* re-emerge in his son. This is clear when the chorus warn of the state of *orgē* in which Haemon appears to be (766), addressing Creon seemingly with the aim of influencing a softening of his stance. But Creon is still just as much subject to the forces of passion and haste, too, and he replies: 'let him keep on acting and thinking too big for a man' (768). The overall effect of the *agon* between Haemon and Creon is to demonstrate an entanglement of character psychologies that cannot be easily separated by references to biological age. It seems that a youth-like psychology is likely to emerge from the midst of emotional turbulence (most usually fuelled by anger at the inability to realize one's idealized self-image) if one is not able to check inflamed *thumos* with internal reasoning or external advice. Likewise, age is not necessarily a reliable marker of ability to make decisions in a manner appropriate to those who govern. The key to understanding what this passage might tell us about views on youth involvement in politics is Haemon's point concerning intellectual maturity, that participation in political decision-making is appropriate for those who can control their emotions, regardless of age. All characters, bar Tiresias and Haemon, up until 765, provide unwitting evidence in their speeches for why they *should not* have political involvement, but not purely on the basis of age, rather on the basis of intellectual instability, exacerbated by the refusal to seek advice that would help correct their enrapture to *thumos, tachos* and *orgē*. There is the danger of producing a circular argument here, but a simple formulation appears to be this: a youth-like mind, not fully capable of escaping haste and passion, cannot make rational decisions, and those who are incapable of overcoming the effects of passion on their *thumos* are destined to retain a youth-like inability to control *dianoia* that can only be corrected by the external-to-unconscious application of reason, or where this is not possible, because of the uncontrollability of *thumos*, the application of external counsel. In this respect, in *Antigone*, Haemon and Creon can be considered to have reversed the levels of intellectual maturity expected of those from different age groups, older versus younger. Or so it would seem.

This view of Sophocles' handling of both youth and the intractability of Creon is immediately challenged by the end of the episode and the following choral ode (781–806). After Haemon's departure, Creon at last concedes some ground as, when the chorus ask if he will really kill both Antigone and Ismene, he replies: 'not the one who played no part; you are right' (771). This sudden collapse of resistance to counsel is both unexpected and difficult to explain.[19] The effect is to show how Creon has finally relented, but in a way that only emphasizes his cruelty towards Antigone and the brutal condescension of his son.[20] The king acts as a tyrant who recognizes he has overstepped the boundaries of what his subjects are prepared to tolerate, and so makes a strategic concession. But he is still too fuelled by anger and self-righteousness to concede the really crucial ground, that of the burial of Polynices. Whatever the motivations for this change of mind, the chorus are credited by Creon as partly involved in his decision not to kill Ismene and their interventions do appear to have had an impact. Throughout the debate, and eventual degeneration into a slanging match between Creon and Haemon, the chorus appear to maintain a neutral position and argue for the validity of both father and son's perspectives on the turmoil in Thebes. What is more, whilst acknowledging the potential for misunderstanding because of their age, they do point out Haemon's good counsel. Once the third stasimon begins, however, the chorus, rather than continue this approach, adopt a tone curious in comparison to that of their earlier neutrality. Now it is Eros to blame for inflaming the *thumos* of Haemon, having, 'stirred up the kindred strife between these men' (795). The power of Aphrodite too, say the chorus, is irresistible and: 'even I am carried beyond due limits, and can no longer restrain my welling tears' (803–4).[21] But this can hardly be the same influencing force to which they suppose Haemon to be subject: they plainly feel pity or sorrow, rather than amorous love, for Antigone. This inconsistency is just one challenge to interpretation that this passage presents. Just as puzzling is the use of Eros as a metaphoric descriptor of the untrammelled emotional force possessing Haemon, a view that cannot be easily reconciled with the chorus' earlier judgement that Haemon has spoken well, so well that Creon should learn from his son. The sudden denial of Haemon's rationality could be the result of a number of factors: as a reaction to Haemon's sudden angry exit, due to fear of antagonizing Creon further or purely as an authorial device for re-introducing Antigone that, 'add[s] powerfully to the pathos'.[22] It could also be said that the influence on the chorus' own *thumos* by Aphrodite, as conceded at lines 803–4, results in the restriction of their perceptions to see any other possible explanation, other than inflamed *thumos*, as a cause for behaviour. The same argument could be made for Creon, that his all-consuming *thumos* has made him unable to apply rationality to his decision-making, only emotional forces. Audience responses are notoriously difficult to estimate but the consistent characterization in the play makes it likely that the chorus' erratic and sometimes hypocritical behaviour would be relatively transparent to those seated in the theatre. It is quite possible to imagine one popular interpretation of Haemon's character to be of a relatively rational young man caught between the tyrannical-obsessional ravings of the older Creon and the self-confessed senility of the yet still older chorus. And yet, the overall impression is of a group of old men lamenting in a conventional, traditional way in response to what they see as the typically uncontrolled *thumos* of youth, liable to uncontrollability when faced with the traditional defining characteristics of *neanikos* psychology: love and anger.[23] Their earlier intervention in support of Haemon is perhaps an exception brought about by the immediacy of Haemon and the persuasiveness of his speech. Once he is absent from the stage, and the older Creon is the sole auditor, the chorus lapse back into a traditional mindset. The positive voice of youth can only be heard when youth are present to argue their case, otherwise the traditional conceptualization of youth remains unchallenged.

The chorus' failure to properly recognize the human and rational from the divine and irrational continues, demonstrably, in the following fourth episode. Antigone, in what is a line heavy in irony, says: 'see me, citizens of my fatherland, taking my last road' (806). The irony is multiple: this testament of her treatment, the chorus' witness, amplifies their failure to adequately deploy *euboulia*; her use of the word '*politai*' emphasizes the political disempowerment of the supposed 'council of elders'; and by using *patrias*, Antigone's words suggest that the politics of Thebes is synonymous with the dysfunctional family of Oedipus. The chorus miss the point entirely and appear unable to see beyond the simply poetic, suggesting: 'Have you not, then, won renown and praise as you depart for the cavern of death?' (817–18).[24] It is as if they echo a purely Homeric understanding of psychology, that honour and heroic legacy are the primary concerns, a misunderstanding that jars violently with all that has gone before in the play. It is not long until Antigone is provoked by the chorus into an angry response, comparable to that of Haemon before his departure from the stage at the end of the second episode. The chorus, still failing to comprehend Antigone's psychological state, continue with their faulty and insulting comparisons, saying: 'it is a great thing for a dead woman even to have said that she shared the fate of the demigods' (836–7). The chorus then place all the blame for the disastrous state of affairs in Thebes on Antigone, addressing her using the word *teknon* and so emphasizing their view of her failure as due to her youth, later blaming her downfall on her *orga*, her 'self-willed temper', in another stereotypical condescension of youth (852–75). Time and again, the perception of young people in the play by the older chorus, appears unable to break out from popular negative constructions, regardless of external empirical evidence to the contrary.

With Antigone's fate sealed, the arguments of the younger characters appear to be defeated in the political arena, even though morally superior to the spurious arguments of Creon and the chorus. However, the entrance of Tiresias, at 988, throws sudden doubt on the outcome of the play, and presents an insurmountable challenge to the validity of Creon's process of *dianoia* and the legitimacy of his rule. Tiresias' opening words are typically prophetic: 'we have come on a shared path, two seeing with the eyes of one; for it is thus, with the help of a guide, that the blind must walk' (988–90).[25] The advice is thinly veiled: that the correct path is one taken through cooperation, not by a narrow unilateralism. The theme of duality is embodied, literally, in the presence of Tiresias' guide, a young boy. The effect on the spectator of this tandem-character is striking, the use of a young boy as guide, telling. Rather than give the impression of Tiresias as just another old man with an opinion, the mutual dependence of the very young and very old effects the complete removal of this dual character from the discussion of deliberation and valid psychological states for taking decisions from the perspective of age groups. Tiresias-and-guide appear completely outside the framework of age relations (befitting the prophet's generic role as mouthpiece for the gods) and are thus external to the societal values placed on roles associated with age. The inter-dependency, and exceptionality, of the two-as-one is emphasized at 1012–14, when Tiresias comments: 'I learned from this boy ... for he is my guide.' Tiresias, with his inestimable age and association with divinity, is transcendentally, rather than conventionally, virtuous. At first glance, Creon's response confirms his acceptance of Tiresias' counsel, saying: 'I have not neglected your advice in the past' (993), a strangely accommodating statement that is notably at odds with the evidence for his (one way) discussions with all other characters of the play. In fact, the Greek word used here that is translated as 'advice' is *phrenos*, a term that can be used to mean 'thinking' but is also, literally, a part of the body (the midriff or diaphragm, correlative with the English term 'guts', suggesting the application of a form of intuitive rationality) and was associated widely with the physical seat of human emotions.[26] Creon, therefore, is not willing to concede to Tiresias the position of full counsel, but he does accept that he has been open to his 'thinking', as an indirect concession. With *phrēn* closely related to an emotional process, Creon admits only to being influenced by Tiresias' own, perceived, emotional state of being. When Tiresias makes his argument that Creon is poisoning the city by his *phrenos*, he offers direct advice, saying: 'consider these things then, my child', and, 'it is most pleasant to learn from one whose words are good' (1023–32). The advice, offered in this overtly age-specific way, is too much for Creon to bear and he responds with a similar fury to that he earlier directed at Haemon. Just as in that earlier exchange, he is also quick to retaliate along age lines, replying: 'old man, you are all like archers shooting at me' (1033),[27] with a tone it would be probable to assume is both sarcastic, in the use of the nominative 'o presbus', meaning old but commonly understood to mean venerable, and intended to highlight the potential faultiness of Tiresias' judgement based on age (cf. 681–2). This turnaround from the opening pleasantries between the two offers further evidence for Creon's fragile *thumos*; a psychological state apt to degenerate into an uncontrollable state of *orga* at any slight suggestion that he reflects on his own faulty *dianoia*. Still, Creon doesn't reject outright Tiresias' suggestion that: 'the best of possessions is good counsel' (1050).[28] Rather, he retorts with an insult, an angry response that seems designed to help him avoid engaging with real debate. But this won't throw Tiresias off track, and he then delivers invective worth quoting in full for its summarizing qualities:

> Boy, take me home, so that he may direct his anger at younger men, and learn
> to keep a quieter tongue and a better mind than the mind which now he bears.
>
> 1087–90

Quite simply, Tiresias frames Creon's entire current psychology in relation to age. He refers to four generations (the boy, younger men and indirectly to himself and Creon) and so the entire male population at Thebes. In this full spectrum of masculinity it is not the boy or the young men who are febrile in respect to their *thumos* but the ruler of the city. Worse still, this anger has led him to lose control of his *logos*, Tiresias says he must keep a quieter tongue. Creon's wayward speech has resulted in an inability to participate in proper counsel, and all of this has combined in an aggressive and erratic pattern of *phrēn* leading to the perilous situation in which he now finds himself (as revealed by the preceding prophecy).

Creon's and, to some extent, the city's fate has been sealed by the combination of behaviour and irrationality that has been clearly labelled early in the play as *neanikos*. Ironically, for all the positive presentations of the young but un-youth-like, it has taken the oldest inhabitant of Thebes to point this out directly to Creon in a way that actually has some sort of psychic impact. Creon almost immediately afterwards exclaims: 'my mind (*phrenas*) is troubled' (1095).[29] Age, again, is related to thinking and maturity: Tiresias only delivers his knock-out blow prophecy after his attempts at gentle persuasion are ineffective. It is this superior ability that sets him apart from the chorus, a maturity of *phrēn* that allows tactical deployment of different types of argument. The older chorus are locked into a mindset reflecting the ancient values of honour and shame that are only distantly related to the more personal values of human justice Antigone represents. In this respect, the chorus and Creon represent an older, more traditional psychology, one that elevates personal honour above all other concerns. Haemon and Antigone, on the other hand, seem to promote views on justice that are less grandiose and more tolerant of a plurality of perspectives. Indeed, it is the social construction of the psychology of youth that is used by the older characters to explain the behaviour of Antigone and Haemon, and yet the actions and speeches of the younger characters are demonstrably countervailing of this popular negative view of youth, being predominantly measured and controlled rather than impulsive and emotional. The *neanikos* move to the use of insults by the older men, and their obsession with shame and honour, cast them in the psychological role of youth. The constant reiteration of the importance of justice and popular opinion by the younger cast reveals the emergence of a new adult psychology of politics, of plurality (if not democracy) and universal justice, rather than personal honour. Effectively, the play can be considered to mark the point at which the fully fledged democracy of Athens attempted a complete cultural articulation of the ideals of the new political system over the older order.[30]

The case then begins to build for the character of Haemon as symbolic of the qualities required for deliberation in a healthy and diverse political system besieged by the forces of tyranny (Creon) and the rigid, traditionalist views of the chorus. This proposition faces another serious challenge by the play's final climactic section, beginning with the shattering news delivered by the messenger that Haemon has taken his own life. At 1177, the messenger proclaims: 'He [Haemon] killed himself, in anger with his father for a murder,' before recounting the scene within the cave to which Creon had banished Antigone, and to where Haemon had travelled after departing the scene in anger at 765. According to the messenger's story, before Haemon's suicide:

> The boy, glaring at him [Creon] with wild eyes, spitting in his face and making no reply, drew his two-edged sword. His father rushed out in flight and he missed his aim. Then the wretched boy, enraged with himself, pressed his body down upon the sword.
>
> 1231–9

This extreme behaviour has traditionally been explained as an eruption due to the grief that Haemon felt for the death of Antigone and shame at his attempt on his father's life, together manifesting itself in the punitive self-death that will cause pain to Creon.[31] Emphasis has been placed on Haemon's action, but the preceding lines – the messenger's reported speech by Creon – deserve close attention too. Only in this way can the underlying drivers of Haemon's *dianoia, phrēn* and psychological states, and their relation to intellectual maturity, be correctly understood. It is, ultimately, external forces that lead to Haemon's suicidal behaviour, the definitive self-enacted social exclusion, and these are from two sources: the imposed values of Creon, and the values of society at large. The messenger reports that Haemon's actions follow Creon's words: 'unhappy boy, what a deed you have done. What came in to your mind? What disaster destroyed your reason?' (1226–9). Even after the change of heart that Tiresias appears to have effected earlier, Creon continues to look for some external source for all that is wrong in Thebes: Antigone's death, supposedly, is Haemon's fault. Creon continues in his refusal to engage with Haemon's opposing views, stating, indirectly, that this is because his son's reason has been destroyed. What is more, Creon again uses age-specific language, referring to Haemon as 'boy', and even worse, in the following line, as *teknon*, or child. Relations between father and son appear not to have progressed beyond those of lines 631–765, Haemon's defiance is rendered by Creon into simple unreasoning rebellion by an emotional young man whose views are the product of faulty *dianoia*.

Suicide in tragedy is a fairly common event but *Antigone* is unique in the triple killing that occurs at the play's ending. Superficially, and to modern eyes, the deaths of Antigone and Haemon, by their own hands, could seem to prefigure later famous suicides, such as in *Romeo and Juliet*, as the paradigm of young doomed love. It can be said that Sophocles, like Shakespeare, presents a world in which his lead characters cannot properly integrate into their societies with all their restrictions and taboos, and thus suicide is an inescapable fate.[32] Social exclusion in some form *is* a contributing factor but the motivations for suicide are more than solely due to romantic grief, especially for Haemon. A brief excursus on suicide is necessary to further contextualize Haemon's behaviour at the end of the play when he makes an attempt on his father's life before turning his sword on himself. In the classical world suicide was considered in a very different way to that in which it is understood today, and between different ancient cultures suicide was distinguished by method, gender, agency and motivation.[33] Suicide could be, and was, considered as honourable, or even heroic, in certain circumstances in classical Greece (the example of Sophocles' *Ajax* being paradigmatic in this respect). Haemon's actions must not be viewed against the predominant, post-Christian conceptualization of suicide as a serious taboo, a view that came about many hundreds of years later. Suicide in ancient Greece was a highly gendered concept by practice and male suicide by means other than a weapon would have been extremely dishonourable, making Haemon's use of a sword significant.[34] The fact that this is the sword that moments earlier would have struck his father imbues the symbolism with an additional generational dimension: Haemon's defeat in using reason to persuade his father is as a defeat in battle and the only honourable course of action for the defeated soldier is death. It is not clear how exactly Haemon strikes himself, but the manly way of administering the mortal wound would be to plunge the sword into the guts or *phrenes*.[35] As discussed above, this is the physical seat of the psychological, which has been a central thread of discussion in the play. Haemon symbolically and physically destroys his bodily and psychic *phrenes*. The masculine aspect of Haemon's suicide can also be understood within the general context of the character's suggested marriage, or anticipated marriage, to Antigone. The suicides of Eurydice and Antigone have been explained as a response to the impossibility of these characters' integrations into society.[36] The same can be said of Haemon in respect of a number of barriers to integration, particularly integration to adult male society. If Haemon is to marry Antigone, then he would have a number of important roles to carry out. Most pressingly, in the dramatic context, he would be compelled to help bury Polynices, as failure to do so would be an irreparable stain on his reputation as the only existing male relative.[37] In Creon's dismissal of Haemon's questioning of the decision not to bury the body, Haemon's future capabilities as a male head of household are hugely undermined. Haemon's ability to forge an independent path, with his own thoughts and ability to make decisions, is also challenged by Creon. Effectively, Creon is obstructing his son's path to full adulthood by denying him the ability to marry and carry out his duties and by denying him a voice within society. Creon is only able to see Haemon as a difficult son, rather than as an individual in his own right (the cave in which Haemon and Antigone take their own lives can be seen as a desperate recreation of an *oikos* in which they would have shared an adult life together, if only they were considered as adults).

By the play's end, the young protagonists are dead, as is Haemon's mother. The society that is left – after the pre-narrative deaths of Polynices and Eteocles and, as we latterly discover when we hear about Eurydice's suicide, Haemon's own brother Megareus (1303) – seems to be one that is dominated by older men and is well on its way to annihilation as a consequence of this generational absence. Sophocles presents a society that has failed its young people, even when they have demonstrated the validity of their membership of that society through intellectual maturity and the foresight to see the consequences of their actions (their inability to integrate due to the tyranny of Creon), and the actions of others (the punishment of Creon through the destruction of his family line and resultant inability to maintain a tyranny). Sophocles creates an astonishing world, one markedly different from the less favourable views of youth in tragedy that have gone before, and, as I will demonstrate in later chapters, will return in the later years of the fifth century. It is astounding that Haemon can be considered as such a sympathetic character when his actions in the play show a young man who undertakes a litany of outrages against his father, including attempted murder. But this superficial view of Haemon as a wayward youth simply will not do: the wider context of the play reveals a young man using all means available to him to prevent his father from carrying out further atrocities that will harm the whole community at Thebes.

How, then, would the ancient audience of this supposedly prize-winning play have reacted to this characterization? There is continued and unresolved debate around the dating of *Antigone*, and the marginal consensus that the play was performed at around 442–1 has been challenged in recent years.[38] In some ways, the exact date is of relatively minor importance when considering the general state of being at Athens in the mid-fifth century BCE. In this respect, it is the general political and social realities of Athens of the period between the Persian and Peloponnesian Wars, the *Pentecontaetia*, that is important, and the three decades of Periclean hegemony in particular, that is 462–431. This is a period of relative stability in Athenian history. This is not to say that there were no periods of turmoil, far from it. The continuing fall-out from the Persian Wars, sowing the seeds of Athenian imperial expansion and a concomitant growth in the hostility between Athens and Sparta, meant that military engagements between the city and other *poleis* continued with regularity throughout this period. But the nature of military action, with Athens in an increasingly ascendant position, meant that there was little real danger of a repeat of the destruction of Athens, the terror that was visited on the city before the battle of Salamis in 480. Athens was a city high on confidence, flush with wealth from the relocation of the Delian League treasury in 454 and experiencing a form of democracy that severely weakened the power and influence of aristocratic families to the benefit of the wider citizenry in Athens.

These notable historical features, I suggest, led to changes in society that enabled a softening of the traditional views of youth. In earlier, pre-democratic Athens the traditional view of youth was that young people were celebrated for their physicality but viewed in less favourable terms when considering their intellectual abilities and control of their emotional states. The democratic reforms introduced by Cleisthenes at 508/7, followed by the introduction of ostracism some decades later and the reforms of the Areopagus by Ephialtes in the late 460s all contributed to a strengthening of democracy that directly undermined and weakened traditional patriarchal power structures. Formerly, these restricted the greatest political power to a number of families who would pass this power down through their own family/generational lines. The result of the political changes was the dispersal of political power through the community and a diminishment of obvious hereditary political power.[39] As a consequence, the younger generation (aristocratic youth, that is) had come to be seen, and identify themselves, as a distinct group within society, rather than as a sum of individual would-be heirs to power from political dynasties. The great paradox here is that it was Pericles, supposedly the political protégé of Ephialtes, who would become the most prominent name of these new democratic values and that his rule, which arguably resembled a tyranny in his consolidation of power and length of authority, defined this period of stability.[40] The impression of relative security (social, political and economic) presented itself most obviously in less intensive military activity, resulting in a weakened emphasis on youth as part of a large war machine that would have been the case during the Persian Wars (and is evident from Thucydides during the Peloponnesian Wars). Furthermore, the changes to citizenship requirements, introduced by Pericles, according to which full citizenship could only be bestowed on those with Athenian mothers and fathers, led to a much tighter definition of identity with the state and consequently a further diminishment of identity by family.[41] In combination, identity would appear to have become something that was defined by other social factors and, in relation to present discussion, age groups, or more specifically Mannheimian 'generational units' would have been one such identity defining category. This, I suggest, may have been a honeymoon period for youth, since a distinct category was beginning to take shape and benefit from relative stability that softened societal views of a political marginal group that would attempt to assert and justify its involvement in political decision-making.

It is against this backdrop that Sophocles' *Antigone* was probably performed, where a combination of new social factors, generated by political changes, may have allowed a softening of traditionally negative views on youth. At times of political crisis, young male characters like Haemon would be considered as representative of danger to traditional authority and yet youth in the play appears not as a destructive force, but as a possibly redemptive one. The supporting conceptual struts of Athenian democracy included the idea that genuine *euboulia* and subsequent measured decision-making emerged from respectful and reasoned exchange between diverse groups who shared political authority. Such ideas appear manifest in the speeches and actions of the young characters while the old authoritarian and narrow politics of Creon, supported by the older chorus, are symbolic of the danger of disenfranchising younger members of society. This picture is all relatable to the stability of the real world represented by the figure of Pericles. Through the character of Haemon, Sophocles demonstrates that intellectual maturity is not necessarily linked entirely to age and that the failure to recognize a young man's virtuous abilities poses a risk of failing to integrate that person into society. This social exclusion, subsequently, leads to radical behaviour in the young who then turn to conform to age stereotypes in the most extreme way, and in so doing contribute towards their own annihilation and the destruction of their society. The tragedy of *Antigone* is the unavoidable death of youth when they cannot be integrated into their community, specifically through acceptance into adult society. The risk reflected in the real world is that political disenfranchisement of the young, at a time when there were more young people in Athens with a greater sense of group identity and no major war requiring their sacrifice, had potentially very serious consequences for society. The democracy therefore had to find a way to accommodate this new social category. All this happened in a period dominated by the figure of Pericles who, to begin with at least, represented the thrusting power of a new generation. Whether it is Creon's *psychēn te kai phronēma kai gnōmēn* or the traditional virtues set out in Plato's *Symposium*, if these values appear to be somehow prohibited to young people, due to the condition of age, then that community takes on a, perhaps, intolerable risk by imperilling how well young people integrate into society, if, indeed, they choose to do so at all.[42] At least one modern adaptation of *Antigone* has drawn the titular character as a would-be suicide bomber of the Islamist type. Even more so now with the emergence of religious extremism, it is easy to relate the characterization of youth in the play to real-life examples of young people who are propelled, lured even, into extreme behaviours. In our own time, as in that of Sophocles, a failure to take seriously the next generation within society can have the most perilous of consequences.[43] That is not to treat as heroic tragedy the nihilism of death cults, but to understand how the ground can be prepared for the inevitability of their emergence.

The Cult of the Young Warrior
in Euripides' *Heraclidae*

Euripides' *Heraclidae* is a regrettably understudied play, having only recently received partial rehabilitation from a state of summary disregard in the nineteenth century.[1] The play's marginal status within the Euripidean canon could be explained away by the undoubted structural problems and a large number of possible lacunae.[2] Yet the play offers a compelling picture of the political and social tensions in a *polis* facing war, is often darkly humorous and, unusually, presents a fictional Athens in a less than positive light. These facets of the play can be seen as a dramatic mediation of the tensions at a historical Athens that would shortly send its young men to fight and die. But the play also carries a paradox. It contains speeches on the importance of protecting the young whilst, at the same time, conveying themes that seemingly promote martial values in young men, to the extent of endangering their lives, in order to protect the glory of former times or generations. And echoes of Athens' glorious triumph over Persia at Plataea, Salamis, and particularly Marathon, reverberate throughout the play. They do so directly, through the setting of the action at Marathon, and more obliquely through the central theme of comparison between current status and past achievement.[3]

Close reading of *Heraclidae* also reveals the possibility that Euripides has smuggled a highly subversive, and to youth hugely provocative, sentiment into the play's action. This subversion, manifest in the play's invocation to youth to fight whilst following a narrative arc that renders youth useless, creates uncertainty about what, exactly, should be expected of each age group at a time of war and depicts indirectly the tensions inherent in generational relations. Euripides, through *Heraclidae*, presents an idealized view of the role of youth in a time of war, both shaped by political expediency and fixed within Athens' own mythological-historical view of its defeat of Persia in Attica (that is, that contemporary politics shapes the national historical narrative for utilitarian purposes) whilst also subtly destabilizing this ideal. The play offers vital material that documents that youth in tragedy, or concepts associated with youth, are presented in response to the dominant political mood of a play's historical context, whilst in turn forming part of, or questioning, Athens' own evolving self-definition and mythologizing historical narrative, one which was reinforced through dramatic performances.

In a tradition that's likely to have begun after the second Persian invasion of Greece, Athenian children orphaned during war, or more precisely those whose fathers had died in military operations, were paraded in front of their community at the City Dionysia.[4] Of the many Athenian festivals, the City Dionysia is generally considered to have played the greatest role both in promoting the dominant Athenian ideology, because the festival was open to non-Athenians; and in strengthening self-identity, largely through the inclusion of major first performances of tragedy.[5] The war orphans were supported by the state, by payment for their education and in receipt of dole, thought to be one obol a day, a small but not insignificant amount, and this support lasted until they reached adulthood at eighteen. The set of ritualistic processes in which the liminal space between childhood and adulthood was traversed, the *ephēbia*, has disputed origins and it's uncertain if it was a feature of fifth-century Athens.[6] But what we do know is that those war orphans who had turned eighteen in the year up to the City Dionysia were not only paraded as part of the opening procession into the theatre at the foot of the Acropolis. They were specifically honoured too. Their names were read out in front of a packed audience in the theatre and they were given a panoply – that is a set of hoplite armour – then finally shown to seats of special honour, ready to watch close up the drama that was about to be performed.[7] At times of war, the presentation of these newly qualified hoplites would have taken on a special significance. Their presentation would have had some characteristics of a military review of those about to be sent to fight. This significance would have been no more evident than at the onset of the Peloponnesian Wars. While the concerns of young warriors may not have been addressed directly by the characters of all tragic plays, in Euripides' *Heraclidae* the audience would see the dramatization of the complex expectations placed on young men in a time of military crisis. Here they are notably absent from the action but large groups of young warriors are a tangible off-stage presence.

The opening stages of the Peloponnesian War were tentative in nature, as the Athenians retreated from the lands surrounding the city and concentrated efforts on naval engagements, where they had military superiority. But this policy was put in major jeopardy as a plague swept through Athens, decimating the population and killing the pre-eminent political leader, Pericles. As the city recovered, civic and ritual life continued. We don't know the exact date, but it seems likely that sometime between 430 and 427 BCE, the City Dionysia saw the first production of Euripides' *Heraclidae*.[8] The play, rarely staged in modern times, sees Athens asked to defend the children of Heracles against an army from Argos, that is, from the Peloponnese. Set at historically important Marathon, the play is dominated, largely, by older characters and the city is led by Demophon, an anxious and indecisive leader who all but disappears from the action around 600 lines in. Like most Greek tragedy, the role of young male citizens forms a major theme, primarily in relation to the need for generational continuity in order to further propagate a heroic narrative. But unlike most Greek tragedy, young people are absent from major speaking roles, a potential prolepsis of a city whose 'flower of youth has invaded the House of Hades'.[9] As the newly qualified young hoplites sat down to watch a play in which young men like them are absent, yet often referred to, what, then, would they have made of the drama?

The staging of the play at Marathon is important in relating expectations of this group of young warriors to a pre-eminent mythic and historical past. As far as we know this was the only tragedy set in this location and Marathon also had well-known associations with Heracles, the Heraclidae and Theseus.[10] The battle of Marathon was recounted as the Athenians' ability to face superior odds and triumph against a Persian enemy on home soil, and for a just cause. So when the 192 Athenians who fell in battle were buried, they were entombed in a commemorative structure that celebrated them as heroes, rather than as war dead, as was usually the case.[11] Moreover and notably, Herodotus has it that Sparta had refused the Athenian request for aid, due to their own activities in a religious festival, the Karneia, which prevented them from engaging in military action (interestingly, a festival that was apparently overseen by a group of five unmarried youth). This period is attested most fully by Thucydides and from his work we have sections of major importance that correspond to the historical period: from the first year of war and Pericles' funeral oration, through to the Mytilenian Debate and stasis in Corcyra. These sections cover the period from the summer of 431 to the end of the summer of 427, the most likely period during which Euripides would have composed the play if it was performed at the City Dionysia at the earliest in the spring of 430 and no later than the same festival of 426.[12] According to Thucydides' account, the role of young men would have been at the forefront of both the Spartans' and the Athenians' minds in 431–430. In Book ii, 20.2, Thucydides suggests that the Spartans even planned their military strategy around the large population of young men in Athens who had yet to experience war, and so might rashly rush out to battle. Indeed, the city was said to have: 'a population of young men that had never been exceeded' (2.20.2) in line with Pericles' policy of withdrawing the population of the Attic plain behind the city's walls. Regardless of the likelihood that Thucydides would have been an unreliable reporter of Spartan intentions, this passage suggests that the response of young men to their first taste of war was of concern in Athens, as projected on to the mind-set of the opposition by Thucydides. In a curious following passage (2.22.1), Thucydides explains that the young had not yet had experience of their lands ravaged by an invading force, and that the old men could only remember the invasion of the Persians, decades earlier. The question must be asked: where were these old men when the Spartan king, Pleistoanax, invaded fourteen years earlier, as stated in the preceding passage (2.21)? Whatever the explanation, when Thucydides refers to 'The Athenians', as in 'The Athenians remembered the case of the Spartan king Pleistoanax', he is clearly referring to a particular age group. It seems likely that group was those actively involved in public office, that is, those over the age of 30 but below the age of veteran of the Persian Wars. Although this view of youth is mildly critical of the behaviour of the young soldiers, and their youthful inexperience and liability to manipulation, young men clearly constituted an important part of the military capability of the city. This military capability is later put in a generational contact when, at 2.35–6 Pericles in his famous funeral oration sets out the intergenerational aspect of Athenian exceptionalism, that each generation has added to the glory of the city:

'They [former generations] certainly deserve our praise. Even more so do our fathers deserve it. For to the inheritance they received they added all the empire we have now . . . And then we ourselves . . . have added to the power of our empire.'

2.36.2–3

This may appear a common enough platitude, but what is said is that each successive generation is dependent on the one that precedes it for material wealth, and for the following generations for honouring the glory of their forefathers.[13]

The role of the young men, then, is to grow up to fight, and possibly die, in battle to protect the city and, according to Pericles, to sustain the imperial interests of Athens (those interests that helped fund the enduring image of Athenian glory, such as the Parthenon). This rather depressing view of youth, albeit perhaps necessary in war when the existence of a city was at stake, is reflected back to Demophon in *Heraclidae* by the Herald who, in a lengthy opening speech to the king of Athens says:

You will certainly get abuse from your citizens if you get into difficult waters for the sake of an ancient man, almost a tomb, a nothing, and these children. You will have at best only the hope of soon having the children as allies.

165–8[14]

These remarks could be seen to represent part of the view of youth as an Athenian might imagine would belong to a non-Athenian society. This is in sharp contrast to the more nuanced view of the role of young people in Sophocles' *Antigone*, where age is considered alongside intellectual maturity, i.e. partly as a social measure, rather than purely biologically determined. But when considered alongside Thucydides' account of 431–426, these words suggest that youth were thought of primarily in terms of military utility at this time, that is, in terms of young men's physical contribution to the city's survival. With Athens relatively secure, before any major, direct engagements with Sparta and with the empire still intact, the war had yet to focus the effects of political crisis on society itself. Athens was still unified and groups within the city, including those associated with a younger generation, had not fully factionalized, as would be the case before the disaster of the Sicilian expedition some twenty years later. As such, while youth were not yet considered to represent an internal threat to the political hegemony held by older citizens, the general perception of Attic youth exhibiting natural recklessness would have no doubt been at the forefront of the minds of the *stratēgoi*. Demophon later refines the Herald's view of the relevance of each generation, saying: 'For the birth of noble offspring is terrifying to enemies, young men who remember the maltreatment of their father' (467–70).[15] Demophon presents in this speech the ideal form that intergenerational loyalty should take, and its effects. The (superficially) gentle reminders that can be found throughout the play of how youth should behave in a city preparing for war take on a different tenor when considered in the wider intergenerational context. Demophon, on his entrance, at 120, says: 'Since you, old though you are, were quicker than younger men (*neōterous*) in running to a cry for aid …' Although this line undoubtedly has a comic effect when addressed to the chorus of old men, the fact that they are old men of Marathon would no doubt set off comparisons in the minds of the audience between the heroism of the *Marathonomachoi* and the standard of young warriors of the day.

This passage and others are effective because of the lack of young men in the play. Heracles' eldest son, Hyllus, is away scouting enemy positions and the youth of Athens, referred to, often indirectly, are absent from the stage (120). Indeed, in a scene with a similar humour, Alcmene warns Hyllus' servant, before she knows who he is that: 'If you lay a hand on these children, you will have a shameful struggle with two old people' (652–3). Just as in the scene of Demophon's entrance, the comic effect is enhanced by the latent observation that Alcmene and Iolaus are apparently vulnerable without the young of military age, in this case Hyllus, attendant to protect them. This is in contrast to many other tragedies where youth occupy principal roles. But, like the handling of other themes in the play such as the moral certainty of Iolaus' case, this scene sets up in the audience false expectations of frail, defenceless older characters reliant on younger men to protect them (and it is the young men, referred to in special terms, who are specifically named as part of the Argive army and, it is implied, the Athenian army too). Shortly after Iolaus' sets out Demophon's (depreciating) genealogy, an angry exchange breaks out between the Herald, who attempts to take away the heraclidae by force and Demophon who, against all conventions, threatens to strike him (250–87).

This scene sets the tone for much of the remainder of the play, as the very young and very old prepare for their possible annihilation at the hands of a foreign army. The following section, against this backdrop, is highly significant, and merits quoting at length:

> There is no finer gift for children than to be born of a noble and virtuous father. . . . We, for example, had fallen into the utmost sufferings but found these friends and kinsmen, who, alone in the whole inhabited expanse of Greece, defended these children. Give them your right hands, children, give them, and you likewise to the children, and come close.
>
> 297–311

The issue of greatest significance here is the emphasis on the importance of intergenerational continuity, specified by the reference to parentage and the physical gesture of linking the hands of the children and the old men of the chorus. In speech and action, the two generational boundary points form the impression of the life cycle in totality. But this impression is not as straightforward as it might seem. The old men of Athens are present, and the young children of Heracles, but the young men of fighting age are absent. It is these people whose lives are at the greatest risk from the Argive army and who have the greatest burden of responsibility. And, of course, the old men of Marathon, if considered to represent the heroes of past Athenian military victories, would have been responsible for some severely generationally limiting actions of their own. In short, the passage presents the inconsistency that is at the heart of *Heraclidae* and casts a shadow of Athenian popular thought about youth and their role in war. Young men must aspire to match the achievements of their forebears by embarking on military action, and these endeavours are also thought by Athenian society as essential in helping to secure the future of the city. But those who shoulder this responsibility are to a great part removed from the decision-making that shapes their fate. Youth are essential yet politically powerless, expendable yet necessary for the furthering of the glory of the empire.

The absence of young men in *Heraclidae* also offers a resonance of the massive mobilization of those of relatively recent military age that must have taken place ahead of the first Spartan incursions into Attica. But the absence of youth in the play is problematic if taken as a direct historical parallel as, according to

Thucydides, Pericles' advice was for the residents of Attica to withdraw from the countryside into the city, a traditional tactic of the Athenians, and this would have resulted in the presence in Athens of a large number of young men ready to fight. In this case, the absence of young men could be better understood as a proleptic suggestion of the death and battle to come, and a reminder of what was at stake. A more astonishing possibility is also imaginable, and that is the play was performed in front of an audience swollen in number by the young men who would have been drawn into Athens from the countryside ravaged by the Peloponnesians. The real and dramatic off-stage presence of large numbers of men in their youthful prime would have been a remarkable act of staging. Thucydides suggests that a large garrison consisting of the youngest and the oldest in the army was responsible for the final defence of the city and this likely mobilization of inferior troops does make the following passage regarding Iolaus' desire to fight take on a highly historically relevant appearance.[16] In Athens, old men would be expected to rally to the defence of the city walls and it is likely that this duty would have been communicated as an appeal to the memory of former glory. As conscription at Athens continued up to the age of 59, it is just about possible that this veteran garrison would include some men in their late sixties and early seventies who would have seen action at the battle of Plataea in 479.[17] There would certainly have been some veterans of Plataea alive in the audience. Reflected and dressed up in a comic idiom, it is possible to read the protracted interaction between Iolaus and Hyllus' servant (680–747) as offering an ironic parallel to the demands about to be placed on old men in a real war.[18]

Finally the decision is made to take to the field against the Argives and Iolaus exclaims that he will take up arms too, the chorus warn, 'there is no way for you to get your youth (*hēbēn*) back again' (707–8). The use of *hēbēn* here is significant. The first time this term is used in relation to youth in the play is when the Argive Herald threatens Athens with 'a large army of young men (*hēbēn*) in Argos' (283).[19] As appears time and again in *Heraclidae*, the army is composed of, and known primarily as, a force of young men. The significance of the use of the stem *hēbē* over more common terms, such as *neos*, is twofold: firstly it relates semantically to the goddess Hebe, personification of youth and mythological wife of Heracles, a figure who was closely associated with the martial values of youthful physicality, and thus places Ioalaus' actions within a heroic context.[20] At line 740–1, Iolaus uses the semantically proximate *hēbēsanta* when he says: 'Ah!, I wish, arm of mine, you could be such an ally to me as I remember you were in your youth [*hēbēsanta*], when you destroyed Sparta with Heracles!' And second, the term has been known in relation to social transformation, such as the rites of passage known a little later as the *ephēbia*, when the upper limit of adolescence is reached and the transition to adulthood, through martial training, begins. In this respect, the term relates closely to an associative field that contains military and social transformative properties. Admittedly, much of the scant evidence for the *ephēbia* belongs to the following century but it appears likely that some sort of ritual of entering manhood and military training would have been understood in the fifth century.[21] The use of the term, then, is a sign that a threshold is about to be passed, albeit in a reversal, from physical immaturity (or in Iolaus' case, infirmity) to martial competence. In this passage, with the Argive army massing, the term is used against a threatening backdrop, and deploying a word that relates to the stage of transition into adulthood adds impact when used in a context of violence where that transition for the young of the city is under threat. Thus, when the herald threatens to unleash his army of *hēbē* he is warning that the young of Athens are threatened with a sudden unavailability of the transition of the *ephēbia*, i.e. death. The impact of this apparently systematic use of the term suggests the positioning of young men's role and status within the heroic framework of martial values and mythological characters that embodies these values (Hebe and Heracles), whilst highlighting the instability and vulnerability of youth. This use by Euripides may have reflected the historical context of the opening salvos of the Peloponnesian War during which there would have been open exhortations or rallying calls to the defence of Athens by young men (and old men) at a time of great threat to the city. Unlike in *Antigone*, these young men are not given a voice and perhaps this is because of the narrow set of expectations placed upon them in wartime. Whereas in *Antigone*, Haemon's character is defined by his engagement with debate and willingness to participate in the politics of the city (as a reflection of the softening of traditional anxiety about the recklessness of youth in a period of unparalleled stability and confidence), the muteness of youth in *Heraclidae* reflects the new prevalent mood: young men of military age were expected to fight and not to question why. After all, they were unable to fully participate in the politics of Athens and excluded from the *Boulē*. They represented a large, militarily important cohort with direct representation solely in the *Ekklesia*, without any executive influence, due to age restrictions, or participation as councillors, as jurors or magistrates. As we shall see in later chapters, the arc of portrayals of youth in tragedy (from negative to positive and back to negative again) reaches its nadir in *Orestes* and *Bacchae*, in which youth are presented at their most negative, and this negative presentation is given the greatest prominence in tragedy, when Athens was in the midst of tumultuous revolutions and counter-revolutions.

The incredible scene of the rejuvenation of Iolaus, at 799–866, is perhaps the most memorable passage of the play and certainly its dramatic crux. Almost any commentary on the play makes reference to the cult of Iolaus and how both the hero and his worship were associated with youth. This is important as it helps modern readers appreciate what associations the play's audience would have made when witnessing the famous messenger scene. But this is not a straightforward endeavour: there is a complex inter- and extra-textual tangle of references to youth and Iolaus in the ancient sources, pre- and post-dating the most likely date of the production of *Heraclidae*, making any modern interpretation of the passage of Iolaus' rejuvenation vulnerable to influence by knowledge of later sources.[22] It is easy to see Euripides' handling of Iolaus as simply reflecting a well-established tradition of presentations of Iolaus as associated with youth. But the later dates of various attestations of Iolaus' youth cult, and Pindar's placing of Iolaus at Thebes rather than Marathon/Athens, make it possible that Euripides' presentation is an innovation, partly fuelled by the play's historical context in which the old and the young were the last line of defence of the Athenians. It is almost impossible to disentangle the various myths and the retold and modified stories about Iolaus. All that can be confidently claimed is that there were strong associations of Iolaus with Thebes, unsurprising given the city's association with Heracles, and that Iolaus/Heracles appears to be closely connected with young men, at least in the martial values that they both embody. That Heracles was married to Hebe, the personification of youth, in his personal mythology, further intensifies the connection between Iolaus/Heracles and youth, and this rings out with absolute clarity in the scene of Iolaus' rejuvenation.[23] Perhaps some local appropriation by an Athenian audience of Iolaus' miraculous transformation can be interpreted through Iolaus' joining of the Athenian army, but it is Hyllus' servant (presumably, both as a slave and as owned by a non-Athenian, ethnically not Athenian himself) who leads the old man into battle. So, then, the Athenian role in the relationship appears to act primarily as democratic host to a persecuted hero and his charges, rather than as playing a part in the aetiology of the cult of Iolaus. The greater and more heroic the figure, and his associated history, that seeks refuge at Athens, the greater the reflected glory on the host city. Iolaus represents the greatest of former martial glories whilst suffering from the vulnerability of old age. The absence of Heracles as his powerful ally, and the threat of death of Heracles' children would erase the lineage and continued glory, of Heracles' feats.

But as is the case throughout the play, this simple formulation comes with an ironic undertone. As we shall see shortly, a sudden revelation at the end of the play creates a dramatic inversion in the moral narrative. The full speech is précised by the messenger's startling report to Alcmene that: 'he [Iolaus] has changed back from an old to a young man again' (796). In this section, unlike the descriptions of the young soldiers of the Argive army, or Iolaus' recollections of his past, the term used to mark Iolaus' miraculous transformation is '*neos*', as if to make clear that whatever he has temporarily become, he cannot truly re-become an *ephēbe*, due to the transitional nature of this category as from adolescence to manhood. The messenger continues to report the formation of battle lines and Hyllus' challenge of Eurystheus to single combat, sacrifice and preparation for battle before a brief description of the battle itself and the beginning of the rout of the Argive army (799–842). At this point the messenger tells of Iolaus' boarding of Hyllus' chariot and his prayer to Hebe and Zeus, asking that 'he become young [*neos*] for a single day' (851–2). But it appears that it is Hebe and Heracles, not Zeus, who apply the divine transformation:

For two stars stood above the horses' yoke and hid the chariot in a shadowy cloud. Those more skilled about such things say that it was your son and Hebe. And out of the murky darkness Iolaus showed the youthful mould of his young arms.

855–6

The terminology used is again telling. Iolaus is described as possessing a youthful mould, that is, he appears a young man. But his 'young arms' reflects the language used to describe young men entering military age. If he is a young man by miraculous appearance only, his actions are primed to be consistent with the martial values expected of young men in military training at the time of war. Consequently, the Messenger goes on to report, 'Glorious Iolaus captured Eurystheus' four-horse chariot at the Scironian rocks, and having bound his hands with cords he comes leading the formerly blessed general . . .' (859–63). The physical act that captures Eurystheus could only be carried out by young arms of military prime, even if divinely gifted. His appearance as a young man (*neos*) is superficial, his actions as a temporary member of the *hēbēn*, substantive. But this transformation is illusory in another respect. Although Iolaus, through the agency of the gods of youth in Hebe and Heracles, has won the war, he has unwittingly set himself up to lose the battle for a secure future for the Heraclidae, as Eurystheus is about to reveal.

Alcmene is unsurprisingly ecstatic at the news of Iolaus' defeat of Eurystheus and the capture of her former tormentor. In a section of speech that neatly captures the rewards that await the younger generation if they can match the glories in battle of their predecessors (in this case, only available through the proxy of the old/young Iolaus), Alcmene foresees: 'Children, now, yes, now you will be free of your troubles, free of the accursed Eurystheus! And you will see your father's city, take possession of his landed estates and sacrifice to your ancestral gods' (871–6). These joyful predictions are quickly curtailed by a rising fury as Alcmene questions why Iolaus has not put Eurystheus to death. Perhaps sensing that he has acted rashly, becoming as a youth in his thinking as well as in his renewed physical prowess, Alcmene says, 'But with what clever motive did Iolaus spare Eurystheus from death? . . . For in my judgement this is no clever thing' (880–2). It could be the case that Iolaus is simply more cautious than Alcmene, and does not suffer from the direct generational threat of losing his grandchildren that Alcmene does, but he is clearly as disgusted by Eurystheus' actions as Heracles' mother. Both characters use the same language when referring to the Argives as '*ho misos*', or hateful thing.[24] But, Alcmene's bloodthirsty wish that Eurystheus, '. . . must die vilely . . . you should be dying more than once' (957–60), is also consistent with the general theme of justice dispensed by the old, regardless of whether their justice is at odds with the laws of the city. And this judgement and justice, i.e. the political power, is prosecuted by those who have not been put directly at risk through military action, a reiteration of the generationally weighted balance of political power and exposure to danger. When Eurystheus replies to Alcmene, he restates a peculiar prophecy, so far unarticulated in the play: '... I shall lie forever beneath the earth, a foreign resident who is well disposed to you and a saviour to the city, but most hostile to the descendant of these children when they betray this favour of yours and come here with a powerful army' (1032–5). It is not an exaggeration to say that this sudden revelation changes everything. For an Athenian audience, feelings of moral clarity and loyalty to Iolaus can no longer be easily sustained. Undoubtedly, the audience would cast their minds towards their current array of allies, and what hidden future they might bring about for the real world Athens. But it is only really at this point that the *Heraclidae/* Sparta myth emerges in the play. At the point when a simple and heroic resolution to the plot seems imminent, the theme of shifting allegiances and the suggestion of generational decay (at least from an Athenian perspective) is strongly reasserted. It is as if the ability to create new glories, wrought from the fusing of the cultural memory of former glory with the body of youth, has begun to fade as the magical rejuvenation of Iolaus begins to dissipate.

The play ends abruptly, with the chorus convinced of the need to execute Eurystheus. Although one wonders how much the news of the prophecy has swayed their reaction, the chorus appear casual in their complicity with the circumvention of Athenian law by Alcmene in relation to Eurystheus' fate (1021, 1053–5). Most disturbingly, this comes even though they and the servant earlier imply the authority for political decision-making lies elsewhere (964, 1018). The figure of Demophon is nowhere to be seen and apparently has no involvement in this major decision. Indeed, Demophon has been absent from both the action and speeches of the play from around line 600, playing no part in the major political decisions or in the military clash with the Argive army. As is the case earlier in the play when Iolaus and the chorus decide between them which course to take, the chorus and elderly Alcmene appear the most influential political actors: the old appear to have total political control, having temporarily appropriated the image and physical attributes of youth.

For all these points, *Heraclidae* is still considered a minor star in the Euripidean firmament. It is true that the play does lack a real tragic core as the sacrifice of Macaria and the late narrative twist of Eurystheus' ironic legacy in death are not developed enough to have much dramatic or emotional impact.

The play's comic content, however effective in creating thematic juxtapositions, also contributes to a tempering of the play's tragic intensity. Perhaps these perceptible weaknesses are due to the play's very particular historical context, and because the production was so fundamentally tied to the political climate. This should not be surprising, given that the possible date range of first performance would make this play a strong contender for the first of the Peloponnesian War period, a conflict that Thucydides describes as more significant than any other conflict in the history of Greek civilization.[25] If considered on these terms, *Heraclidae* is an extremely important testament to the dynamic relationship between tragedy and empirical reality in classical Athens, and a significant record of the pressures on a society that was acutely aware of the possibility that not just its current imperial interest, but also its glorious past were under threat. Simultaneously, the city would rely on the next generation to put themselves at risk to secure both the past and future, and in such large numbers that even if successful, there would be serious generational imbalances to come. Indeed, the end of the play is quite shocking in this respect. There are none but the old on stage, Alcmene, the chorus and possibly Iolaus, and their decision-making is highly questionable, and in the case of Alcmene ultimately self-defeating. No mention is made of the sacrifices of Athenian youth who were committed to battle, unnecessarily it seems and without a clear mandate, to borrow a loaded modern phrase. And even if youth had played an important role the glory is claimed by the old as a reflection of Iolaus' former heroic *aretē*. The message from the play's gerontocratic cast could not be clearer: youth's role is to fight and die without question. The skill of the playwright revealed in this rehabilitated reading of *Heraclidae* is this: it presents a dramatic superstructure that appears to revel in a utilitarian view of youth at war, progressively iterated through the continual measurement of current actions to past achievements, whilst simultaneously questioning the base relations between young and old in society by setting up standards it will be impossible for youth to meet. All the while, throughout the performance, an audience of young men preparing to go to war for the first time in their lives would have been looking on. One can only imagine they did so with a dawning realization of their new grim reality. And yet no interpretation of tragedy can be so simple. After all Athens was not, by comparison to Sparta, a gerontocratic state and, as we have seen, young warriors were given special honours.

One must step back from the text to assess the wider significance of the play within a festival that both celebrated and questioned what it means to be an Athenian. The play problematizes the role of young hoplites in society: how can they both heroically die for their city and sustain generational continuity? But it also problematizes the old, and through them the heroic-historical narrative of former martial glories. The question that remains in my mind at the play's end, is: 'how dangerous is it to set expectations of young people so high, especially when their unvoiced role is largely to risk their lives in combat?' Put another way, does the tangle of themes and historic resonances in *Heraclidae* make one think about how contemporary events shape our understanding of national historic and mythic narratives and how they shape ongoing popular conceptions, such as in relation to the role of youth in society? Is it the case that Euripides is providing the audience with a medium that allows the observation of the shaping of both cultural memory and social construction? The playwright's linking together of three separate narrative strands: the Bronze Age legend of Heracles; the Persian Wars; and Spartan incursions into Attica suggest this is the case. Of all the Athenian festivals, the Dionysia, where the play was first performed, would be the place at which such reflection would be possible. It is difficult to find modern parallels in terms of annual events that commemorate the war dead and question how we continue to engage with our own national myths. I would argue that the UK's annual Remembrance Day event, usually televised from the Cenotaph in London, does not allow for the interrogation of the nature of our own cultural memory of the First World War and honest reflection on what commemoration of that conflict means in terms of generational relations (similar observations could be made in relation to Veterans Day in the US, or ANZAC Day in Australia and New Zealand). We do not have a City Dionysia to allow such reflections. I would suggest that such monuments/events to shared cultural memory must be reinvigorated by *and for* each new generation through intergenerational discussion. *Heraclidae*'s continuing relevance, I suggest, is not in its dramatic power or tragic intensity. It is in the play's ability to provoke in an audience the ability to observe the dynamic nature of shared cultural memory and how this is transmitted through the generations.

Youth and Limitations on Personal Authority in Sophocles' *Philoctetes*

A decade after the call to arms of Euripides' *Heraclidae*, a series of tumultuous military and political events had left Athens stunned. The catastrophe of the total and unequivocal defeat of the Athenian expeditionary force at Syracuse in 413 sparked a backlash against what might have remained of the younger political faction at Athens. Blamed for the decision to sail against Sicily, and castigated as reckless, younger male citizens were denied access to positions of greater political power when a *Proboulē* of only older men was appointed to oversee decision-making.[1] This conservative administration was not to last and was replaced by a far more retrograde regime when the oligarchic coup of 411 asserted the political dominance of a group of four hundred of the wealthiest citizens of Athens. The coup, according to Thucydides, was partly facilitated by a group of younger men who met in the 'political clubs' (*hetairiai*), apparently constituted by groups of wealthy citizens with oligarchic tendencies (see the similar account of the drinking clubs that led to the mutilation of the Hermae; 8.65).[2] These young men assassinated the democratic leader, Androcles, whilst at the same time the leaders of the oligarchic party took to taking an escort of a gang of 'Hellenic Youth' with them in order to intimidate political opponents into silence (8.69).[3] In Thucydides' account, democracy was restored, ironically due to the efforts of Alcibiades, once a frequenter of the *hetairiai*. The remainder of his account, ending abruptly in 411, speaks no more of youth in Athens. It was just two years later that Sophocles' *Philoctetes* was performed, winning first place in the City Dionysia, according to the transmitted text's hypothesis. The production's temporal proximity to the restoration of democracy, and the hyper-politicization of the festival at which it was performed, could well have affected the play's reception.[4]

The play is dominated by the relationship between the young Neoptolemus and two older characters, Odysseus and Philoctetes, and is the only tragedy extant in complete form to feature Neoptolemus as an on-stage character.[5] The innovation by Sophocles of giving equal, if not greater, prominence to Neoptolemus over Philoctetes in his version of the story of Philoctetes' retrieval is highly significant.[6] It changes the myth of Philoctetes' abandonment and recovery from simply a story of the utility of Odysseus' *dolos* (trickery or guile) in enabling the fall of Troy to a play about education and guardianship and the nature of noble descent. This significance is also historical: the actions of young men had been critical in shaping recent Athenian history, the influence of sophistic education was at a peak, and traumatic political abrasions, caused by the friction between factions representing democratic, consensual and communal action as opposed to familial hereditary, noble and oligarchic ones, had led to revolution and counter-revolution. These factors have not escaped scholarly attention and Sophocles' *Philoctetes* has a substantial bibliography.[7] The relationship between Odysseus and Neoptolemus has been much discussed in relation to a perceived father–son dynamic and the nature of competing education systems and the values they represent.[8] But less often discussed is what the two men have in common: a desire to control Neoptolemus' actions and his capacity for self-determination.[9] That these special interests in the nurturing of youth into manhood – Neoptolemus' *paideia* – are so clearly present in the play, again speaks to events of the years immediately before *Philoctetes'* production. The actions of young men, both political and physical and both before Sicily and during the oligarchic revolution, served interests other than just their own and Thucydides (8.65, 8.69) suggests these others could be older men. *Philoctetes*, as we shall see, can be read as a play that asks how best young men can be mentored and supervised whilst not allowing the mentors or supervisors potentially unbounded instrumentality of youth.[10]

From the very beginning of the play, the action is set within a framework of political authority. At line 6, Odysseus is quick to point out that he has abandoned Philoctetes as he was: 'acting on the orders of my masters', a claim that subordinates his decision-making capacity to that of simple executor, with policy determined by a higher authority. It is within this political hierarchy that Odysseus then addresses his directive to Neoptolemus, stating: 'it is your task now to serve in the remainder of the enterprise' (15). This command and control structure is not surprising given the military nature of the visit to Lemnos. Odysseus sets the initial abandonment of Philoctetes in the definite past, determined by an authority at a remove, and accomplished by a middle-range male figure. Neoptolemus' conclusion of the enterprise takes on the appearance of a son completing the work of his father, who began the endeavour at the instructions of a grandfather figure. The military/paternal lines of authority are exactly commensurate with each other in this case and, throughout the prologue, as we shall see, Odysseus makes great efforts to assert this structure on his interactions with Neoptolemus. The limitation that Odysseus places on Neoptolemus is not just in restricting his actions but in the information to which he allows the younger man access. Closing his prologue, Odysseus says he will impart further detail of the endeavour once Neoptolemus successfully completes his initial scouting mission, offering to reveal: 'the remainder of my plan, and the two of us may act together' (24–5). Neoptolemus, in return, acquiesces to Odysseus' requests and dutifully reports back that he has spotted Philoctetes' cave-home. Having agreed to send his own sailor away on Odysseus' bidding, without questioning this assumed authority over his own kinsman, Neoptolemus reminds Odysseus of the promised extra information, saying: 'and now, if there is something else you wish to say, go on' (49). It is here that the age-related restriction on Neoptolemus' political authority is first and most fully articulated. Odysseus, rather than provide the background information as promised, reminds Neoptolemus of his place within a paternal/martial/political structure: 'Son of Achilles, you must be stalwart in your mission, and not just by bodily exertion. But if you hear something that comes as news to you, you must serve those as whose servant you are here' (50–3). What appears at first to be rather formulaic dialogue, containing standard statements on loyalty and the reminder of familial/heroic lineage, can also be read as the clarification of the minimal control and independent agency that Neoptolemus is offered in cooperating with Odysseus. It is quite clear that, since Neoptolemus is the son of Achilles and thus junior to Odysseus in age and rank, he must toe the line both in action and in words, and the entire endeavour is designed by his superiors, to whom he is completely subordinate. Furthermore, the reminder of his heritage, juxtaposed with the warning not to be swayed by unexpected news, reinforces the intractability of Neoptolemus' relationship to Odysseus, and that his orders must be carried out without question.

The following speech by Odysseus finally lays out the extent of Neoptolemus'
subordination and leaves no doubt that the task, to capture Philoctetes and his
bow, must be achieved by trickery. But Odysseus also weaves into the speech
the lines: 'You have not sailed under oath to anyone, or under duress, nor as a
member of the first expedition', adding then, 'But I can deny none of these
charges' (72–4). The effect is to explain the impossibility of Odysseus
approaching Philoctetes whilst also framing Neoptolemus' actions to date as
completely autonomous. But by stating Neoptolemus' relatively late involvement
in the Trojan Wars, clearly a consequence of his younger age, Odysseus makes
it clear that the young man is as yet of unproved value to the Greeks, implicitly
limiting his status within the confines of Odysseus' expectations and within an
age hierarchy. Odysseus goes on to concede that the 'evil scheme', '*technasthai
kaka*', is contrary to the nature of Neoptolemus. But he begins this sentence by
addressing him as *pai*, or boy (79–80). When Odysseus suggests some
autonomy to act, or at least to mentally wrestle with the deception he has been
asked to deploy, the implicit overarching message is that Neoptolemus is, after
all, a young man and should do as instructed. But while Neoptolemus is young
he is no fool and reflects back Odysseus' words, addressing the older man:
'*Laertiou pai*', or 'Laertes' boy' (86) when he objects to the dishonourable nature
of the scheme. Referring to his father's nature, or the *phusis* he has inherited, he
states clearly his wish: 'to act honourably and fail completely rather than act
dishonourably and succeed' (94–5). This passage introduces the first signs of
conflict between the two men and Odysseus will not be challenged so easily.
He replies: 'Son of a noble father, I too, when I was young (*neos*) once, had a
reluctant tongue but an active hand' (96–7). This response seems designed to
move the discussion away from examination of the moral questionability of
tricking Philoctetes, as well as subverting Neoptolemus' natural tendency
towards a heroic course of action. Indeed, Odysseus claims that Neoptolemus'
objections are simply reflective of those of a *neos* and that his youth, by its very
nature, will propel him on to reckless activity rather than considered strategy.

It is important to also reflect on use of *neos* here as the only example of this
term in the entire play. While it is not unusual for young men to be referred to
as child or boy, deployment of the term *neos* often also signifies that the young
men in question are of military or political age. In *Antigone* or *Persae*, for
example, *neos* is used as a signifying term for a psychological state, in part, and

is used to emphasize aspects of the characterization of these plays' younger male characters, Haemon and Xerxes.[11] Similarly, the term *hēbē* is deployed extensively in *Heraclidae* and serves to emphasize active martial responsibility. The absence of the term in *Philoctetes* suggests that the psychological traits of youth are of little relevance to the action. Indeed, if the play does reflect the prevailing Athenian dominant view that young men should be severely limited in their political authority, it is perfectly understandable that the primary emphasis should be on examples of how young men can be controlled, rather than offering insights into youth psychology. The use of 'boy' or 'child' over 'youth' give the age relation aspect of character interactions a much more pronounced sense of the different levels of political power. If we are to believe, as I am inclined to, the traditional date of *Antigone* in the 440s, the historical distance between *Antigone* and *Philoctetes* is great, taking Athens from her apex of confidence, power and wealth, to a time of great uncertainty, diminished imperial breadth and depleted resources. Over such a period, it is perhaps not surprising that tragedy should reflect a critical need to control a shaken society, rather than a more liberating (for young men, at least) portrayal of the potential political power and competency of *neoi*. It is also noteworthy that Odysseus applies the noun to his own past, but does not use it to describe Neoptolemus. It is as if to confirm the receding political autonomy of young men.

The tactic is clear to Neoptolemus. 'Are you not merely ordering me to utter lies?', he throws back (100). Thus starts a fractious exchange between the two characters as Odysseus again slowly introduces new information to persuade Neoptolemus to act on his instructions. Odysseus senses that he cannot rely solely on his position as superior in order to get Neoptolemus to act as he wishes and carefully replies to the provocative answers of the younger man. Comparison with the exchange between Creon and Haemon in Sophocles' *Antigone* is instructive. In that play, Sophocles shows Creon not to be in control of his own wits as the dialogue on Antigone's decision to bury Polynices spirals towards conflict. Here, the older man's control of the dialogue is masterful, shaping the conversation in a way to demonstrate that his suggested course of action is necessary in order for Neoptolemus to win the honour of enabling the fall of Troy. Set against the historical context, one in which the lives of many young men had been shaped or curtailed by the dialogue of older men, not just through the decisions to take the battle to Syracuse but also through the tumult of revolution, the manipulation of Neoptolemus by the older man would resonate with many in the audience. Unlike the historical context of *Heraclidae*, Athens would not be inundated with young men drawn in from rural areas of Attica. Quite the opposite, Athens of 409 would most likely be depleted of its younger men, many of whom would have been killed or captured near Syracuse.[12] But there is also a strong pseudo-democratic element to this section of the play. Odysseus claims to reflect the collective will of the Greek Army, not just the two kingly leaders. Neoptolemus, by contrast, is driven by the need to be true to his nature and his heroic heritage. In short, his allegiance is to himself and his family. It is tempting to interpret this characteristic as representative of a narrow way of thinking, one that was subversive to democracy and which had been recently expressed by one of those men who, perhaps, benefited from the political violence of younger men. A key figure in the oligarchic revolution, and a very persuasive orator, Antiphon (Thu. 8.68) was reported to have claimed primacy of one man's advice over that of the many (Aristotle, *Eudemian Ethics* 1232b7) and this view appears contrary to the advice and guidance offered by Odysseus.

Consistent with his approach throughout, Odysseus exits the scene issuing final instructions for Neoptolemus, whom he now refers to as child, *teknon* (130) and reveals that a sailor disguised as a merchant (as we later discover), will be sent to out to Neoptolemus if he is too slow in his efforts. Again, the young man is to all appearances given a great deal of responsibility but the use of the disguised sailor, as proxy for Odysseus, demonstrates the limitations in which Neoptolemus is permitted to operate. Whatever prize he might win, it will only be achieved through close supervision by an older man. The opportunity for the policy of Odysseus to be put into practice arises as Neoptolemus, accompanied by the chorus of his sailors, approaches the squalid home of Philoctetes. The chorus also refer to Neoptolemus as *teknon*, but this initially appears simply as a kindly expression of a group of older men as they then submit to his authority, asking how they can serve (141–3). But after they are provided with instructions to accompany Neoptolemus with which they comply, when they hear Philoctetes offstage, they interrupt with an abrupt: 'quiet, boy' (201). Like the older Odysseus, they too then appear in possession of information vital for the task, describing the cries they hear and where they might locate Philoctetes. Before the play's namesake arrives on stage the chorus

utter a warning to Neoptolemus urging: 'child, have ... further thoughts'
(208–10). Their meaning is that Neoptolemus must mentally prepare for
the imminent encounter with Philoctetes, but as sailors to the princely
Neoptolemus, their interruptions and constant address of their master as
teknon/pai would seem to undermine his authority. Furthermore, their direct
advice and control of the flow of information to Neoptolemus is suggestive of
a strong paternalistic characterization. Of course, choruses consisting of older
men who give advice to a main character are not uncommon. *Antigone*, again,
is a case in point, where the angry stichomythia between Creon and Haemon
is unsuccessfully mediated by a chorus of Theban elders. There, the chorus
comment on what they judge to be the truth of what is said and rebuke the
younger Haemon at times, though it is significant in that play that they avoid
using *pai* or *teknon* when addressing the young man. And yet the interventionist
attitude of Neoptolemus' sailors doesn't so much qualify his speech as
predetermine it by the degree to which his actions and words are shaped by
their direct influence. Effectively, Neoptolemus, whilst issuing orders, is
managed by his older subordinates.

As the chorus finish giving their guidance, Philoctetes enters the stage and
begins an exchange with Neoptolemus that sets out their dramatic background:
Philoctetes recounts the tale of his abandonment by the Greeks, and Odysseus
in particular, and Neoptolemus offers a greatly modified version of his history,
underscoring a personal, violent fallout with Odysseus (219–390). Just like
Odysseus, though, Philoctetes is quick to refer to the young man as *teknon* or
pai. However, whereas Odysseus' use of these terms fits within a convincingly
realistic linguistic style, Philoctetes' use of the same terms in *Philoctetes* is
markedly different. Significantly, in Philoctetes' speech from lines 254 to 316,
the terms *teknon* or *pai* are uttered eight times by Philoctetes, seven of which
are direct references to Neoptolemus. More remarkable still is the opening half
of this speech, in which the terms are used to refer to Neoptolemus four times
and at exact intervals of eight lines.[13] Such precise use of spacing must be part
of a design; it appears unlikely that such sustained repetition could be the
result of pure chance. The impact on the initial framing of relations between
the two men is significant. First, Philoctetes appears as much older than
Neoptolemus, the repeated use of 'child' or 'boy' is reminiscent of a standard
utterance made by one who is used to being the eldest. But the apparently

structured use of the terms creates the impression that Philoctetes can *only* view Neoptolemus via the prism of age relations. This dialogical device could be deliberately engineered partly for dramatic purposes, allowing the impending betrayal of the apparently much older man to appear all the more brutal. But second, the regular repetition also reflects earlier language used by Odysseus and so carries the hidden (from Philoctetes) encoding of Neoptolemus' position as a junior member of the Greek army, and a vehicle for the delivery of his superiors' policies. Such use of verbal repetition in Sophocles has been discussed by many[14] and even if the exact significance must be assessed on a play-by play-basis, it is clear that this type of linguistic pattern is particular to this playwright. Critically, it brings into his work recognizable aspects of Homeric language and when combined with heroic characterization strengthens the presentation of values of the Homeric context in a work.[15] The Homeric, and heroic, content of Sophocles' work is well attested and clearly relates dramatic action in Sophoclean tragedy to the aristocratic values of the Homeric world.[16] In the context of *Philoctetes*, and the play's innovative inclusion of Neoptolemus to allow the exploration of the best political management of youth, this intertextuality is highly important, as we shall see, when Neoptolemus' deception is finally revealed to Philoctetes.

Once Neoptolemus has established the basis for the deception, that he too had been treated outrageously by Odysseus, he answers a series of questions from Philoctetes on the fate of the various famous Greeks at Troy. The roll-call of the dead or missing is stupendous, even without the death of Achilles: Ajax is dead, as are Patroclus and Antilochus.[17] And yet Odysseus, Agamemnon and Menelaus survive, not to mention Thersites, a character so clearly oppositional to the heroic ideal as to cause great anguish to Philoctetes. Whilst avoiding temptation against drawing direct historical parallels and identifying a particular political position with the playwright's handling of speeches, it is difficult not to see correspondences of a more general kind with contemporary Athenian history. The reminder of the death of many young warriors is likely to have resonated deeply with a contemporary Athenian audience who were still entangled in a conflict that had no obvious end, or promise of outright victory, and who had recently experienced the horror of the decimation of the Athenian army at Syracuse.[18] Neoptolemus finishes recounting his deception and indicates that he is about to leave, provoking Philoctetes to protest against the latest abandonment: 'for your father's sake, for your mother's, my son . . . do not leave me alone' (464–70). Philoctetes' words do not immediately sway the younger man, but they do cause the chorus to advocate his position. Neoptolemus relents, ungraciously stating, 'well, it certainly is shameful for me to appear more hesitant than you in efforts to meet a stranger's need' (524–5). The response is emphatic as the older man rejoices, 'most welcome day, dearest man, and kindly sailors', before instructing Neoptolemus: 'let us go, boy' (530–3). Philoctetes thanks the older men and Neoptolemus but then reduces his role to that of guide. But his use of the term 'dearest man' (*anēr*) does appear to include reference to Neoptolemus and highlights an interesting point. This is the first time in the play that Neoptolemus has been referred to as an adult, and only after he has agreed to, and is on the verge of, carrying out the actions requested and advised by the older men around him.[19]

It is at this point, with part of the deception successfully achieved, that one of Odysseus' proxies, disguised as a merchant, approaches to covertly direct events towards the planned outcome. Along with advice from the chorus, and direction from Philoctetes, yet another older male figure arrives to curtail the authority of Neoptolemus. The quick interchange between the merchant and Neoptolemus not only demonstrates the penetration of Odysseus' political power, exercised here from a distance, but also introduces critical new information in the story of Helenus' prophecy of the fall of Troy. Although it would not be clear to the characters on stage whether or not this information formed part of the deception, it is an established element of the Trojan War myths and to an audience this revelation is further evidence of Odysseus' ultimate control of information. This technique of holding back information for selective deployment is effective, pushing Neoptolemus and Philoctetes towards swifter action, and the episode ends with their departure imminent, albeit to a destination unknown to the older man.

The section following the stasimon, innovatively placed as the only major choral ode in the play, and creating two distinct sections, 'is remarkable for its vivid representation of intense physical and psychological pain'.[20] It is the point at which the full horror of Philoctetes' affliction is brought out into the open, harshly exposing the acuteness of Philoctetes' suffering. The searing cries of pain that Neoptolemus witnesses close up, shortly after successfully acquiring Philoctetes' bow by deception, rends his dissonant psychological state in two.

Exclaiming: 'Oh! what, then, am I to do?' (895), after helping Philoctetes to his feet, the young man is completely unable to reconcile the two polar forces that are represented by the principal older men of the play. On the one hand, to Neoptolemus, the aristocratic, personal code of Achilles falls like a shadow across Lemnos, the figure of the father constantly framing his self-conception: 'All is disgust when one abandons one's own nature and does what is out of keeping with it' (902–3). But Odysseus' influence is still strong and the sense of obligation to the Greeks is equally as compelling. When Philoctetes attempts to take back his bow, and Neoptolemus refuses, he says: 'No, it is impossible. For duty and expediency compel me to obey those in command' (925–6). It is here that Philoctetes, furious at his betrayal, roars: 'You fire, you monster through and through, you vilest model of awe-inspiring villainy...' (927–9). The actions of Neoptolemus burn like flames and are now seen clearly by Philoctetes as the rash and headstrong characteristics of an immature youth, certain enough to begin an endeavour but lacking the confidence to see to the end one firm course of action or another. This explosive verbal attack serves to intensify the pressure on Neoptolemus to change tack, but it also enmeshes the speech within a Homeric co-text. A useful analysis has been made of the use of the vocative 'Ō pur [fire] *su kai pan deima kai panourgias / deinēs technēm' echthiston* ..., which Sophocles has Philoctetes direct at Neoptolemus (927).[21] The apparently play-specific use of the term 'fire' can be considered as a direct reference to the language of Homer, encouraging the audience to compare Neoptolemus' actions against those of his father in the *Iliad* when the term is used to describe Achilles as glorious, terrifying and destructive (18.205–14, 19.375–80, 21.522–5).[22] And it has been argued too that this linguistic formulation also underscores a narrative view: 'Neoptolemus is fire as a state of transformation, a young man who changes over the course of the play.'[23] But fire is also an element to be controlled and Sophocles has shown in *Antigone* not only how an inflamed *thumos* can lead to catastrophically reckless action, but how this condition is most often related to young men.[24] Neoptolemus is thus to be judged by the standards of two periods, the contemporary and the Homeric. The Homeric values, brought to the surface through the use of language, frame his actions within an acutely paternalist milieu whilst the contemporary audience are offered a play that appears to show just two ways of controlling young men, in an equally politically neutering way, reflective of the anxious view of the political role of young men in post-Syracuse post-revolution Athens.

The contrast with the presentation of Haemon and Antigone in Sophocles' earlier play is remarkable, but this is unfortunately not often considered in the vast scholarship on *Philoctetes*. When scholars erroneously make a value judgement of Odysseus' behaviour, criticizing his manipulative and utilitarian view of Neoptolemus, they should remember the Homeric heroes' conception of the utility of all youth, demonstrated in Menelaus' instructions to Antilochus: 'We have nobody younger than you, Antilochus . . . why not race out and see if you can bring a Trojan down.'[25] The justification for such dangerous utility of youth, ostensibly for the good of the martial community, is expressed as an exhortation to perform honourable actions or deception in order to achieve a goal. Although the justifications in the *Iliad* and *Philoctetes* are different, the Iliadic, paternalist, appropriation of youth as apparatus is clear in *Philoctetes*. Just as youth are considered as little more than a phalanx in *Heraclidae*, and in complete contrast to the individual sketches of youth in *Antigone*, in Philoctetes the young Neoptolemus is a tool to be manipulated by the older men on and off stage. Philoctetes goes on to beg the return of his bow in perhaps the most pitiful section of speech by a Sophoclean hero before finishing with the oddly tentative curse, 'may you perish – but not yet, till I see if you will change your mind again. And if not, may you die a cruel death' (960–1). Neoptolemus' state of youthful inconsistency offers the possibility of further changes ahead. And this possibility is strengthened just moments later when, in response to the chorus' query on what to do next, their master equivocates before asking of the chorus: 'Ah, what am I to do? I wish that I had never left Scyros. So distressed am I by what is happening now' (969–70).[26] It is difficult to imagine a more recognizable characterization of a young man still wrestling with self-identity, unable to fully become an adult of the world of his father or of Odysseus. But for complete clarity of characterization, and to underscore that *paideia* is an issue in the play, Philoctetes says: 'You are not evil, but you came, I think, after learning shameful lessons from evil men', to which Neoptolemus says (to the chorus): 'what are we to do, men?' (971–4). Sophocles leaves no room for doubt: this young man requires the guidance of older men to make any sort of firm decision. What seemed like manipulation by Odysseus to begin with, now looks like necessary micro-management of a typically inconsistent youth.

At this point Odysseus returns to the stage, accompanied by two sailors. Having, apparently, secretly watched events unfold he rages: 'You villain, what are you doing? Will you not give this bow up to me and come back?' (974–5).[27] Tellingly, the stichomythic exchange that follows is exclusively between Odysseus and Philoctetes, the young man at the centre of the action is denied a voice as the older men argue between themselves – even when, again, Neoptolemus is addressed directly. Philoctetes pleads: 'Give me back my bow, boy, let it go' (981). Odysseus, in an attempt to assert his authority replies, 'This he will never do, even if he wishes. And you must go with it, or they will take you by force' (981–3), and reinforces his power of command by claiming, 'It is Zeus, let me tell you, Zeus, the ruler of this land, Zeus, by whom this has been decided. And I am his servant' (981–90). After a lengthy speech by Philoctetes, where he places the blame for Neoptolemus' actions on Odysseus' influence and curses him for his actions, Odysseus changes tack in the face of Philoctetes' refusal to leave Lemnos. Using an appeal to what might be left of Philoctetes' pride, he says that instead Teucer, or even he himself, could wield the bow, making Philoctetes' role in the capture of Troy redundant. The change of approach is designed to sting Philoctetes into action and the point hits home, the outraged Philoctetes replying, 'Are you going to present yourself, decked out with my arms, among the Argives?' And turning to Neoptolemus he pleads: 'Son of Achilles, will not even you say anything more to me?' (1062–6). Odysseus instructs Neoptolemus to ignore the appeal, and the moral uncertainty of moments ago, before Odysseus returned to the scene, appears to have vanished. When Neoptolemus finally speaks, almost 100 lines after being addressed by Philoctetes, he addresses only the chorus directly, instructing them to stay with Philoctetes in the hope that he will change his mind while the boats are readied for departure to Troy. His personal authority has apparently evaporated in the face of Odysseus' political dominance and Neoptolemus follows him offstage.

The battle for control of Neoptolemus' loyalty has so far taken place entirely on stage with the arguments for expediency and glory presented by Odysseus and fealty to the Achillean honour code by Philoctetes. Neoptolemus' responses to these attempts at control, including many examples of indecision or uncertainty, have likewise played out in front of the audience. Between lines 1081 and 1222 Philoctetes and the chorus, through a *kommos*, poetically restate their entrenched positions, ending with the repeated threat by Philoctetes that he will attempt to kill himself. Meanwhile, offstage, the psychological conflict within Neoptolemus appears to have transformed into a singular certainty on what course of action he should take. The audience are not privy to this transformation, nor is any solid explanation given in the dialogue that follows the return to the action of Odysseus and Neoptolemus. As they enter the stage Odysseus asks why Neoptolemus has turned back, sparking off a stichomythic exchange in which the young man condemns the use of deceit and the older man fixes the necessity within the designs of the Greek army (1228–50). In this fairly straightforward repetition of his initial doubts as to the justice of Odysseus' plans, it is unclear what has galvanized the young man's decision to side with Philoctetes. What is clear is a new-found determination and rejection of Odysseus' authority. As the exchange becomes increasingly aggressive the influence that Odysseus asserted just moments before, less than 200 lines earlier in the play and not obviously at some temporal distance, has lost all potency. Resorting to explicit threats, Odysseus says: 'It is not the Trojans then, but you, we shall be fighting' (1253), recasting Neoptolemus as a traitor. By tossing back an impertinent, 'let be what will be' (1254), this threat is met with blatant insubordination. The potential for physical violence, always present in the play, comes a step closer to realization as Odysseus reaches for his sword to signal use of force against Neoptolemus. The young man does likewise and forces Odysseus to back down, saying resignedly, as he exits the stage: 'Well then, I shall bother you no longer. But I shall report this on my return to the whole army, who will punish you' (1254–8). The direct challenge by the young man on his commanding officer, by both word and deed, is remarkable in a play where all threats of violence have focused on Philoctetes. Comparison with the conflict between Haemon and Creon in *Antigone* is again useful. There Haemon attempts to slash his father when he interferes with the young man's discovery of Antigone's suicide. As Creon flees, Haemon drives his blade between his own ribs and dies, enraged at Antigone's death and his failed and shame-inducing attempt on his father's life. Within a play that is largely sympathetic to the young characters that are denied any influence on the policies of their city, this scene demonstrates the catastrophic consequences of persistent interference in the decision-making of the young by the old. Against this literary-historic backdrop, Odysseus' withdrawal before real violence occurs can be considered a tactical withdrawal rather than an undignified rout.

But the contrast also offers insight into the different historical contexts of *Antigone* and *Philoctetes*. *Antigone*, produced years before the beginning of the Peloponnesian War and in a period of supreme confidence and stability at Athens, allows the full consequences of the disenfranchisement of youth to be played out dramatically. The city had not, to any great extent, endured the mass loss of young lives such as was experienced during the wars that would later threaten to unravel the fabric of Athenian society. By the time *Philoctetes* was first performed a generation had been decimated at Syracuse and the subsequent revolution and counter revolution had involved political violence, possibly originating in the age-group defined *hetairiai* and aimed to impress older mentors, carried out by young men. Odysseus' actions, then, reflect a realistic strategic management of *neoi*, and demonstrate the limits of control of those who, perhaps, were well aware of their value to Athens.

The closing stages of the play show Odysseus' management of Neoptolemus to have had some lasting effect as the young man continues to plead with Philoctetes that he should leave Lemnos and join the Greek army at Troy if he should wish to gain glory, find respite from his wounds and fulfil a prophecy (1325–47). Philoctetes, as predicted by Odysseus, is stubbornly impervious to these inducements and persuades Neoptolemus to escort him back to Oeta. Fully aware of the probable retaliation for this treachery by the Greek commanders, Philoctetes even offers his services in defence of Neoptolemus if his homeland is attacked. But there is something amiss with Neoptolemus' quick decision to sail for home. Abandoning greater glory to satisfy a personal honour code is understandable enough, but Neoptolemus' sudden disregard for the prophecy of Helenus is altogether more perplexing. There are only two or three possible explanations for this turn of events. First, it could be that he does not really believe in the validity of Helenus' prophecy. But if this is the case, by introducing Helenus he is using a form of deception to persuade Philoctetes to travel to Troy. Second, he sincerely believes the words of the prophecy and is ready to depart with Philoctetes, aware that fate will lead them back to Troy no matter what part they take. This too is a deception on Neoptolemus' part. A final possibility is that he simply forgets the prophecy. Causation is impossible to establish, as with all fictional characters, but if Sophocles' characterization of the young man is consistent, and there are no other examples to the contrary, two further possible conclusions can be drawn.

Either Neoptolemus has taken on some of Odysseus' traits and exercised deception in his dealings with Philoctetes, or he is demonstrating quite faulty thinking. At the end of a play that many have read as presenting Neoptolemus as a pupil becoming a heroic adult, in the mould of his father, these two possibilities would show that the picture is not so simple. When considered alongside the possibility that the play is ultimately about the control of young men, and how to manage their political or autonomous ambitions, this final unconscious revelation by Neoptolemus suggests that Odysseus has had the measure of his mentee all along. Not only is Neoptolemus acting out of a selfish impulse to satisfy his own heroic self-identification, but his ability to think through the issue at hand has been shown as questionable.

Finally, as the two characters are about to exit the stage, a dramatic intervention is made by the *deus ex machina* Heracles. Appearing, most likely, on top of the stage building he says: 'I have left the heavenly regions and come on your account, to tell you Zeus's plans for you, and to check your steps ...' (1413–5). Heracles speaks with absolute authority, leaving no doubt that his control over the paths of the two men is incontestable. The prophecy of Helenus is again inferred and Philoctetes is then told of the healing of his sickness and the glory of taking Troy that await him. In contrast to Odysseus' selective presentation of information to Neoptolemus, to cajole him into action, Heracles lays out in exact detail what the future holds. There is no room for doubt, the two men are commanded to leave for Troy and they are given no choice in the matter. Both Neoptolemus and Philoctetes immediately agree to submit to Zeus' will, as expressed by Heracles and the older man says a final, oddly fond, farewell to Lemnos. After all the conflict and uncertainty, the original objective of Odysseus, to bring Philoctetes and his bow to Troy has been achieved. Odysseus, the ultimate strategist, perhaps could see all along that which was bound by the gods to happen. In this light, his withdrawal from the action at the point of potential physical conflict with Neoptolemus looks retrospectively like a sound decision. But Heracles does not just simply ensure a positive, and inevitable, ending for the play, his intervention reflects the theme of political authority that colours interactions between all the characters. The final, and ultimate, hierarchy is confirmed in these closing lines. The gods control all mortal actions and Zeus, via the proxy of Heracles, has supreme authority. On the mortal plane, the Greeks, whilst at war, are a single community, commanded by Agamemnon and Menelaus, and their wishes are expressed via the proxy of Odysseus. The martial command and control structure of authority (regardless of how Odysseus might use the peer group pressure of the army as a form of *peitho*),[28] far from the revived democracy of the audience members, is reflected in the mortal and divine worlds. In this structure, the most junior members of the pantheon or the army are subject to the most stringent control. Heracles is, of course, the most appropriate divine figure to bring resolution to the play. It is his bow that will take Troy and his heroic nature both speaks to the characters of Philoctetes and Neoptolemus and relates to the events that lie ahead. But as an immortal, not an Olympian, he is a junior divinity and speaks with the proximate authority of Zeus, not of his own, whilst also associated through myth and cult to youth, as we saw in *Heraclidae*.

For a modern audience, and for some scholars, the final picture of youth, in the form of Neoptolemus, is in many ways comparable with contemporary experience of how young reach a level of maturity.[29] This view is reflected in the lengthy literature on the different educational models supposedly used by Odysseus and Philoctetes in tutoring the young man. Whilst there may be some truth in these views, the historical context must be acknowledged. The Athens of the period might have found some new confidence in her ability to defeat the Spartans and their allies, but the demographic impact of the defeat at Syracuse, and the political consequences of the removal of a large number of younger citizens, would mean that the social constitution of the polis would be fundamentally different from earlier days of democratic Athens. In the modern Western world, fortunate not to have recent experience of such horror, it is difficult to imagine the acute value young people would have in revitalizing a decimated population and concomitant importance that would be placed on their careful nurturing. In the case of *Philoctetes*, while arguments can be put forward for how young people's education must be managed, represented by the attempts at guidance of Neoptolemus' actions, this includes their management within a political system that required them to put their lives at risk. Before 413, young men were allowed to take some part in the decision-making on the level of risk they would be exposed to. But the decision-making that led up to the decision to launch the attack on Syracuse, greatly influenced – at least according to Thucydides – by a younger political faction (see

Chapter 1), had resulted in disaster. The threat to a community, whether this is the Greeks at Troy or those in the Athenian audience, of young people taking decisions that would lead to military defeat on an epic scale, was not just a martial or party political issue, but one that would have existential consequences. *Philoctetes*, read against this context, offers a reflective narrative of the acute anxiety felt in society of the role of young men at a time when a new generation of hoplites was emerging but with severely curtailed political autonomy. If for aristocratic women in this and other periods, theirs was a gilded cage, for young male citizens, it was a cage bonded by blade and spear. The political upheaval of the period could not hide the fact that without young people surviving the drawn-out war with Sparta, society could not properly function. And whatever political system was to govern Athens, without the existence of subsequent generations of citizens no party could survive beyond the dwindling ranks of their own gerontocracy. This paternalistic system is also reflected in *Philoctetes*, through the power relations between the male, mortal characters, between Zeus and Heracles, and between the all-powerful older divine figures and the young mortal ones. The impression that is left is of a play that reflects a society that was riddled with contradictions and divided opinions, between oligarchs and democrats, sophists and conservatives and between young and old. But most fundamentally, late fifth-century Athens, although with democracy restored, was still dominated by a paternalist core that determined how society was shaped and controlled.

Friendship and Generational Loyalty in Euripides' *Orestes*

So far, we've seen how the plotlines of extant tragedy are taken from a wide variety of myths (and in one case, *Persae*, directly from historical events) but there are two dominant clusters that are repeatedly drawn upon. The first is those stories associated with Thebes and the family of Oedipus. The second is the myth of the Atreidai. This second group is particularly important for discussion of how Athenian tragedy is shaped by historical events due to the precedent set early in tragedy's history, in Aeschylus' highly political *Oresteia*, that established Orestes' association with Athens and the city's political institutions.[1] Sophocles' *Electra* and Euripides' *Orestes, Electra, Iphigenia at Tauris* and *Iphigenia at Aulis* all cover events relating to the Atreidai and, through the admittedly patchy evidence available, look likely to have been written towards the end of these tragedians' careers.[2] Mining the same vein of myth, it is unsurprising that these plays display similarities in plotline. In all except *Iphigenia in Aulis*, a central triadic relationship between two young men and a woman results in conflict that ends, or threatens to end in murder. There are striking similarities in the relationships between these plays' principal characters, the alliances they form in the face of adversity and their preparedness to use violence to achieve their aims. Foremost in this group, it is perhaps Euripides' *Orestes* that presents the most interesting picture of youth in tragedy. This is a play that not only makes a highly innovative departure from the myth of the house of Atreus but features three young characters who form an exclusive group in order to implement a highly aggressive plot.

Between the restoration of democracy in 410 and the Athenian defeat at Notium in 406, a renewed sense of confidence seems to have been established in the city (albeit beginning with a period of political recriminations and show trials). Historical sources for 408 do not reveal any new tensions at Athens, other than those noted in the previous chapter on the different views on how aggressively the Athenian imperial strategy should be pursued and there appears to be relative social and political continuity, if not stability. While the supporters of the oligarchic revolution had been defeated politically, the networks of influence that sustained oligarchic sympathies in Athens would have persisted. One visible manifestation of this network were the *hetairiai* – often glossed as 'clubs' – perceived after 411 as associations for oligarchic conspirators.[3] The most well-known picture of *hetairiai* is sketched in Thucydides, at 8.65. There, he records: 'Some of the younger men had formed a group amongst themselves and had murdered a certain Androcles . . .'. The description of an exclusive group, created in order to carry out violence, appears earlier in Thucydides' work, at 3.82, when he describes that membership of a *hetairiai* (*hetairias*) required loyalty to your peer group rather than kinship in times of civil war. The reference in Book 8 makes specific mention of the group formed by young men, amongst themselves, to create a self-selecting peer group defined by age, violence and a political aim. The political aims of these groups are made clear (at 8.54), when Pisander is said to have made initial contact with such groups or clubs in order to set the ground for the oligarchic revolution of 411. Given the nature of these groups, their exact internal dynamic is unclear but, undoubtedly, they were designed to further the aims of their membership, completely contrary to the democratic system. And time and again, such as in famous association with the mutilation of the *Hermae*, these groups appear as agents of the rendering of political impulses into acts of violence. These *hetairiai* were exclusive and impenetrable by those outside the group, and perceived as being non-democratic violent associations, representing the re-emergence of a destabilizing political force. While young people had been disenfranchised from political processes they appeared to have created covert political organizations. It could take just a spark to provoke these groups to violent action. It must be acknowledged that such groups appear to have existed long before this historical period and may not have been the exclusive domain of aristocratic cohorts. Their composition, however, does appear to have been largely based on age and social equality, forming, in other words, a generational unit.[4]

West points out that critics tend to read *Orestes* with this political topography, and Thucydides' commentary, too foregrounded in their analysis. Importantly, he warns, correctly, that references to Thucydides, such as these above, are used erroneously by scholars to explain the presentation of themes. Yet time and again tragedy proves resistant to neatly exclusive interpretation. As we shall see, one must fully credit the performative nature of tragedy and recognize that in this play the audience 'whose emotions he [Euripides] had enlisted on Orestes' side' would be sympathetic to the young characters.[5] This is an important point: the text must be seen in light of the lived experience of the audience. But as is the danger with any modern view or reading, Euripides' texts can be interpreted in many ways and West makes his own error when attributing a particular viewpoint to Euripides. Whether Orestes *et al.*'s case is just is irrelevant. Reference to Thucydides serves to demonstrate that the behaviour of the group would have been recognizable to the audience as the actions of young people in a time of political crisis. I place no moral value on their actions, and argue that Euripides does likewise. But it is important to remember that the literary Orestes is a figure who was generally treated sympathetically by Athenian tragedians and is placed by Euripides, in this play, in hostile territory.

Following the oligarchic revolution of 411 such groups appear in Thucydides exclusively in relation to oligarchic political activity, and post-revolution Athens appears to have been rife with *hetairiai* consisting of young people.[6] While most groups with older memberships appear to have been designed primarily to assist in litigation for political ends, in contrast, the groups with younger members appear to have been centred on social activities. Moreover, these groups used violence and sacrilege towards religious rites as a way of expressing their identity and as pledges of continuing allegiance to the group.[7] Calhoun, writing in the sixties, makes comparison with the 'Hellfire Club' (or more accurately, 'clubs') of the eighteenth century, the secretive associations of upper-class men, and is representative of many scholars in translating *hetairiai* as 'clubs'.[8] A more recent parallel could be the notorious Bullingdon Club, the Oxford University drinking society, and this, too, would reinforce the class-inflected categorization that distorts the view of these groups in the modern and ancient world.[9] Formed of a generational unit, mixing social aims and support for mutual benefit, and with an identity shaped by often violent opposition to wider society, these groups are gangs by any other name. It appears only their aristocratic connections that allow the term 'club' to be applied without contest, revealing the fundamentally class-based interpretation that scholars unwittingly apply. When such group characteristics are related to the core of Electra, Orestes and Pylades in *Orestes*, the dramatic characterization features all the elements of these historical 'youth gangs'. By age and status, identity formed through violence, already committed against the immediate society of the family, and for mutual benefit, all three are tightly bound to one another.[10]

In Euripides' play, the opening monologue is delivered by Electra who sets out the mythic background to her present circumstance at Argos. Retelling the story of the curse of the house of Atreus, she admits her part in the killing of Clytemnestra and foresees the sentencing to death by stoning by the people of the *polis*. Her admission sets the action within a mythic sequence that is most famously realized in tragedy by Aeschylus' *Oresteia*. Produced exactly fifty years before *Orestes*, the trilogy includes the three central characters of *Orestes*: Electra, Orestes and Pylades. In Aeschylus' version of the myth, Electra too, actively helps plan the murder of Clytemnestra but is absent from relatively early on in *Choēphoroi*. Pylades, who would become a central figure in *Orestes*, is a near mute figure in the *Oresteia*, making a single contribution in the *Choēphoroi*, albeit a significant one.[11] The *Oresteia*, unsurprisingly, is focused on the actions of Orestes, at least in *Choēphoroi* and *Eumenides*. The plays can be seen to track Orestes' passage to maturity: from his boyhood in exile in Phocis, he returns to Argos as an adolescent in order to carry out the murder of his mother, finally reaching adulthood with his first political duties when he triumphs at the Areopagus at Athens. This transformation serves mainly to create a charter myth that expressed for the Athenians several discrete strands in their democratic identity – the proper role of the Areopagus, the participation of citizens in juries, the role of women in religion but not in legal or political arenas and the alliance with Argos. Following a period of political turmoil, the end of the play raises questions about the redefinition of the court of the Areopagus after Ephialtes' reforms and provides an aetiology for the establishment of the cult of the Erinyes. In this sense, the play is a directly political one, mediating the contradictions, primarily the accommodation of ancient traditions within a modern democratic polity, which underlay the grand politics of the day.

In Sophocles' *Electra*, Pylades is an entirely mute character. Orestes appears briefly to set the scene at the beginning of the play but then withdraws until two-thirds of the way through the action to help bring the play to a mythically compliant ending. Electra, Orestes and Pylades do form a group of sorts in the *Electra* by Euripides and Pylades is present, again as a mute character. Unlike Sophocles' *Electra*, however, Orestes and Electra share much more stage time and Electra takes a central role in devising the murder of her mother, interrupting Orestes' plotting at 647 to say: 'I shall arrange the killing of my mother.' The play contains some fairly horrific content, such as the luring of Clytemnestra to her death by making her think she is visiting a newly born granddaughter. But a sense of adventure, the exciting pursuit of a risky strategy, is palpable throughout, making the play similar to other, possibly, later plays by Euripides, such as *Iphigenia in Tauris*, *Helen* (412 BCE) and indeed, again, *Orestes*. While *Helen* does not contain the characters in question, *Iphigenia in Tauris* certainly does. Although Electra is absent, Iphigenia presents a third part of a triad of characters that form a group in opposition to all those around them. While Orestes and Iphigenia are clearly the principal characters, Pylades is, for the first time in tragedy, present as a fully developed participant, one who makes regular important contributions to the dialogue. Together, the three plot a bold and successful escape from Tauris, until their plans are discovered and they are set to be chased down by the barbarian king Thoas. A *deus ex machina* appearance by Athena is all that stops their endeavour ending in capture and execution. This structure is extremely close to that of *Orestes*. This play, in comparison, can be seen as *Iphigenia in Tauris* (IT) on home turf, with an exclusive group formed, based on shared cultural ties, in order to challenge the local community. But also like *Iphigenia in Tauris*, the play contains a clear sense of adventure, accelerated by near brushes with death and disaster. *IT* has been described as the archetype for all adventure narratives featuring the entertaining escapades of 'two guys and a girl'[12] and the same sense pervades *Orestes*. Euripides in writing *Orestes*, even more so than *IT*, makes this adventure story one based on the development of a youthful group that might be considered to use violence gratuitously, rather than out of necessity. If *IT* is the progenitor of travelling adventure stories, *Orestes* is correspondingly the archetypal 'youth against the world' stories, in which the audience is presented with characters with whom they may not naturally identify but through whose focalization we are won round.[13]

While *Orestes* lacks the exoticism of *Iphigenia in Tauris*, the Greek setting allows for the crystallization of a more directly political message. Rather than in a barbarian country, the action takes place in a Greek city now hostile to the youthful principals. The stakes are the same for the triadic groups but the consequences for Argos are much more severe than those faced by Tauris' King Thoas. The vigorous opposition to wider local society (supported by the creation of an exclusive group that offers the participants hope of controlling their future, created as a result of absolute political disenfranchisement) is characteristic of both *hetairiai* in Athens and Orestes' group in the play. The inter-communal violence threatened by the young aristocratic group, in response to their impending execution by the Argive democracy, and the symbolic execution of the younger generation by their own city, so reminiscent of recent Athenian agonies, carves out a unique place for *Orestes* from the same narrative fundament as *Iphigenia*. The transposition of the group conflict from barbarian territory to home soil comes as no surprise if *Orestes* (as is probable) can be dated later than *Iphigenia* in tragedy's chronology, following the revolutions at Athens that provided an historical context for stasis between political factions.[14]

Orestes is effectively composed of two acts. The first half presents a sympathetic analysis of the psychic impact on Orestes and Electra of their matricide, as well as the torment of impending execution. The second part appears, superficially, quite different as the protagonists launch a daring plan of escape. But from Electra's opening monologue onwards, the language used in the first half sets the inevitability of the action of the second. The feverishness of Orestes, first articulated by Electra and then the young man himself, anticipates the febrile nature of the dialogue that is later shared between Electra, Orestes and Pylades. Unlike in Aeschylus' *Eumenides*, or the *Electras*, the matricides have not left the scene of their crime. But the city has been their prison since the murder of Clytemnestra some six days past. As Electra says, while Orestes sleeps fitfully nearby, 'This city of Argos has decreed that no one is to give us hospitality of roof or fire, or speak to us, matricides that we are. And this is the appointed day when the community of Argives will divide its vote on whether the pair of us must die by stoning' (46–50).[15] The position they find themselves in is impossible. Electra and Orestes are outcasts within their own city, unable even to seek the relief of exile. For Orestes the punishment for matricide is even more severe. As demonstrated in the introductory monologue by Electra, he is internally and psychologically terrorized by the Erinyes and faces physical annihilation by the city of Argos (34–8).[16] But the pair hold out hope that the approaching Menelaus might help them overcome their problems. It is this hope that sustains their stoic resolve through the first half of the play, and the betrayal of that hope, as we shall see, that acts as a catalyst for the young people's group to devise and implement a daring plan to strike at the heart of those who have betrayed them. It will be this betrayal, and the group's reaction to it, that marks the point at which political power in Argos appears to have become gerontocratic and the play from that point becomes in part a warning of what might come by implanting anything resembling Sparta's societal structures in Athens. Both the isolation and the tainted status of the (yet to be fully formed) group are underscored when Helen enters the stage at 71 and asks Electra, outrageously, to take some flowers to Clytemnestra's grave. She says she cannot go herself because, 'I am ashamed to show my person to the Argives' (98). Moreover, she will not send her young daughter, Hermione, as: 'it is not seemly for girls to go out in public' (108). Helen is far from respectable in the eyes of the local population, but even she has a place to maintain within society. Electra, on the other hand, is completely outside society. From Helen's perspective, Electra is able to undertake the most shameful activities (walking unescorted in public, placing flowers at the grave of the mother she helped to murder) without fear of incurring further shame, such is the fullness of her ignominy. While there in undoubtedly an ironic undercurrent to this exchange, Helen is all but comparing her own presentation in literature to that of Electra, the two women's relative social status is made absolutely clear. Electra has no further to fall.[17]

When Orestes finally wakes up from his fevered sleep it is clear that consciousness offers little comfort. But he sees some sliver of hope of escape from the death penalty when Electra reveals the imminent arrival of Menelaus in Argos. Orestes, physically and psychologically wrecked, receives the news with desperate expectation: 'He's come, light of deliverance for my troubles and yours, our kinsmen who owes gratitude to our father?' (242–3). Menelaus represents one last shot at persuading the Argives not to stone the two of them. The news, however, offers very temporary respite as the Erinyes return to torment him. Invisible to all others, their impact is evident in the young man's convulsions. Filling with terror, Orestes begs his dead mother: 'don't threaten me with those blood-eyed, snaky maidens!' before pleading with Apollo, 'O

Phoebus! They'll kill me, the bitch-faced, fierce-eyed priestesses of the nether ones, dread goddesses!' (255–61). These lines are resonant of Orestes' reaction to the arrival of the Erinyes at the end of Aeschylus' *Choēphoroi*. There, he also reacts in terror and makes an appeal of sorts to Apollo.[18] But while, in Aeschylus, the arrival of the Erinyes pushes the plot towards Orestes' exile from Argos and his trilogy's resolution at Athens, in Euripides' play Orestes has no opportunity to flee. Cornered, terrified and desperate, Orestes' subsequent speech becomes highly aggressive and confrontational, allowing a brief glimpse of what is to come. Twisting to break free of the Erinyes' invisible grip, Orestes demands: 'Give me my horn-drawn bow, Loxias' gift with which he said to defend myself against the goddesses if they terrified me with raving fits. There's going to be a deity shot with mortal hand if she doesn't move away out of my sight! Can't you see the feathered shafts speeding out from the far-shooting bow?' (268–74). Orestes sees no other option in his fever of anger and seeks release through violence over his enemies.

But while this brief episode demonstrates the acuity of the Erinyes' psychological impact, comparison with other tragic figures shows that the aggressive response, his battle against all including deities (*theomachy*), is not one widely shared by older characters suffering similar psychological torment. In Sophocles, Philoctetes seeks death in his delirium and Ajax, in his name-play, once recovered from his divine madness, sees only suicide as a means of escape.[19] While there are some typically Sophoclean aspects to these characters' reactions, both of these examples are of older men who find themselves with limited options to respond when marginalized within society. In *Bacchae*, as we shall see in the following chapter, the young king Pentheus, inflamed by opposition to his authority, threatens violence against the disguised Dionysus (the charge of *theomachy* is made against him repeatedly by Tiresias) while acknowledging that he is acting against the gods too. Yet he falls so completely under the spell of Dionysus that he is unable carry out his threats in any effective way.[20] Moreover, at no point does Pentheus believe he is not in control of his city and central to society. Other young characters who are similarly constrained and angry, most notably Antigone and Haemon in Sophocles' *Antigone*, also commit suicide. It is true that Haemon makes a half-hearted sword swipe at his father, but Sophocles has him then make a heroic exit in suicide. This (probably) much earlier play is in many ways sympathetic to young people, reflecting an Athenian society relatively tolerant of political participation by youth (see Chapter 3), and traditional associations with youth and older authority are reversed. When considered against these other tragic examples, Orestes in Euripides' play presents a unique case of a young man, psychologically pained, excluded from society and with few options to influence his future, who reveals an innate tendency to violence.

By the end of the play, the aggression that Orestes reveals in his delirium transforms into a dominant characteristic. When Menelaus finally arrives his reception is less than effusive in warmth and sets the tone for Menelaus's questioning of Orestes. Having already heard the news of Clytemnestra's death, the king proclaims: 'it is not monstrous that monstrous things be suffered by those who have done them' (413). Clearly, his judgement is against the actions of Orestes and his dialogue becomes increasingly one of distanced interrogation, rather than supportive conversation. With the facts established, that the Argives are set to vote on the execution of Electra and Orestes, the young man lays out his expectation for his salvation, saying: 'My hope runs to you for refuge from my troubles' (448). But before the older man can reply the chorus alert Orestes to the imminent arrival of his grandfather, saying: 'See now, on aged legs the Spartiate struggles this way, Tyndareus' (456–7). With the arrival of the old man three generations are brought together. The following passage of dialogue, first between Tyndareus and Menelaus and then Tyndareus and Orestes, reveals the extent of Spartan political power based on age. In a play that can be seen as pitting aristocratic youth against egalitarian democracy, the intervention by Tyndareus demonstrates the corrupting impact of gerontocracy on a local democracy. In essence, this section of the play imagines the political restrictions that would be placed on Athenian youth if a Spartan model of age relations were to be adopted.[21] Menelaus is quick to demonstrate his deference to the older man, greeting him with: 'joy to you, old sir . . .', to which Tyndareus replies: '. . . joy yourself, Menelaus, my son-in-law' (476–7). Their age-related statuses thus established, Tyndareus launches an immediate attack on Menelaus' relations with Orestes. When Menelaus justifies his support for Orestes in terms of kin obligations, the old man says: 'You have become barbarised, being so long among barbarians' (485).[22] Replying, at 490, that compulsion by law to take prescribed action should not be the sole option amongst the intelligent, Menelaus goes so far as to accuse Tyndareus of faulty thinking due to his old age. So far, this reflects the age-politics of Athens: Menelaus, as the middle-range aged male, claims his superiority of intellect in contrast to the old man. But this argument is stopped dead by a masterful speech by the old Spartan. Beginning with a summary of how Orestes has contravened Greek laws, Tyndareus goes on to illustrate his point with an example of how the cycle of kin-killing could spiral to destroy a community. He then places an emotional value on Orestes' killing of Clytemnestra, saying: 'my poor old eye runs away in tears', then, swiftly states that the gods are not on Orestes' side. Summarizing his argument, the old man adds the threat that Menelaus will be banished from Spartan soil if he fails to support the verdict of the townspeople (491–541). In this speech, Tyndareus delivers forensic oratory worthy of a law court, as opposed to Menelaus' fairly feeble defence, stating his case in relation to the legal, emotional and normative justifications for Orestes' punishment. But he also prejudges the final verdict of the democracy of Argos, asking Menelaus to leave the young man to be stoned to death, and adds a threat to Menelaus himself if he should disobey.

Orestes, seeing that Menelaus' attacks on Tyndareus' reasoning due to his age have proved ineffective, begins his defence by bringing into the open the age dynamic that is at play. The defence begins thus:

> Grandfather, I must say I am afraid of answering you in a situation where I am bound to hurt and annoy you. Assume our debate is not hampered by your age, which deters me from speaking, and I will go ahead; but in reality I am inhibited by your grey hair.
>
> 544–50

With his obvious disadvantage stated from the outset, Orestes sets out his corresponding arguments to justify his actions. Mirroring Tyndareus' claims, he sets out his case along similar lines. First, Orestes argues that his actions have set a precedent that will prevent the murder of husbands by their wives, then states the emotional torment he has suffered in weighing up the consequences of his actions. Finally, he points out that Apollo directed his actions (550–99). On every point, he offers a direct response to each of Tyndareus' accusations and demonstrates, regardless of his youth, well developed arguments as one would hear in political debate.[23] However, Tyndareus' response to Orestes is even more aggressive than that directed moments earlier to Menelaus. Damning Orestes' insolence, Tyndareus says: '. . .

you shall fire me the more to go for your death' (608–9). Tyndareus now speaks with palpable fury, the kind of elderly wisdom offered to Menelaus transformed into barely controlled raging. 'I shall go to the Argives' convocation and bring the city crashing down on you and your sister whether it will or no, so that you pay the penalty of stoning' (612–14). In the face of Orestes' counter-arguments, the old man will brook no opposition, whether it be from the young man or members of the Argive Council. The challenge to his gerontocratic authority is met with his restatement of the absolute power he is accustomed to holding over those younger than himself.

As Tyndareus leaves the stage, Orestes sees the opportunity to put his case to Menelaus again in the hope that the absence of the older man will allow him to make a more successful appeal. But it is already clear from Menelaus' posture that his support for Orestes is waning. Distractedly, Menelaus allows Orestes to make another speech and the young man offers appeals to the older, comparing the support Agamemnon gave him with the assistance he now seeks, and saying how he doesn't seek the death of Hermione as restitution for the death of Iphigenia (640–79). If the anticipated response is to galvanize Menelaus into martial support of Orestes, the speech is a failure. Menelaus says his company of arms is too weak to physically challenge Argos and that the best way to support Orestes is through intelligent speech in his defence. To Orestes, this amounts to a betrayal. On recent evidence, Menelaus is no match in words for Tyndareus, but more importantly the older man appears to show no loyalty to the memory of his brother, the man who gave his daughter's life in order to pursue Menelaus' expedition against Troy. Shouting at Menelaus after he exits the stage, Orestes, understandably, berates him, 'You good for nothing but to make war for a woman, you most worthless when it comes to succouring your kin, do you turn your back on me and run away?' (718–20). Menelaus' actions are anathema to Orestes: not only is he to be left to face death, along with his sister, but his family ties have been betrayed. And critically, Menelaus' refusal to reciprocate the support his brother gave him at Troy demonstrates the betrayal of the age-group to which they both belonged. Orestes, valuing deeply the bond with his own generational unit, is devastated.

From here on in, the only support will be from Electra and Pylades, and all others will be viewed as opponents to their cause. By contrast, when Pylades approaches, he immediately confirms his loyalty to Orestes, saying: 'How are you ... favourite of my age-group, of my friends, of my relations, for you're all these things to me' (732–3). His unambiguous devotion to Orestes is in stark contrast to Menelaus' half-hearted assurance that he will argue against the execution. In a frantic, conspiratorial exchange, the two friends discuss the impossibility of escape and Menelaus' weak attempts at assistance. Amongst this discussion, Pylades reveals that he too is in great danger, having been exiled from Phocis by his father, Stophius, for his role in the killing of Clytemnestra. This revelation, along with Electra's earlier admission of active participation in matricide, draws the three characters into an exceptionally well-defined group. All three stand accused of the crime, and all three have been cast out by their communities and, it now seems likely, their kin. The two decide together that Orestes should face the citizens of Argos and present his defence. Risking his own life, Pylades agrees to accompany his friend for moral support and in case Orestes is struck down by the Erinyes again. The closing lines to this section, spoken by Orestes, sum up the strength of their allegiance, and make it clear that it is only one's own *hetaireia* that counts when faced with such adversity: 'There you are – get yourselves comrades [*hetairous*], not just family! An outsider who becomes fused to you by his character beats ten thousand relatives as a friend to possess' (804–6).[24] Over the next two hundred or so lines the chorus lament Orestes' bitter circumstances, Electra returns to discover that her brother has gone before the Argive Council, and a messenger, in the form of an old man, appears to deliver the news that they have been sentenced to death (807–1012).[25] Although the outcome was not unanimous, the majority voted for Electra and Orestes to be killed by stoning and Menelaus failed even to attend the deliberations. The sole concession won by Orestes' own defence is that the pair of them may commit suicide rather than face a public execution. But that action is sanctioned only if it takes place on that same day. Euripides' handling of the plotline, now well and truly innovated away from the established mythography, not only places the protagonists in a position of extreme peril but sets the clock ticking on the resolution of the play, by their suicide or otherwise.[26] The arguments of an old man, then reported by another old man, look set to result in the deaths of at least two young people. There is no realistic possibility of escape and the young group will be hunted down by the people of Argos if they fail to carry out the suicide by the day's close. Their situation appears impossible and the two siblings bicker over how to accept and then carry out the judgement, grimly, going so far as to long for death by the same sword and to be buried together.

The play could end from here in a similar way to Sophocles' *Ajax* or *Antigone*, but as suggested towards the beginning of the play, Orestes' inclination is towards action against his opponents, even if they are divinities, rather than Sophoclean heroic self-sacrifice. Pylades, who has as little to lose as the other two in the group, intervenes to steer the play in an unexpected direction. Assuming, at first, that his friend is merely attempting to restate his loyalty, Orestes says: 'Let your father have you back, don't die with me' (1075). To Pylades, the bond is stronger between the *hetairoi* than between family members and he sets out his plan. From this point on *Orestes* is unlike any other extant tragedy in its depiction of youth as a closed group, opposed to all around them and intent on causing the maximum chaos in order to gain revenge and demonstrate their agency in a society that appears to have denied them any political power. Pylades' plan is simple, yet devastating. He proposes that the two of them should kill Helen, as a way of exacting revenge on Menelaus. The exchange, when Pylades explains how this might be done, is very similar in structure to the earlier section in which Pylades persuades Orestes to attend the meeting of the Argives (1100–30).[27] Pylades' plan is outrageous: the two friends are to enter the palace where Helen is currently residing, lock up any attendants and track down Menelaus' wife, all along pretending to be in deep lament for themselves, readying for suicide. The aim is to lay hands on Helen and kill her (in the text, at 1107, Pylades states that they are literally to slaughter Helen in sacrifice [*sphaxantes*]). The language here is extreme. There is no euphemism or downplaying of the violence they intend. But the image of Helen as sacrificial victim allows the audience the chance to make a number of different associations. First, it links the cycle of revenge and killing back to the curse of the Atreidai, as well as the sacrifice of Iphigenia, and demonstrates how Orestes' actions are part of a horrific family narrative. Second, the use of this specific term makes reference to a sacrilegious act they are about to perform. They are to put on a performance of lamentation when in reality they are about to inflict terrible violence on Helen. Intentional or not, this section brings to mind the accusations made of some *hetairiai* after the destruction of the *Hermae* (as well as the scene earlier in the play when Orestes threatens to shoot the Erinyes). Then, some young male members, likely to have included Alcibiades, were accused of profaning the mysteries through a false and sacrilegious parody of the rituals.[28] Indeed, such is their destructive intent that Pylades ends his exposition of the plan by revealing the final act: that they should set the palace alight if they are unable to find Helen, bringing down the symbolic structure of power in Argos whilst killing themselves. Pylades offers a view that can only come from within the group, and erroneously looks towards their future mythologizing through the *kleos* they will win (1151). Orestes, in what must be partly a comic speech, then turns to Pylades and says: 'Oh, there's nothing better than an unmistakable friend …' (1154–5). This restatement of commitment to friendship serves to validate the outrageous plan put forward by Pylades. The group has set a course of action, all they then need is some firmer hope that they will find a way out of the morass. Orestes ends by wishing, '… if we could just get hold of one thing. Good fortune would be ours … if some unexpected salvation were to drop down from somewhere so that we killed without being killed' (1172–4).[29] Enter Electra into the conversation. Until this point, she has been waiting quietly whilst the two friends devise the strategy. On hearing her brother's words she interjects, saying: 'I think I have that very thing – salvation for you and Pylades, and also for me' (1176–7). As Pylades has done, Electra reveals her contribution to the group's assault on the community, proposing the kidnap of Hermione and her use as a hostage to win safe passage after they confront Menelaus with the body of Helen.[30]

All three of the group have now made contributions to the plan and are fully committed to the cause. To reinforce this loyalty the three then chant what can be considered 'a formal invocation of Agamemnon, Zeus, and *Dike* as a prelude to the assassination attempt.'[31] The formulaic nature of this chant establishes a ritual for the group. Each in turn claims responsibility for their actions and, through these ritualistic utterances, confirms their loyalty to each other. Orestes admits to the matricide, Electra to providing the weapon and Pylades to his encouragement of Orestes in the murder. The group chanting appears to galvanize each group member, the song propelling them along their path to destruction.[32] The section ends with a summary by Pylades of the exact nature of the group: '… for the trio of allies face a single trial, a single settlement: one sentence for all of us, either life or death!' (1240–5). The frantic following section of the play involves the frenzied attack by Pylades and Orestes on

Helen's attendants, reported by a Phrygian escapee (1493–5),[33] their failed attempt at the murder of Helen, the capture of Hermione and the setting alight of the palace. The action, largely narrated by the Phrygian, is fast-paced and explosive. The scene's contrast with the opening sections of the play is stark, but not entirely unexpected. The slaughter of the household attendants by Pylades appears to be the real enactment of the destruction Orestes fantasized about in his delirium at the beginning of the play.

The final scene must be the one that made *Orestes* one of the most popular of all plays in the classical period. Appearing above the stage, in an area of the set usually reserved for gods or those about to commit some horrific act (such as Medea in her name play), Orestes' and Pylades' re-entry to the action would have been a real *tour de force* of dramatic production. With Menelaus hurrying to the palace, having been informed of the pair's actions and under the impression that Helen has been slain, Orestes and Pylades thus appear on the palace roof. This re-entry must have been quite some sight: Orestes has Hermione hostage, his sword to her throat, whilst Pylades holds aloft a flaming torch as smoke begins to rise from the building. Orestes looks down on Menelaus and addresses him: 'you there', before threatening: 'I'll smash your head in with this coping stone' if he attempts to enter the building (1567–70).[34] Unsurprisingly, Menelaus is furious, returning Orestes' threat, saying that if he harms Hermione, 'you'll regret it – that is, unless you escape on wings' (1592).[35] But this threat is quickly shown to be empty, as Orestes makes to slit Hermione's throat Menelaus pleads with the young man not to carry out the act (1598).[36] But the price Orestes asks of Menelaus is perhaps too high, demanding that Menelaus fulfil his promise to persuade the Argive Council to not only rescind the death penalty on Electra and Orestes, but also to reinstate the young man as king of the city. With Orestes as spokesperson, the young group are demanding complete control of Argos by use of the most outrageous acts of violence. Of course, this plan is completely unrealizable, and Orestes' demands show the levels to which the group have created their own parallel reality outside the Argive community. Orestes then immediately instructs his co-conspirators to set the whole palace ablaze, in contradiction to his implied promise to Menelaus. Menelaus regains some composure, seeing that Orestes is completely unhinged, and sets about breaking down the door to the palace.[37]

With the disaster seemingly inevitable, the conflagration looks likely to take down the entire cast of participants; but Euripides deploys a *deus ex machina*. The already busy stage is joined by Apollo and a mute Helen, most likely also on the upper platform of the *skēnē*. The god reveals that all the events since the beginnings of the Trojan War are of their design and he sets out the future lives for Electra, Orestes and Pylades; Helen, Hermione and Menelaus. Peace is to be made through his direction. The end is very similar to that in *Iphigenia in Tauris*. The angry older man is easily bought off, the young man is reassured that he was right in his actions all along and the female protagonist is allocated a not entirely satisfactory future life.

The play dramatizes a world in which disenfranchised youth groups are formed in opposition to wider society resulting in their energies being channelled through covert groups which the historical context shows results in violence. The conditions that necessitate the actions of Orestes and his gang, subsequent to the matricide, are thus caused not only by the group's own actions but by a failure of society around them.[38] The play also shows specifically how the application of gerontocratic politics, when applied to control of youth groups, acts as accelerant to the flames of generational opposition. The scene is complicated by the clear conflict between democracy and aristocracy but it is the power of the oldest man, Tyndareus, which ultimately prevails until the intervention of Apollo. A member of the audience, with recent memories of the mutilation of the *Hermae* and the actions of gangs of young men during the revolutions, might well have reflected on how a city must be kept in political tension, but that outlets for pressure must be inbuilt, including political integration of *hetairiai*. For a democracy to function effectively it must be completely inclusive of the *dēmos* in totality. And while the threat to this stability comes from oligarchic groups, the imposition of gerontocratic values will only help propel democracy towards dissolution. Without the proper inclusion of young people in political processes, this cycle is likely to continue. Euripides, in his final direct address to the people of Athens before his self-imposed exile to Macedonia, presents the future of a city without solidarity. In the face of Spartan aggression they must stand together or fall. In *Orestes*, Euripides shows what might be. In *Bacchae*, he accurately dramatizes what will.

Euripides' *Bacchae* and *Iphigenia in Aulis*

A Gap in the Generations and Political Failure

Euripides' *Bacchae*, and the play's two companion pieces (as performed together), *Iphigenia in Aulis* and *Alcmaeon in Corinth*, were produced at a point in Athens' history that was to witness the collapse of her imperial power and the half-century-long experiment with mass, direct democracy. In 405, the almost certain date of their posthumous production, Athens was under siege, her fleet destroyed and with it access to the supply of grain through the Bosphorus in the east. Unsurprisingly, *Bacchae* and *Iphigenia in Aulis* contain highly negative portrayals of those in power and their political decision-making (*Alcmaeon in Corinth* exists only in fragments, and it is practically impossible to reconstruct accurately the content, *a fortiori* to determine any contemporary political resonances).[1] In both fully extant plays, the 'mob', led by a charismatic individual, is cast as the force that defeats individual decision-making, whilst young characters are well placed to change the course of events but fail to do so. With Pericles long dead and Alcibiades an outcast from Athens, historical sources, encoded with their authors' biases, suggest massive miscalculations in policy and executive decision-making that irreversibly damaged Athens.

While in *Iphigenia in Aulis* the full range of generals are involved (Menelaus, Agamemnon and Odysseus, albeit off stage in the case of the last), decisions to act are made rashly, reneged on, reaffirmed and then enacted, seemingly without the application of any firm control by those in authority. In *Bacchae*, there is even less sense of control of events by Thebes' nominal authority, the young king Pentheus. And in this play the absence of a middle range of male citizens reinforces the sense that the city's ability to formulate policy that is supported across generations has been lost. Pentheus, it will be argued, is shown to be the apparently lone representative of the final generation of a dynasty that by now has become morally and authoritatively regressive, internally opposed solely by ineffective old men. First, a note on the concept of middle-range absence. The absence of male citizens or rulers between the ages of qualification for the *Boulē* and exemption from military duty (thirty to late fifties) in *Bacchae*, and as demonstrable in many other tragedies (from Aeschylus' *Persae* onwards), has clear mythological antecedents. The myths of the cyclic epic *Nostoi* (only partially available through fragments and later sources[2] and in non-cyclic form as constituted by the *Odyssey*) offer an array of stories in which male authority figures leave their *polis* to fight abroad and endure a difficult homecoming. Most famously Odysseus, in the *Odyssey*, not only struggles to return but leaves behind his young son, Telemachus, who fails to effectively oppose a gang of unruly suitors. When dramatized by tragedians, the adaptations of the *Nostoi* myths are an articulation of the risk to one's authority, such as in the fate of Agamemnon in the *Oresteia*. In *Bacchae* it is something of a mystery as to where Pentheus' father and his uncles are.[3] But this play offers an echo of a Homeric homecoming setting where the authority figure fails to return. This tendency towards failed homecomings in literature is, perhaps, an imaginative portrayal of the (presumably frequent enough) occurrence of very real failed homecomings as the outcome when a war fought overseas is lost.

A brief summary of the political context will help to establish the environment from which these plays came. A number of surprising Athenian victories followed the Sicilian debacle of 413 and these events appeared to reinvest the Athenians with a sense of control over their destiny (see previous chapter). For a time, the city had regained enough confidence to refuse a number of opportunities to reach an armistice with Sparta. The post-Thucydides sources are a tangle of accounts, often drawing on the same material from the fragmentary *Hellenica Oxyrhynchia* and heavily infected by political bias (Xenophon, in particular).[4] But it can be gleaned that the political turmoil that preceded and followed the Sicilian expedition appears, whilst seemingly having receded, to have had a continuing political impact. Following the battle of Arginusae in 406, a vitally important naval victory for Athens, those politicians remaining in Athens (not including Alcibiades, who was deposed from public office earlier in the year)[5] took the decision, circumventing proper judicial process, to execute the Athenian generals who had overseen the fighting, ostensibly for their failure to save surviving Athenian sailors who were cast adrift in stormy seas. In Xenophon's view of the debate,[6] the city's politicians offer no strategic direction and the authorial voice has it that decision-making is subject to obvious manipulation by figures such as Theramenes. Of course, Xenophon's well-known negative opinion of democracy colours this account, to the extent that the most famous democratic politician of the era, Cleophon, is practically written out of his history. But the fact that the generals were all sentenced to death without a proper trial is absolutely certain.

What is also clear is the dysfunction of political decision-making in Athens, disabling the city's ability to see beyond internal political threats, thus reducing the ability to address properly the wider issues at hand. This briefest of summaries shows that Euripides would have most likely composed his final works while Athens was in a state of perpetual political turmoil, even during occasional successes in the Ionian theatre of war.[7] Indeed, a state of political paralysis is represented in both *Iphigenia in Aulis* and *Bacchae*, where erratic decision-taking results in the failure to apply any clearly rationalized line of policy. Euripides, through the plays in question, seems to suggest (not unlike Xenophon) that without a stabilizing influence, moderating the indecision of weak political leadership and the irrational power of 'the crowd', a society is well on the path to complete breakdown. In *Iphigenia in Aulis*, Euripides presents the version of the myth of Iphigenia's sacrifice in which (the transmitted text has it) Agamemnon's daughter escapes death when Artemis dramatically replaces her body with that of a deer. While this substitution is interesting in itself, it may well be the most problematic of a number of later interpolations in the play.[8] Instead, it is the discussions between the Greek generals that lead up to the dramatic climax that are most relevant to an analysis of the playwright's handling of political themes during the final stages of his career, and of Athens' 'golden' period. Whilst the playwright could not entirely foresee the imminent collapse of Athenian military strength, the play contains elements of the tensions within society that would contribute towards the later failure of political and military leadership.

At the play's opening Agamemnon is in great distress, having agreed to sacrifice one of his daughters, on the instructions of the seer Calchas. After initially refusing to allow his daughter to be killed he was persuaded by his brother, Menelaus, to carry out the murder and sent for his daughter under the pretence that she was to be married to Achilles.[9] He has now fully comprehended the moral and political consequences of his acquiescence to his brother, and Agamemnon orders an old man to send new instructions to Clytemnestra, asking her not to send their daughter to the Greek camp at Aulis.[10] But the message is intercepted by Menelaus and he furiously confronts Agamemnon. The two argue, and it looks as if Agamemnon will not be swayed from his decision to refuse the sacrifice, when a messenger announces the arrival of Clytemnestra and Iphigenia at the camp. Agamemnon's resolve then breaks, and he concedes defeat to Menelaus. Oddly, the hitherto implacable Menelaus, seeing the torment his brother is suffering, offers to reverse his decision to lead the Greeks to Troy, and to disband the massed armies of the various *poleis*. Surprisingly, Agamemnon refuses the offer and decides to persevere with the original plan to sacrifice Iphigenia, whilst continuing the pretence of preparing her marriage to Achilles. When asked by Menelaus why he would do such a thing, Agamemnon says that he feels compelled by the Greek army, who are poised for war. Agamemnon clearly feels a weakness in his authority and Menelaus recognizes this anxiety, saying: 'do not fear the mob [*ochlos*] too much' (517). The brothers can hardly be presented in a more negative light, since neither even shows the strength of character to acknowledge his own agency, blaming both fate and pressure from the martial community for their proposed murder. While the play's other characters are much more sympathetic, the interactions between Clytemnestra, Iphigenia and Achilles being at times heroic and moving, these individual figures also show indecision and a clear hostility to the rank and file of the army. At 1357, Clytemnestra, as the army encircles, states: 'a crowd is mad for crime' (*to polu gar deinon kakon*). Although Odysseus is picked out earlier on as a particular threat, when he is effectively accused of being a demagogue, it is the faceless mass of ordinary soldiers that the various aristocratic characters suggest is the greatest threat. Achilles, at first a steadfast opponent of the proposed sacrifice, is obscenely quick to accept Iphigenia's decision to allow her sacrifice to go ahead, having been cowed by the massed ranks of the Greeks. As has been put perceptively, Achilles' actions demonstrate the 'failure of an adolescent to change the world of the adults, a failure that results in the loss of his name and personality'.[11] This failure in action and consequential loss feature as a central characteristic of youth in *Bacchae* too.

Iphigenia in Aulis appears to contain three major political themes. One is the absence of serious political authority. Both generals have mobilized a large number of soldiers, already sent them far from their homes and have them ready to die for Menelaus' cause. But they are paralysed with indecision when the issues they face become more complex. Moreover, once they do settle on a particular position it is because they appear forced to do so, blaming fate or the weight of expectation from their fellow Greeks. In short, the play demonstrates the inability to formulate proper policy without generals in possession of true leadership qualities. Second, throughout the play the ranks of soldiers, specifically named as a 'mob' (*ochlos*), or as an undifferentiated group (*to polu*), are presented as a threatening, irrational group with whom neither general can satisfactorily engage. The picture is very similar to that painted by Thucydides in Book 8 of his work where he uses this negative term (*ochlos*) to refer to a large group of sailors.[12] Third, the old messenger and the young Achilles are both able to influence the course of events but fail to do so adequately. This theme, of the impotence at each end of the generational scale, underscores the political failure of the middle-range. The overall effect is to show an environment in which control over society has been lost, in part due to a lack of leadership, in part due to the power and fury of the mob, further incited by a demagogue and exacerbated by the inherent failure of young and old to take appropriate, decisive action. And if the Greeks are to even reach Troy they must make a symbolic sacrifice of the next generation in the form of Iphigenia; all the more relevant to contemporary Athens where similar arguments appear to have played out (when many young lives had been sacrificed at Sicily to no advantage, the citizens having been propelled down this route by a young political faction). The small group of aristocratic characters who are given a voice in this play, as contrasted to the voiceless mass of soldiers, appear oddly powerless against a rough democracy of the military camp. This is not to say that Euripides intimates a particular sympathy with the oligarchic or democratic side, since both sides appear monstrous, but an Athenian audience would no doubt have left the performance reflecting on the nature of political decision-making not just witnessed on stage, but in their lawcourts, *Boulē* and *Ekklēsia* too.

These political themes, as well as ones associated with the killing of young people by their parents, are even clearer in *Bacchae*. And it is in this play – and it really is very stark – that Euripides points to a kind of societal-generational failure, represented through the absence of a male middle-range citizenry. In the play's prologue Dionysus offers a view of his recent and distant history (his journey from Asia and the story of his birth) before turning to immediate events. He has arrived to demand that he is honoured as a god, threatening to lead his maenads into battle against the (male) Thebans if he is not satisfied. He is explicit in his aims, and about his potential recourse to violence should things not go his way. Indeed, he has already launched a pre-emptive strike through the madness that he has inflicted on the female population of the city. And the account of the fall of various cities to his cult appears as evidence for the absolute control he has enforced elsewhere: these cities' identities are now defined by their submission to the cult. On one reading, this is a most sinister introduction to a play, and to a character.[13] Dionysus is, perhaps, the most discussed mythological figure in classical scholarship and he has long been associated with the powers of chaos and destruction.[14] Here, too, Dionysus appears as the embodiment of social and political dissolution and, given his divinity, the prognosis for Thebes and Pentheus cannot be anything but poor. No doubt some in the audience witnessing the play at its first production[15] would be long familiar with the reality of siege warfare, as experienced both when defending allied cities and colonies, and as part of a besieging force. It is feasible that they would have experienced a sense that what they were about to see on stage was similar to the threats they had experienced and inflicted elsewhere. They had also seen 'siege' plays set at Thebes, most recently Euripides' own *Phoenician Women* of just four years earlier, in which dialogues had been delivered from the ramparts themselves, in striking *teichoskopia* scenes. Now, before the seven gates of Thebes stands an agent of the destruction of political and social systems, as well as the physical form of the city. His story of his journey from Asia Minor to Thebes (little more than 40 miles away from Athens and 'the negative model to Athens' manifest image of itself'),[16] may similarly have triggered resonances of personal experience in war in the minds of the audience.[17]

The sense of menace and intent to act is reinforced during the parodos, when a large number of chorus members, in role as Asiatic maenads, enter the stage.[18] Their ethnicity again underscores the geographically specific source of the threat to Thebes and their ecstatic chanting, including a 'specific exhortation to proceed',[19] imbues the scene with a febricity, an atmosphere of cult fervour that is impermeable to external intervention. Although metrically very different, the effect given is similar to that in Euripides' *Orestes*, when in stichomythic exchanges two young characters provoke each other into embarking on a murderous campaign.[20] The *folie à deux*, as performed in *Orestes*, is in this instance presented as a *folie à plusieurs*.[21] But, as we shall see, such an exclusive, fantastical understanding is also evident in the relationship between the two elder statesmen of Thebes, Tiresias and Cadmus. As the chorus gather outside the gates of Thebes – on stage surely a sight immediately recognizable as a besieging force – the response from the first Thebans to appear is surprising.[22] Tiresias arrives, clearly in a state of excitement and says, calling for Cadmus to join him, 'He himself knows what I have come about, and the agreement I made with him, an old man with an older one, to make *thrysoi* and wear the skins of fawns, and to crown our heads with ivy shoots' (174–7).[23] The joyfulness of Cadmus, too, is immediately clear. Emerging from the on-stage royal house, Cadmus exclaims: 'O dearest friend – for I recognised your voice when I heard it, a wise voice of a wise man ...' (177–8), before making explicit his acceptance of the Dionysiac cult, echoing Tiresias' words that they speak one old man to another, repeating that the seer is wise and stating that they both have forgotten their ages. They feel they are no longer *gerontes*, they are now both young men.[24] Indeed, such is the transformation that when they both decide to travel to join in the Bacchic revels by walking, rather than by chariot, in order to demonstrate their complete subservience to the cult and so give the greatest honour to Dionysus, Cadmus asks of Tiresias: 'shall I lead you like a child, although we are both old men?' Not only have they become young, they have completely regressed to a prematurity (193).[25] This regression, seemingly bypassing a young adult age at which they would be youthful, and yet mature enough to have mastery of their wits, is part of the Euripidean model of political incompetence at Thebes.[26] But it also reflects the realities of Dionysiac worship in historical Athens. At the annual festival of Anthesteria, celebrations revolved around wine, the liquid intoxicant most associated with Dionysus. Such was the importance of wine that the entire community, including slaves and children, were expected to imbibe on the second day of the festival, the day of 'the Jugs', or *Choes*.[27] In a fascinating passage in Plato's *Laws* (Book II, 666b–c) reference is made to rejuvenation through worship of Dionysus, and the ritual drinking of wine, by an Athenian speaker. Intriguingly, Plato has the Athenian suggest a recommended wine drinking limit for different age groups: nothing for under eighteens as they: 'must be on their guard against the madness that is habitual in youth'; moderate amounts for under thirties; and for those approaching forty and older, as much as they want in order to gain the beneficial rejuvenating effects.[28] As Pentheus enters the stage, it becomes clear that, in terms of those with political influence, there are just the young and old at Thebes, and the Dionysian intoxication of the old has severely curtailed their capacity for offering sensible counsel.[29] In annual ritual, such abnegation of ordinary responsibility is accepted for a few days across the community. However, such festivals did not involve permanent physical destruction, just temporary dissolution of social distinctions. In historical Athens, the community celebrating the Anthesteria did welcome into the city a foreign power, in the form of Dionysus, but as part of celebrations that would cement community cohesion. In *Bacchae*, in part, Dionysus has already introduced a forced conversion of the womenfolk to his ritual. Against this backdrop, the older men appear all too quick to embrace the new religious hegemony, perhaps due to their drunkenness of spirit, whereas Pentheus, as we shall see, suffers from the intoxication of youth and, like Achilles in *Iphigenia in Aulis*, will lose his personality (after making a similarly precipitous *volte-face*).

At this point, it is worth considering what actual psychological effect submergence in a group might have, and how this translates to the political realm. It is easy to lapse into the view of groups as simple 'mobs', as can be interpreted in the case in *Iphigenia in Aulis*, where a clear class bias in speeches of the aristocratic main characters defines the rank and file soldiery in an undifferentiated negative light. Writing in the early twentieth century and building on earlier work, most notably that of Gustave Le Bon,[30] Freud makes some interesting observations on the common view of group psychology at the time:

> Since a group is in no doubt as to what constitutes truth or error, and is conscious, moreover, of its own strength, it is as intolerant as it is obedient to authority. It respects force and can only be slightly influenced by kindness, which it regards merely as a form of weakness. What it demands of its heroes

is strength, or even violence. It wants to be ruled and oppressed and to fear its masters. Fundamentally it is entirely conservative, and it has a deep aversion to all innovations and advances and an unbound respect for tradition.[31]

This description of typical group characteristics was not completely supported by Freud, but he did believe it was one that would be familiar to pre-modern societies. In *Bacchae*, those principal figures in Thebes who are doing all they can to demonstrate their loyalty to the new group, Tiresias and Cadmus, quite clearly share an intolerance to dissent, a sense of the absolute morality of their choices, are in awe of Dionysius' power and reject the contemporary political realm for an ancient cultic one. Moreover, again using Freud, through Dionysus they appear to be engaged in a 'death-drive', 'an urge in organic life to restore an earlier state of things'.[32] That is, through acceptance of Dionysus' divine authority they are rejecting the king's temporal political power and through this they hope to achieve some form of rejuvenation, albeit one that an audience might correctly guess will end in some form of dissolution, or, in the Freudian conceptualization of the death-drive, a return to nothingness. This description so far fits the commonplace view of the unthinking, destructive mob. But both Le Bon and Freud agree that group psychology is greatly influenced by the qualities of those who occupy a leadership position within the group, or as they call it 'prestige'. These prestigious individuals can effect in a group – by strength of character, and facilitated through the suggestibility of the group – a dynamic that is: 'capable of high achievements in the shape of abnegation, unselfishness, and devotion to an ideal.'[33] In essence, groups can be creative as well as destructive and these differences depend on individuals with great influence who are already part of the group.

In Euripides' play, Dionysus aside, there appear to be no individuals charismatic enough to mitigate the totality of submergence into the group: Pentheus' weakness of character (regarded by the older Thebans as due to his youth) means he cannot effectively challenge Dionysus. Moreover, Pentheus is not even in control of his own city. For the Thebans, this group psychology, as per Freud, is the same as the psychology evident in those suffering neurosis (and possibly that demonstrated in the Athenian *Ekklēsia* such as in the treatment of the generals after the sea-battle, discussed above): 'a hysterical symptom is based upon phantasy instead of upon the repetition of real experience, and the sense of guilt in an obsessional neurosis is based upon the fact of an evil intention which was never carried out.'[34] Although Pentheus (only at first, it must be said) assesses the situation accurately, the expectations of the old men and that of Pentheus, once he is under the yoke of the god, are based on pure fantasy, demonstrating a kind of childish wish fulfilment. Youth, then, in this view of group psychology, can only play a destructive role in these plays. They are not, by ancient standards, psychologically equipped to fulfil the 'prestige' role, due to their tendency towards indulging an enflamed *thumos*. Furthermore, as is the case in the earlier *Orestes*, and historically in the case of the *hetairiai*, youth groups are essentially constructed in opposition to society. In the Le Bon model, that Freud critiques, youth groups can never be creative. Applying this perspective to *Bacchae*, Pentheus will either be completely subsumed into the group, losing all sense of self, or will act in total opposition, propelling society towards complete breakdown. Indeed, the young king eventually suffers the first, after taking part in the second.

Returning to the play, Pentheus also enters the stage in a state of agitation. But he is far from ecstatic when faced with the encroaching Maenads. To him, they are clearly a threat, having encouraged the entire female population of the city to relocate to the mountainside in a frenzy. It is not just the female depopulation that enrages him, it is the behaviour of Tiresias and Cadmus, 'the sight of your old age without sense', (252) that is doubly infuriating. When he says that they are only free from imprisonment because of their old age, it is because he considers them as senile, rather than as deserving respect as old men. While the chorus, who by now appear inside the city (it can only be assumed that one of the old men has opened the gates for them), react with anger, saying: 'what impiety!' (263), Tiresias adopts a patronizing tone, when addressing Pentheus, that quickly descends into insult:

> When an intelligent man chooses a good basis for his speech, it is no great task to speak well. But you have a fluent tongue as if possessed of understanding, yet in your words there is no sense. A man whose capability comes through boldness and who is able to speak proves a bad citizen, for he is without sense.
>
> 267–71

Through Tiresias, Euripides offers a commonplace formulation for creating the basis of good political engagement, but one which is very much fixed within an age-related framework. In Sophocles' *Antigone*, this formulation, the requirement of mastery of thought processes (*dianoia*) and speech for properly controlled discussion of political issues and the correct approach to decision-making, is demonstrated through arguments between Creon and Antigone, and Creon and Haemon and shows how the older man has allowed an enflamed *thumos* to distort his political views. Sophocles presents an inversion of the conservative view of young people, and at a time of confidence in Athenian society demonstrates that a faulty 'youthful' approach to political involvement and leadership is not necessarily linked to age, but to a state of mind. Here, Tiresias re-presents the conservative view and makes it clear, from his much older viewpoint, that Pentheus' judgement is unsound because of the young king's age; addressing him as young man (*ō neania*). Tiresias completes his address to Pentheus by laying out Dionysius' lineage, his contributions to mortal wellbeing and his power. In his final reasoning for succumbing to the cult, the seer compares the desire for honour that Pentheus feels, and that which Dionysus demands. Superficially, these arguments appear sound. But considered within the immediate context of the play there is reason to question Tiresias' judgement. First, Dionysus does not come seeking equal honour. In the prologue, Dionysus says: 'For this city must learn to the full, even if it does not want to, what it is to be uninitiated' (39–40). The god does not simply demand honour, but for Thebes to suffer. His pre-emptive strike on the city, the madness he has inflicted on the women, demonstrates that he is prepared to destroy and dissolve, as well as subdue. And it is the menacing way in which his demands are stated that makes the light-heartedness of Tiresias and Cadmus all the more worrying.[35] The gleeful manner in which the two older men accept the situation looks like complete capitulation to an unstoppable force that is ready to deploy all the powers of a god for his cause. While Tiresias' role as a seer goes some way to explaining his compliance with a new religious cult, it is difficult to understand why Cadmus, who struggled so hard to establish the city, is so easily persuaded to support a force that has already inflicted damage on the social fabric of Thebes. Pentheus' grandfather, however, does suggest that submission could be deceptive, that Pentheus should 'tell a lie in a good cause' (334). But this admission makes his willingness to comply all the more baffling; his accompanying giddiness either the early onset of Bacchic frenzy or a complete submission to the *external* group (if they are not, in fact, the same thing or at least stages in the same process of sublimation). Indeed, Tiresias, leading Cadmus to Cithaeron, where the bacchants are gathered, says: 'we must be slaves (*douleuteon*) to Bakchos' (366).

Their unquestioning acceptance of a potential destructive new cult is at odds with the unquestioning opposition by Pentheus. The opposition of youth to wider society has already been discussed at length in the preceding chapter and Pentheus fits a typical youth role in defining himself by opposing his views to the older characters. In a functioning society, the role of the older men would be to deliberate and advise in a manner that would allow Pentheus to integrate into the community, or at least come to terms with the difficult decisions he has to make (as is the case with Neoptolemus in *Philoctetes*). But there is practically no deliberation and no chance of compromise, and the absence of a moderating influence exacerbates the problem.[36] The interchange between Pentheus and Tiresias (with Cadmus playing a supporting role) provides a view of political dialogue that is fractured into binary opposites: absolute opposition to Dionysus and absolute submission. With the very existence of Thebes seemingly at stake, there appears a stark absence of objective political debate and the pragmatic view of Cadmus, 'to tell a lie in a good cause,' is compressed into a single line, completely obscured by the primary arguments of the two other Theban characters currently on stage. Euripides has the older men describe themselves as feeling young again, even like children, whilst also suggesting that Pentheus' view of things is faulty because of his youthfulness. In short, Euripides appears to have created a fictionalized world in which there is no moderating influence and the absence of a middle range of male citizens from the play indicates where this moderating force might once have been located (though as we have seen through their failure in *Iphigenia in Aulis*, the middle range has to be capable of deliberation and not just present). Instead of a full debate on the consequences of various courses of action, Tiresias and Pentheus stubbornly, rigidly hold their political positions and the result is that a form of political paralysis takes hold.

As is the case in *Iphigenia in Aulis*, this state leads to a loss of political control, as other forces begin to dictate the course of events (here, Dionysus, there the Greek army). As in contemporary Athens (see above), the lack of proper political control resulted in a sort of self-inflicted damage. Surely, the only beneficiary of such political dysfunction (contemporarily the ex-judicial execution of the generals), was Athens'/Thebes' enemies. To meet the threat, unity is required but this is a clearly absent quality. In fact, submergence within the Dionysiac cult has already begun, one fractured part of society at a time. By the time Cadmus makes a more realistic assessment of the impact of Dionysus on Thebes ('just, yet excessive', 1249–50), it is too late. Reacting to the presentation of Pentheus' head by a stupefied Agave, the old man successfully talks his daughter down from her delusional state of revel, displaying the ability to properly counsel and guide that is missing at the play's opening. His words to Dionysus, when he appears *ex machina*, also reflect a more nuanced analysis of the god's actions, questioning the wholesale nature and rapidity of the god's destruction. It is as if the earlier intoxication has worn off and his political understanding has returned, or rather he has progressed back to an adult capacity for sound *dianoia* once he has become individuated from the bacchants. The words spoken by the messenger as he reports Pentheus' death before this scene are telling: 'The best thing is to be moderate (*sōphronein*) and to revere the things of the gods: and I think that this is the wisest possession for mortals to use' (1152–3). As in *Iphigenia in Aulis*, the characters in *Bacchae* fail to display adequately such wisdom. Their hasty actions fuelled by the intoxication of atavistic group thinking or youthful rashness, and unchecked by proper deliberative questioning, bring about the city's destruction.

Conclusion

The Case for Youth Studies in Classics

To risk repetition, the core argument throughout this book has been that not only was Greek – Athenian – tragedy political but that almost without exception tragedy was concerned at some level with the role of youth in society. This role of youth, as demonstrated through all the sources, both in and extraneous to tragedy, was consistently and prominently of great concern to the Athenians of the period. The social was communicated as the political through tragedy, and this articulation took many discursive forms: as anxiety over the shift of power between generations in *Prometheus*; as an exploration of the extent to which young people should be allowed to participate in political decision-making in *Antigone*; as an examination of society's expectations of youth in times of war in *Heraclidae*; as questioning what limits should be placed on youth's autonomy in *Philoctetes*; as an enquiry into how political factionalization along age groups lines should be managed in *Orestes*; and as a demonstration of the consequences of the mismanagement of intergenerational relations in *Bacchae*. If the Aristophanic view is to be believed (a perspective unreflectively adopted by too many scholars), all young people are argumentative, insubordinate and prone to violence. Indeed, it is the case, if the plays surveyed in detail in this book are truly representative, that tragedy contains characterizations of young men and women who are by turns aggressive, disrespectful and bloody-minded. But in tragedy they are also shown to be at times honest, physically brave, intellectually mature, morally courageous and loyal. Their relationships to society are always difficult and this is often due to the manipulative interference of older men in their personal agency. They often face outright hostility from an older generation, and have to constantly struggle to have their voices heard and their achievements recognized.

I believe there are great rewards in a much more nuanced reading than has previously been achieved of the way in which youth are handled in the genre of tragedy, which provides richly divergent portraits of young people, as a correlate of the much more complex way in which youth would have been viewed in contemporary society. I do not argue, as others have done, for a discernible 'generation gap' in fifth-century Athens. I consider such retrojections of this modern concept into the classical period anachronistic as they fail to take into adequate account the contextual factors that determined this use of language (ones that are semantically firmly rooted in the mid-twentieth century). For the post-Second World War generation, in Britain and America at least, the term 'generation gap' was a useful phrase that was deployed to underscore that upcoming generational unit's identity in opposition to the preceding generation, as well as to establish what that earlier generation collectively perceived as the expectations that the new generation failed to meet. These expectations were largely to do with respect for authority and tradition. There were very real technological and demographic factors that facilitated this social phenomenon and intensified the sense of disconnect between the two generations. Since the 1950s/1960s, the notion of a 'generation gap' appears often to be used to describe the popular social construction of the (almost) tacitly-accepted difference in values between generations, and has often been less antagonistic in nature. As such, just half a century after working its way into the popular imagination, the term 'generation gap' has become shorthand for what is conceived as the trans-historically consistent state of mutual suspicion and misunderstanding between each existing and new generation, even though the precise use of the term was first specifically produced, at a specific moment, in response to specific contextual factors.

When one speaks of intergenerational conflict, or opposition, however, the case is quite different. Instructively, there is now a newfound anger amongst many young people who believe a kind of intergenerational theft has taken place, one whereby all publicly funded services enjoyed by the 'baby-boomers' have been withdrawn. This anger appears to be a response to an acute political crisis in which economic contractions have acutely impacted on young people. The subsequent expression of these young people's anger, through protest, has thus been cast in the popular media as wanton vandalism by gangs of unruly youth, as was the case with recent student protests, nationwide riots and a wave of university sit-ins in the UK of the early 2010s. One thinks back to other times of political crisis, such as during the anti-war/radical left-wing movements of the late 1960 and early 1970s, which were partly results of the Cold War, and the very negative popular views of young people engaged in protest (most notoriously in the events at Berkeley, California and Berkeley Square, London). One sees that in the modern period, intergenerational conflict breaks out into near-stasis at times of the most acute political tensions. And at these times the conflict has been transactional, in that the younger generation, since they now have some forms of limited political power, recognize the constraints placed upon them and displace the anger resulting from this recognition into antagonistic action. Correspondingly, some sections of the older generations who still hold substantive political power use the media at their disposal to present these actions as part of an atavistic narrative that presents any political views held by youth or action taken by young people to be simple and unconsidered youthful idealism or recklessness.

It is this form of rupture in the constant of anxious intergenerational relations, caused by political crisis, that I believe was demonstrably present in late fifth-century Athens as a consequence of the Peloponnesian Wars. Furthermore, I have argued that evidence is available for the existence of a kind of youth culture in classical Athens, that is, the empirically discernible existence of recognizably 'Mannheimian' generational units that formed identities based on age and in opposition to wider society. This, I have proposed, could only exist because of the demographic and political changes that weakened vertical dynastic power structures whilst encouraging lateral, democratic ones. Greek tragedy demonstrates the centrality of young people to society and to political decision-making, as well as the tensions arising from the short-lived transition from standard atavistic views on the control of unruly young men to a more sympathetic perspective on the contribution that young men could make, before the collapse of Imperial Athens reintroduced the earlier dominant perception of youth. As a result, young people began to find a voice in both culture and politics, and even perhaps the power to change the course of Athenian history, albeit with disastrous results in Sicily. In short, I have suggested that youth culture may have first developed in recorded literary history not in the 1950s but in the 450s BCE. The fact that this culture then disappeared from view for thousands of years is perhaps for further discussion by experts on other historical periods. It may not have ever really dissipated, but rather have gone underground, never to find literary expression that has survived for us to read throughout later antiquity, the transformation of the world of the pagan Mediterranean into the world of Christianity and Islam, the Middle Ages and the Renaissance, the Early Modern, Enlightenment, revolutionary and Victorian periods. On the other hand it may well be the case that modern perceptions have been so bound up in the notion of youth culture developing in the twentieth century that research has simply not been carried out on other historical periods.

Of the thirty-three extant full plays of ancient Greek tragedy, and the hundreds of fragments, I have investigated only a very small proportion in any great detail. There is consequently immense scope to expand this initial foray to become a larger project that aims to examine exhaustively themes to do with youth in Greek tragedy. One might question why this would be useful. I would answer that a greatly improved understanding of youth in tragedy would be useful in two ways. First, this area is under-researched, and represents a major gap in classicists' understanding of the ancient world. Throughout the discussion I have challenged the prevailing categorization of an undifferentiated 'troublesome youth' that is so often used by classical scholars, reflecting an unquestioning use of this stock character by Aristophanes. In the last half century, great strides have been made in taking seriously the role of women in tragedy, as well as slaves and those not of aristocratic birth, and those of different ethnicity, in order to create ways of reading 'fictional' literature so as to illuminate these groups' historical place in ancient society. And so it should be. But the young people of ancient Greek drama have yet to experience this type of sustained interest and it is this change that I hope to effect, in some small way. A sceptic might say that focusing on the presentation of youth serially in individual tragedies distorts the overall picture. However, wherever possible, I have attempted to integrate the most obvious thematic uses of 'youth' from other plays into my discussion. The sceptic might also complain that plays have been arbitrarily selected, or worse, deliberately cherry-picked in order to support the historical argumentational arc, that young people are treated more favourably in literature (as a response to more favourable treatment in culture and society) during times of political stability. It is true that the plays analysed in detail do come from periods of particular historical importance. But then so do many others that I have not selected. A parallel investigation, for example, could have chosen to follow detailed discussion of the following plays: *Persae, Eumenides, Ajax* (although I am aware that this play is undated), *Hippolytus, Troades,* and the result would be quite similar. The exact plays investigated are less important than the core argument that issues to do with youth are universal in tragedy and highly responsive to the political context. It is also true that I cover much historical ground very quickly, and future research may benefit from a more synchronic approach that could draw out more fully the tensions in society of which social anxiety centred on youth forms a part. But perhaps more critically, it is still incredibly difficult to reconstruct the voices of non-aristocratic youth, and this difficultly severely limits the ability to effectively draw conclusions regarding popular conceptions of youth across social strata. I would argue this makes the argument for further work on youth in Classics all the more persuasive.

Notes

Introduction

1 Butler (2000) on *Antigone*; Devereux (1985) on *Hippolytus*; Devereux (1970) on *Bacchae*; and for a more general ethno-psychoanalytic survey of dreams, Devereux (1976). See also Green (1979) and Kerenyi & Hillman (1987) on *Oedipus*.

2 As argued by Griffin (1998). While Griffin may have set the pendulum swinging too far towards the notion of tragic theatre as purely spectacular and emotional, his views are a useful reminder of the multiple factors at work in tragedy. His conclusion, however, that tragedy has survived because of its remote and strange content (p. 61) seems, at least superficially, to be difficult to reconcile with modern reception theories, such as the essential role of Classics in our self-definition; see Martindale (1993). A general framework view is put succinctly by Anderson, 'Greek tragedy in particular explores several instances of incomplete or irregular transitions [from youth to adulthood]' (Anderson, 2005, pp. 125–6). See also Sommerstein (2012).

3 See 'Youth' entry in Brill's *New Pauly* for the absence of comprehensive research on youth. Cancik & Schneider (2006).

4 Such as found in Bertman (1976), see below.

5 This is not to claim equivalences between tragedy and categorically political texts such as Plato's *Republic* or Aristotle's *Athenian Constitution*. Rather that, as Hall (2010) states: 'tragedy, while representing an instance of suffering in dramatic form, always asks *why* it has occurred' (p. 6). Without wishing to dilute Hall's formulation, naturally, one feels, this question has a shadow: how could such suffering be avoided? From a Marxist perspective, there is a clear link between the cultural artefact and political discourse (Williams, 1977).

6 There are many correspondences between classical Greek and Near Eastern cultural artefacts, which suggests further evidence may be available to experts in, for example, Sumerian or Akkadian literature. See Harris (1992), West (1997) and Haubold (2013) for the extent of cross-cultural transmission.

7 Ethnic 'otherness' was most notably brought within the mainstream of Classics through the work of Hartog (1988) and Hall (1989), as well as framing the theoretical core to Bernal's (1987) controversial *Black Athena*; gender was

introduced rather earlier by a number of classicists such as Pomeroy (1975), Zeitlin (1978), Foley (1981), and Lefkowitz & Fant (1982).

8   Konstan (1995, p. 5). See also Rose (1992) for a more overtly political approach and Hall (2006a, pp. 4–6), for a defence of a reflexive historical materialist approach.

9   Montgomery (2007, pp. 25–71).

10 Granville Stanley Hall (1904, pp. 74–5). Or in the words of the contemporary writer, Karl Ove Knausgaard, 'The chasm at the centre of the world opens only to one who is neither child nor adult, but midway between' (Knausgaard, 2017, p. 107).

11 Kliejwegt (1991, p. 50), who discusses at length the twentieth-century debates on whether the concept of adolescence was understood in pre-industrial times.

12 See Golden (1990, pp. 12–14) on childhood and children, and later pages.

13 See Nash (1978, p. 19, n.13) 'Adolescence generates the widest vocabulary of all; just as "adolescent, youth, juvenile, teenager, and young adult" may all describe an eighteen-year-old today, *neos, hēbē, pais, kouros/koura* may indicate the same stage in Greek.'

14 Pinker (2002, pp. 266–7, n. 87).

15 Such as throughout in Bertman (1976), Strauss (1993) and Forrest (1975) – see below – and in Hall (2010, p. 286).

16 Pilcher (1994, p. 482).

17 Pilcher (1994, p. 483).

18 Mannheim (1952, p. 298).

19 The original essay, from which the book takes its title, was first published in 1968. By the author's own claim, it was the first attempt by a Greek historian to apply the structuralist concepts of Lévi-Strauss to an investigation of ancient Greek society (Vidal-Naquet, 1986, p. 187).

20 The paper was subsequently converted into an article in *Yale Classical Studies* in 1975 (Forrest, 1975).

21 The first use of the term 'baby boomer' appeared in the early 1960s, the decade in which The Who's 'My Generation' first explicitly linked music and social attitudes to a defined cohort, and which could be considered the cultural artefact of Becker's (1963) Sociology of Deviancy applied to an entire generation. 'baby, n. and adj.' *OED Online*. Oxford University Press, March 2017. Web. 25 April 2017.

22 See also Eyben's *De jonge Romein volgens de literair bronnen der periode ca. 200 v. Chr. tot ca. 500 n. Chr*, which appeared a year later in 1977.

23 That is not to say that interest in young people vanished amongst classicists. The year 1988 saw an early example of digital classical scholarship in the form of Thury's catalogue of words associated with youth in Euripidean tragedy (Thury, 1988).

24 For those interested in the homoeroticizing of youth in Classical Greece there is also Schnapp's *Images of Young People in the Greek City State*, but this narrow take on youth seems a fairly arbitrary choice for inclusion in the promisingly titled Levi & Schmitt (eds) (1997) *A History of Young People: Ancient and Medieval Rites of Passage*.

25 First produced as a conference paper in 1996 and then published in Markantonatos & Zimmermann (2012).

26 Lape (2004, p. 243). See also Hall (2006b, pp. 93–126). See Note 5 above for Williams.

27 Hansen (1999, pp. 88–90).

28 Hansen (1999, p. 89).

29 http://www.ucl.ac.uk/spp/publications/unit-publications/45.pdf; see also Audickas (2016). The US system is similarly dominated by older members (average Congress age/50; average Senate age/61; see Manning, 2016, p. 2). The Spartan system was much more rigidly structured than the Athenian both in terms of education for boys aged seven onwards, and in its openly gerontocratic (Cartledge, 2003, pp. 83–9) forms of political office. The minimum age for attendance at the Apella, the equivalent of the *Ekklesia*, was 30 and 60 for the Gerousia, a constitutional function approaching comparability with the Athenian proboule. The verses by Tyrtaeus quoted in Plutarch's *Lycurgus* (6.4) show that culture's political investment in (first) the monarchy and (second) aristocratic elders.

30 Kehily (2007, p. 251).

31 For the decade's interactions between politics, youth and tragedy, see Hall (2004, pp. 1–46) and Zeitlin (2004, pp. 49–75) in Hall, Macintosh & Wrigley (eds) (2004).

32 The links between youth, especially seen as those in morally formative years, and criminality are well attested in post-industrial Europe. Regular 'moral panics' have been documented since the 1800s with groups of working class youths the target of moral outrage (regardless of the fact that the events that caused such outcries – penny theatres, gangster films, gangster rap or video games – are all created by an adult industrial capability). See Springhall (1998). Cohen's (1972) *Folk Devils and Moral Panics* remains a seminal text on the subject.

33 See Halsey & White (2008) on antisocial behaviour and for an extensive literature review on perceptions of youth crime, including commentary on the role of the media in shaping perceptions. Other recent research goes so far as to suggest that older people actively seek out negative stories about young people, in order to positively reinforce their own age-group identity. Knobloch-Westerwick & Hastell (2010, pp. 515–35).

34 Beginning with Frederic Thrasher, sociological interest in youth and conflict, most often rendered as 'gangs', has evolved through various phases in the twentieth and

twenty-first centuries, such as the still-sometimes-fashionable criminological focus, towards a culturally and politically nuanced view of the role of the place of youth in society (Katz & Jackson-Jacobs, 2004). Recent media coverage of murders of adolescents in the UK has resulted in a new wave of interest in this subject, but now within a wider context of social exclusion and 'social mobility' (McAuley, 2007).

35 McDonald (2003, pp. 62–6).

36 Katz & Jackson-Jacobs (2004). This unified, transactional form is nicely expressed in the lyrics of American hip hop band *A Tribe Called Quest*'s 2016 song *Kids*, a composition that, perhaps, looks back to the band's younger selves as a pioneering group in the late 1980s.

37 From *A Winter's Tale* III. iii. 58–62. Winnicott (2000, p. 156).

38 Ward (2012, p. 130).

39 Ward (2012, pp. 157–8).

40 Thrasher (1927). The study almost exclusively discusses working-class and second-generation immigrant groups. The wealthy and/or settled community had, according to Thrasher, no significant gang activity (p. 20).

41 Thrasher (1927), p. 251.

42 Thrasher (1927), p. 251.

43 Bertman (1976, p. 38).

44 Aristotle, *Rhetoric* 2.12.3–14.

45 Isocrates, *Areopagiticus,* 49–51. Note that these atavistic views are very similar to ones in archaic literature, both belonging to historical periods when full democracy was absent. That is, the periods before the reforms of Ephialtes and after the Athenian defeat in the Peloponnesian War.

46 Thrasher (1927), p. 3.

47 To my knowledge, only one piece of classical scholarship has been published to date on gangs and the classical, Fuchs's *The Greek Gang at Troy* (1993). Here gang experience is framed within the context of illegal entrepreneurial activity, not to mention anachronistic individualism, reflective, perhaps, of a barely veiled context specific cultural lens.

48 See Bulmer (1984) for the innovation of an ecological approach to sociological fieldwork, by which the Chicago School won its renown. Thrasher's legacy is demonstrated in the other great early twentieth-century work on gangs, Whyte's (1943) *Street Corner Society*.

49 The provocatively titled *The Criminologist's Gang* (Katz & Jackson-Jacobs, 2004).

50 Katz & Jackson-Jacobs (2004, p. 99).

51 Certainly, there remains doubt as to the authorship of this play, but for present purposes the play is considered broadly as a product of the Athenian imagination

and representative of fifth-century cultural thought, of which Aeschylus was a part. Scholarly opinion on authorship of the play is traceable through Thomson (1932, pp. 1–5), Taplin (1977, pp. 460–9), Griffith (1983, pp. 31–5), Podlecki (2005, pp. 195–200) and Hall (2010, p. 230). For a full discussion on *Prometheus* see Chapter 2 below.

Chapter 1

1 Aristotle, *Poetics*, 3.5.
2 I am fully aware of the contentious claim I make here, and persuasive arguments have been made for Old Comedy to be considered as a dramatic form of equal cultural significance to tragedy (Robson, 2013).
3 This phrase is repeated at 2.79 and 7.328 and 9.93 and is also used to describe Odysseus at 2.281 and Priam at 7.368 and Thoas at 15.281, all older leaders.
4 MacCary (1982) argues for the presentation of an immature Achilles in the *Iliad*, as consistent with a literary mirror to a society in which young/*erga* and old/*logos* were natural binaries. Both Gottesman (2008, p. 1) and Lloyd (2004) identify widespread use of '*kertomia*' by Achilles, a form of speech that is associated with young men.
5 It is always a hazardous task to try and estimate ages of fictional characters but Menelaus' speech at 4.113 suggests that Telemachus must be around 20 years old. At 4.669, Antinous suggests that he has not yet reached manhood, and Odysseus' dog is referred to as having aged 20 years since Odysseus left Ithaca (17.328), having been born around the same time as Telemachus.
6 Griffin (1980, pp. 80–1).
7 Belmont (1967), Austin (1969). See also Lateiner's entry for 'Youth' in Finkelberg (ed.) (2011, pp. 947–9).
8 Felson (1994, pp. 67–91; p. 91).
9 West (2008a, pp. xi–xii). We also have an important ritual song that holds up youth to comparison with other age groups and previous cohorts (Anonymous fragment, Ritual Songs, 870).
10 See also 1063–8 and 1129–32.
11 CURFRAG.tlg-0263.27. The text is clearly mediated by the later writer – what should be '*theoi*' presented in singular form and the use of sets of seven years, a possible hint at early Christian syncretic thought.
12 See Rozier (2015) for discussion of characterization in hexameter poetry set against a generic schema of increasing heroic/divine dislocation from the mortal plane.

13 Vernant (1986, pp. 42–3).

14 Goldhill (2006a).

15 The identity or identities of the Antiphons cited in classical texts are still disputed. For simplicity I treat the various texts attributed to various Antiphons as a single set. See Gagarin (2002) and Pendrick (2002) for the competing views.

16 DK 21B11; KRS 166.

17 DK 21B15; KRS 169, F9 DK 21B16; KRS 168.

18 DK 22B79; W 105; M 92; K 57.

19 DK B117.

20 *Laws*, Book II, 666b-c.

21 DK 22B80; KRS 212; W 26; M 28; K 82.

22 Isoc. *Busiris* 28.5–29.9.

23 Isoc. *Areopagiticus*, 49–51.

24 DK 59B6, KRS 481.

25 DK 59A41, KRS 492.

26 DK 59B17, KRS 469.

27 DK 31B12, KRS 353, W 9, I 18.

28 DK31B22; KRS 388; W 25; I 37.

29 DK 31B26; W 16; 1 28.

30 Most prominent in DK 68B3; KRS 593; T D27 and DK68B191; KRS 594; T D55.

31 DK 68A135; KRS 574, 589; T 113.

32 Pythagoras charged 100 minas, a huge sum, according to Diogenes Laertius' *Lives of Eminent Philosophers*, DK 80A1; B1; B4 but there is further testimonial that emphasizes the civic-mindedness that was also apparently characteristic of his outlook, DK 80B3.

33 DK 82B3A.

34 DK 80A5.

35 DK 80A1; B1; B4.

36 Plato, *Gorgias* 452e1–453a3.

37 DK 82B6. Such moral relativism is played out most outrageously in tragedy in Euripides' lost *Aeolus*, in which the son of the play's namesake, Macareus, argues on relativist terms for the appropriateness of his impregnation of his sister. See Hall (2006a, pp. 74–5).

38 DK 84B2.

39 Xenophon, *Memoirs of Socrates*, 4.4.19–21.

40 DK 87B60; DK 87B61.

41 *Oxyrhynchus Papyrus* 414.

42 Dionysus of Halicarnassus, *Demosthenes* 3.

43 Hall (1989).The passage describing the matrilineal traditions of the Lydians, a clear example of an inverted social norm, to a Greek, presented as a curio. Herodotus *Histories* 1.173–4

44 Although this inability to properly make an independent, fully accountable decision is what allows the sons of the Theban leader, Attaginus, to escape execution on charges of treachery (9.88).

45 Although there seems to be no incontestable evidence for the exact ages of Persian kings, see How & Wells (1961, p. 131); Dandamae (1989, p. 373).

46 Hall (1989), Blok (2002, pp. 225–42).

47 See also the final sections of the *Histories*, which look back on the glory days of Persian army discipline, against their current ill-discipline.

48 Castration of boys has already featured at 3.48 in a hostile passage regarding the tyrant of Corinth, Periander.

49 Interestingly, such assertions are almost all made early in the work, such as at 1.42, 1.72, 1.80, a reflection, perhaps, of the uncontested authority of older men that would be challenged later in the conflict.

50 Clearly in Thucydides, Pericles is a major exception, described as wielding all the power (2.65). This is not a traditional description of a democratic leader.

51 Young and old soldiers are again grouped together at 5.64, this time on the Spartan side. See also 5.75.

52 His brilliant political manoeuvring but reckless disregard for democratic process is immediately demonstrated at 5.45.

53 He is thought to have been aged between 30 and 33 (Gomme, Andrewes and Dover, 1978, pp. 48–9; Hornblower, 2008, p. 101).

54 Thucydides qualifies his description of Alcibiades as 'a man who was still young in years', with: 'or would have been thought so in any other city in Hellas' (5.43), which suggests that political involvement by young people was even more restricted in other *poleis*.

55 Thucydides' own view of Alcibiades is quite favourable, perhaps due to common oligarchic sympathies. At 6.15, the picture drawn of Alcibiades is of a master tactician whose personal misdemeanours made him objectionable.

56 It has been argued that Nicias attempts to open up an intergenerational divide to support his more moderate approach to the expedition to Sicily (Hornblower, 2008, pp.361–2). He is defeated, but there follows the re-emergence of generationally defined invective that follows the *Hermae* incident.

57 Pseudo-Aristotle, *Athenian Constitution*, 29.

58 The prefix 'Hellenic' is generally considered superfluous, serving only to clarify that these are Greek, not Skythian, young men (Gomme, Andrewes & Dover, 1981, pp. 80–1). The oligarchy seems to have been supported by a number of political

'clubs', *hetaireia* (8.81), and while there is little to suggest, at least in Book 8, that these had a particular association with youth, the idea of a drinking club with political associations (oligarchic) sounds very much like that 'gang' that mutilated the Hermae and was exclusively associated with young men. See Lintott (1982, pp. 125–85) and Chapter 6 on *Orestes*, below.

59 Robson (2009, pp. 103–19). The influence may well have been reciprocated, some seeing the comic elements of certain Euripidean plays taking inspiration from Old Comedy (Silk, 2000, pp. 42–97).

60 Konstan (1995, p. 6).

61 Konstan (1995, pp. 102–8).

62 Konstan (1995, pp. 305–12).

63 Konstan (1995, pp. 311–12). Of course, the two are not entirely inseparable. As we have already seen, the education required to become expert in rhetoric required significant wealth, as did the employment of a speechwriter, but direct patronage seems to have become a blunt tool by the beginning of the Peloponnesian War, by Whitehead's account.

Chapter 2

1 For the sake of convenience, I henceforward refer to the play's author as Aeschylus, and the version of the myth of Prometheus it stages as belonging to Aeschylus, rather than, for example, to Hesiod. This practice also conforms to my view of the date of the play's first production (see Note 51 in the Introduction). Ruffell (2012, pp. 13-24) does not commit to one of two dating parameters but does offer very useful discussion on how the play would relate to either nascent or established periods of energetic democracy.

2 Discussion on the nature of the political in Aeschylean tragedy is well-trodden ground, a good summary of which can be found in the preface to the second edition of Podlecki's (1999) *The Political Background of Aeschylean Tragedy*. See Ruffell (2012) for an excellent and more recent doxographic summary, and Storey (2013) for a valuable critique of that work.

3 *Liddell-Scott-Jones Greek–English Lexicon* (p. 1169). D'Angour (2011, pp. 19–27, 87–8). The Greek for revolution, *neōterizein*, too forms part of this semantic cluster. See Davidson (2006a, p. 31, also p. 38 for transfer of power between generations as revolution).

4 Havelock (1950, pp. 19–31) frames civil war within changing technological advances, and in *Prometheus* (and it must be said, in all other textual sources

relating to the myth, such as Plato's *Protagoras* 320d–321e, as well as *Theogony* 535–80 and *Works and Days* 48–58) such material innovations play a central role in the conflict between the Titans and Olympians. The concept of the shock of the new is manifested most obviously in the triumphant blow delivered by Zeus with the use of his thunderbolt.

5   West (1997).

6   West (1997, p. 209).

7   Conacher (1980, p. 8).

8   Conacher (1980, p. 14).

9   In Hesiod's history of the gods, before Zeus overthrows his father Kronos' rule, he gathers together all Olympians and Titans, and pronounces: '. . . that he who was without office or right under Kronos, should be raised to both office and rights as is just' (396–8). The use of terms such as *dikē* and *timē* is indicative of the cosmic order that Hesiod shows Zeus to represent.

10   Reinhardt (1949, p. 69).

11   Reinhardt (1949, p. 131–2); Lloyd-Jones (1971, p. 66). O' Sullivan (2005, p. 140) does point out that most of the claims made against Zeus are by Prometheus but then goes on to say that the Oceanids or Hephaistos are less biased witnesses, a claim that will be shown to have significant weakness below.

12   Reinhardt (1949, pp. 47–8).

13   The English translation used is by Podlecki (2005) that in turn is based on the authoritative reconstructions of the original Greek by Griffith (1983) and West (1998, p. 69).

14   Podlecki (2005, p. 160).

15   By line four of the prologue a scholarly divide opens up on the poet's presentation of Zeus' regime and character. Podlecki (2005, p. 75) translates *pater* as 'father' appended by 'Zeus', to clarify that Kratos is referring to Hephaistos' father in a directly genealogical way rather than 'in some generic, honorific sense' (p. 160). By contrast, Griffith glosses the term as relating to Zeus as 'father of gods and men, sometimes kind sometimes stern' (Griffith, 1983, p. 82) giving the sense of his general political rather than specific familial authority.

16   Herington (1963).

17   The links between the personal and the political in relation to age have been discussed by Strauss (1993) who attempts to demonstrate that relations in the *oikos* directly reflect and are reflected by – and influence and are influenced by – those in the *polis* in relation to power struggles between fathers and sons. While this attempted synchronization is questionable, there is legitimacy in the use of binary opposites to describe relationships in Greek society; works by Hall (1989)

or Cartledge (2002) show that this was how the Greeks would have viewed themselves, and old/young fits into this world view. The legitimacy is because the Greeks themselves thought antithetically. See Lloyd (1966).

18 The authoritative work by Lewis (2009) sets out very good reasons why tyrannies could attract popular support and ends with the uncontestable line: 'there was no one like a tyrant for getting things done' (p.128). Pindar, in *Pyth.* 3.84–6, uses the term *tyrannos* to describe Heiron without making a political point on his method of governance, although it is true that, as a Theban, Pindar did not belong to the same distinctly democratic Attic culture as Aeschylus. See O'Sullivan (2005, p. 151, n.7) for a range of later sources who use *tyrannos* in a formal, status-related rather than morally evaluative way.

19 Austin (1990, pp. 289–306). The modern tendency to assign *tyrannos* a Lydian origin is reasonable, but the case for this classification is by no means overwhelming; see Andrewes (1956, pp. 21–2). West (1997, pp. 579–85) also sees many aspects of *Prometheus* as indicative of influence by cultural transmission from Western Asia.

20 Austin (1990) dates the definitive point at which the association was made as 499 BCE, at the time of the 'Ionian Revolt'.

21 White (1955, pp. 1–18). Taking the example of the tyrannies of Peisistratos and Hippias, White also sees tyranny as part of a developmental progression with the form enabling the movement from Solonian oligarchy to Cleisthenic democracy.

22 'The mafia analogy . . . helps us make sense of the forms of oppression alluded to by ancient sources, and to explain what caused the crises which led to *coup d'etat* by tyrants all over Greece.' Van Wees (1999, p. 1). See also De Ste Croix (2004, pp. 211–12) for the political and economic conditions that enabled tyrannies to emerge as a response to oppression.

23 The reverse view of tyranny as part of a general political deterioration has also been articulated, in ancient and modern times, but generally in a theoretical way rather than from historical observation. See Pl. *Rep.* Book 8, esp. 8.562c–563c. The obvious exception is in Ar. *Pol.*, chapters 14–19, which follows Thucydides' historical narrative view of the Peisistratos' sequence of tyrannies.

24 Cartledge (2002, p. 3).

25 Strauss (2000, p. 67).

26 Dover (1974) offers a comprehensive overview of popular Greek perceptions of youth as 'compounded of extravagance, pugnacity, thoughtlessness, drunkenness and sexual excess' (p. 103); on the last characteristic, cf. Io's account of her pursuit by Zeus, 640–86. See Chapter 1 for this normative view of youth outside of the tragic sources.

27 O'Sullivan (2005, pp. 129–30) makes the comparison of Polyphemus in *Cyclops* to Pentheus in *Bacchae* but even here refers to a line in the play (43) that confirms that the tyranny of Thebes was given to Pentheus by Cadmus, an important qualification of the term.

28 He is linked with inventiveness and patronage of mortals (*Homeric Hymn to Hephaestus*, West, 2003, p. 203), and there is evidence that cultic activity in Athens reflected some shared rituals (Farnell, 1896–1909, pp. 374–95).

29 *Iliad* 1.590.

30 Burkert (1985, pp. 157–8).

31 Griffith (1983, p. 90).

32 Fisher, 1992, pp. 20, 97–9.

33 Hall, 2009, p. 208.

34 Griffith (1983, p. 99).

35 'Outrageous torment' (93). The word *aikeiaisin*, like the accusation of hubris, is a legal term as well as a form of insult (Griffith, 1983, p. 103; and Podlecki, 2005, p. 164). Prometheus thus questions the very legitimacy of Zeus' rule. The term is a lesser accusation than hubris, not carrying the same connotations of public shame-causing but still accuses the target of gross personal violations and violence. It would have been seen as a safer accusation than hubris when the accuser was at a disadvantage in power, influence or age. See Demosthenes, 54; Todd (1993, pp. 269–71); and Carey and Reid (1985, pp. 74–7).

36 As commented by Gantz 'he sees far more than ordinary men, but never the whole truth' (1976, p. 40).

37 Eur. *Bac.* 341–71.

38 Griffith (1983, p. 115).

39 Podlecki (2005, p. 166).

40 Resonant of Achilles' tone of lament for his heroic diminishment at the hands of the higher ranked Odysseus in the *Iliad*.

41 Podlecki (2005, p. 166).

42 Previously deployed by Kratos at 56. Podlecki (2005, p.167).

43 Taplin (1977, p. 262).

44 *Birds* (1347–59), *Frogs* (149–50), *Clouds* (1321–436), *Wasps* (686). Kassel & Austin (1984) *Poetae Comici Graeci* III.2.

45 See Sutton (1993, pp. 1–37) and Gardner (1989, pp. 51–62), although caution is advised on taking a simple view of real-life analogues in comedy. See Aristotle's *Poetics* (1448a18) for an ancient view of comedy representing characters inferior to contemporaries but recognizably believable.

46 Vidal-Naquet (1986); but there were more traditional elements too, such as the community-based presentation of young men at the Koureion on the third day of

the Apaturia (Cole, 1984) or the recitation of the ephebic oath (Taylor, 1918). See Bowie (1993, pp. 45–52 and pp. 102–12) for correspondences between ephebic practices and traits and characterization in Aristophanes, particularly *Knights* and *Clouds*. While we cannot be certain that the *ephebia* existed as a stable process, it seems likely that elements of it did exist in the fifth century and coalesced into a more established set of practices in the following century (Siewert, 1977).

47 Hesiod, *Works and Days*, 110–200.

48 Thu. 6.56–59, Her. 5.55 and 6.123 for a denial of their role in ending tyranny at all. Thucydides' view was not necessarily a mainstream one: the legend of these two historical figures was central to the Athenian ideal of democracy, evident in the erection and later replacement of their statues in central Athens. See Brunnsaker (1971) for a comprehensive survey of statuary dedicated to Greek tyrannicides.

49 Strauss (2000, pp. 28–9) and Xenophon, I.2.56.

50 The line at 1012 'but your excess rests on a cleverness without strength' sounds like the accusation often made by the old of the young – that they are quick to act without wisdom.

51 Conacher (1980, pp. 120–37).

Chapter 3

1 As in Foley's view, 'the gendering of ethical positions permits the public exploration of moral complexities that would not otherwise have been possible' (Foley, 2001, p. 172). This chapter's focus on Haemon extends this discussion of complexity to include age as well as social status.

2 Griffiths (2003, p. 122) points out that, while the term *kērugma* is neutral, Antigone's speech reflects a proclamation 'that is spoken of as if it came from, or on behalf of, the citizens at large', and Ismene suggests this is the case (79). Nevertheless, Thebes is not a democracy and Creon is a tyrant, in the classical sense, so this discussion, relating to deliberation or counsel, should not be considered as synonymous with truly democratic decision-making in the modern conception, but rather as a king seeking advice from a council of elders.

3 Hall (2012b). Hall makes convincing arguments for the centrality of discussion of 'deliberation' in Sophocles' Theban plays and points towards the significance of how these discussions interact with issues around age and political status (Hall, 2012b, p. 304 and pp. 312–13, in particular).

4 Present usage meaning to be both impetuous and youth-like. See Dover (1974, p. 103).

5   See Caswell (1990) for a comprehensive survey of the use of *thumos* in early epic, and Koziak (2000) for an account of the term with a greater emphasis on context and a wider chronological sweep.

6   Hobbs (2000).

7   Hobbs (2000, p. 38).

8   Plato, *Republic*, Book 4. 435b–441c. That is not to say that philosophical terms and concepts are entirely absent from tragedy. They are not. Discussions of *dikē* or *timē* in plays such as *Philoctetes* or in the *Oresteia* bear reasonable comparison with the basic frameworks of discussion in Plato's *Protagoras*, for example. Indeed, there is significant osmosis between the two forms and Aristotle, in *Poetics* (49b27f), discusses, albeit briefly, catharsis as a psychological output that tragedy must affect.

9   Hobbs (2000, p. 46). Hobbs follows this line with a quote from Adler that brilliantly articulates the capacity of *thumos* to lead people to the dark, as well as the light.

10 Foley (1989, pp. 61–85) sets out the argument persuasively in relation to Medea but the strands of argumentation can be traced back to Nussbaum (2001, first published 1986) especially in relation to her chapter on *Antigone*, pp. 51–84. I follow much of Nussbaum's line of argumentation, though focus on the interactions between psychology and age, rather than Creon's inflexibility and failure to understand the complexity of the political circumstances in which he finds himself.

11 See also 1253a and *Nicomachean Ethics* (1112a–1113b) for Aristotle's view on the importance of speech and deliberation in political decision-making.

12 As we shall see, Creon's own ethical framework is such that he measures himself against subjective abilities rather than moral absolutes. I take the four primary virtues to be *dikaiosynē, sōphrosynē, andreia* and *sophia*, following Dover (1974, p. 66), as set out in Plato's *Symposium* (194–7). This incredible passage sets out the behaviours to which young men must aspire and is explicit in linking these ideals to youth, with the *neanikos* Eros held up as the example to follow. The first three full sections of description begin: 'he is the youngest of the gods' (195b), 'so he is young, and sensitive as well as young' (195d), 'he is very young and very sensitive' (196a). Eros is shown to be both young, in relation to the older gods, but also sensitive, which I believe means that he is intellectually mature.

13 See fuller discussion of this line below. See also Griffiths (2003, p. 310). The repeated use of the term *thumos* in this section (1085 and 1088) reinforces the emotional rather than rational aspect of Creon's decision-making. With Tiresias calling Creon 'child' (*teknon*), at 1023, the youth-like state that Creon has regressed to appears even more distinctly defined.

14 Her. 3.36, 7.13; Thuc. 6.12, 6.38-9. At 6.15, a combined anxiety about lawlessness, tyranny and youth is presented in authorial voice. See Chapter 1 for discussion of these passages. Of course, Aeschylus addresses this issue directly in *Persae*, with Xerxes' failure in comparison to Darius' success blamed on the rash actions of the young king. Aesch. *Persae* 739-86.

15 Curiously, the chorus immediately offer support to Creon, unless they have been 'deceived by time' (*ei mē tō chronō keklemmetha*), lines 681–2. This interesting phrase reinforces both the age effect on judgement and the confusing state of the speeches where control over *dianoia* is breaking up in the older man (and the chorus, it can be argued) whilst being better controlled by the younger Haemon.

16 'Cease from your anger and allow yourself to change.' Creon must escape from the pervasive influence of a *thumos* inflamed by anger.

17 This combination of psychic collapse and misogyny is very similar to that experienced by the autocratic Pentheus in Euripides' *Bacchae* (see Chapter 8), another character who exhibits some of the clear faults of youth in his inability to properly control his *thumos*. His inability to engage in proper political discussion is the primary contributor to his downfall. However, the advice given by the older men, Cadmus and Tiresias, is also suspect due to their intractable positions.

18 Griffith (2003, p. 252). While Goldhill (2012, pp. 58–63) is not convinced of Haemon's moral victory in the stichomythia, as he does not persuade Creon to his way of thinking, I would suggest that Haemon's speeches must be weighted by his fundamentally weaker position within the exchange due to age and relationship. Haemon, as Antigone, represents not just himself but the diversity of opinion within the *polis* whereas Creon embodies the dangerousness of narrow and inflexible views closed to influence through speech.

19 It certainly bears comparison with Pentheus' combined softening and decline in *Bacchae*, thus forming part of a 'catabatic king of Thebes' dramatic model, and it is effective in helping to remove further unnecessary dramatic involvement of Ismene (Griffith, 2003, pp. 252-3). Brown (1987, pp. 184–5) considers Knox's view to be an exaggeration, that the scene is necessary to effect the shattering of Creon's heroic mask in order to emphasize the contrasting 'stoic' heroism of Antigone in the following episode (Knox, 1969, pp. 72–3). The various interpretations all remain open to challenge with no apparent scholarly consensus.

20 Aristotle famously commented on Creon's (and Haemon's) inconsistency, his inability to properly act even when he becomes fully aware of the potential consequences of his actions (*Poetics*, Book 7.4.1454a). This inconsistent consistency was viewed by Aristotle as a negation of tragic character.

21 These lines, along with all others spoken by the chorus, take on a very different meaning if a director chooses to use a female chorus, such as at a recent production of *Antigone* at London's Southwark Theatre.

22 Griffith (2003, p. 266).

23 The figure of Eros is heavily associated with youth but is somewhat paradoxical, being both young, as perceived biologically and anthropomorphically in relation to e.g. Aphrodite, and mature, in behaviour. Perhaps, then, the chorus use the example of Eros as an indirect reference to their, and society's, difficulty in understanding the multivalence of youth.

24 The Greek, here, means that it is difficult to accurately judge the tone of the chorus, whether they are offering negative statement (Knox, 1969, pp. 176–7, n.8) or some form of consolation (Griffith, 2003, p. 267). When considered against the chorus' ability to formulate a realistic picture of Antigone's motivations, these different interpretations are irrelevant. In the absolutely clearest terms, Antigone does not wish for praise or glory, only justice, albeit on her own, narrow terms.

25 As a blind character, it is uncertain who Tiresias is addressing on stage, but as a message to the audience, it is clear that his advice is a contribution towards the ongoing discussion of the best approach to decision-making in the *polis*.

26 *LSJ*, 2007, *phren-* 2–4, p. 768. That said, 'intuitive rationality' is not entirely oxymoronic. One must recognize that knowledge produced via heuristics was not necessarily seen as an irrational form of thought, such as in the concept of 'bounded rationality' (Gigerenzer & Selten, 2001). Moreover, divination and prophecy, both abilities associated with Tiresias, would have been understood differently in the ancient world. It is quite likely that a wider field of 'rational' thought or emotion existed in contemporary Athens. See Struck (2016).

27 The identity of 'you all' is open to interpretation, but the effect is to present Creon's petulant behaviour in a *neanikos* light.

28 *euboulía.*

29 Haemon's earlier speeches have a remarkably similar pattern to those of Tiresias. However, while both Haemon and Tiresias depart with insults (cf. lines 764–5 and 1087–8, which are almost identical in tone and meaning), the prophet occupies a different political stratum, elevated by his unique ability to engage with the divine, and he does not share the fears of the chorus.

30 See Chapter 1. For the impact of political changes on group identity, see Osborne (2010, pp. 27–38) and Davies (2004, pp. 18–39).

31 Garrison (1995, p. 115).

32 Shakespeare had almost certainly read the Latin version of *Antigone* by Thomas Watson, *Sophoclis Antigone* (London, 1581).

33 Garrison (1995, pp. 1–33, p. 25) makes the important point that both Herodotus and Thucydides avoid making moral judgements about suicide, rather 'they leave us with the sense not that suicide created "moral revulsion", but that it provided people with an honourable release from an undesirable life.'

34 Loraux (1987) discusses at length the gender-specific methods of suicide.

35 In *The Trachiniae*, Deianira also kills herself in this way (930–1). But as Loraux (1987, pp. 54–6) has pointed out, Deianira is desperate to uphold martial values after she realizes what she has done to the ultra-martial Heracles. At 931, Deianira is said to have struck her '*phrēn*' or midriff.

36 Garrison (1995, p. 119). More generally, Garrison argues that suicide is a response to external social forces and that suicide is often carried out in a way that allows social structures and values to continue, rather than as a challenge (Garrison, 1995, pp. 32–3).

37 Dem. 43.578. From another oratorical source, if indeed the speech was ever delivered, it is difficult to imagine an audience hearing Lysias' *Against Eratosthenes*, especially at 12.96, without reflecting on the tyranny of Creon and comparing his mythology with the actions of the Thirty Tyrants in their refusal to allow proper burial.

38 Brown settles for 442/1 (Brown, 1987, p. 1), as does Griffiths (2003, pp. 1–2). Scullion (2002) suggests an alternative date of 450, largely based on the absence of *antilabē*, a metrical feature of later Sophoclean works, following the suggestion by Lloyd-Jones.

39 There are vast doxographies of scholarship on Athenian democracy and its relation to changes in power structures, but a seminal work remains Josiah Ober's (1996) *The Athenian Revolution*.

40 Interestingly, it was Pericles who acted as *choregos* for Aeschylus' *Persae*, a play that uses highly critical language to describe young people. In 472, Pericles would have been a young man, only just eligible to attend the Boule and most likely still barred from holding higher office due to his age.

41 Davies (2004), a book chapter reprint of the author's 1978 journal article.

42 The dangers of excluding, or at least discouraging groups from full political participation are well set out in Carter's (1986) *The Quiet Athenian*. In tragedy, in *Ion* by Euripides, the titular character articulates such a discouraged view (585–647), powerfully making a case for non-participation in politics.

43 Very recent research suggests that frustrated expectations even within relatively privileged groups can be identified as a factor for extremist behaviour. See Gambetta & Hertog (2016).

Chapter 4

1   Allan (2001, pp. 21–2) suggests the main perceived weakness relate to structure, political intent and characterization and offers a wry ordering of nineteenth- and early twentieth-century critical comments. More favourable treatments began with Zuntz (1955), and have included Burian (1977), Wilkins (1990 and 1993) and, more latterly, Hall, who mounts a vigorous defence of the play's relevance (Hall, 2010, pp. 245–8). See Allan (2001) for a useful, if now dated bibliography. With the theme of 'displacement' (Mendelsohn, 2002, p. 50) added to the play's topoi on the utility of youth at times of war and the fraught nature of international politics, it could be said the play now has great and tragic contemporary correspondences.

2   Such as noted in the commentary by Wilkins (1993, pp. 192–3), or as the subject of an influential article by Zuntz (1947) or in an introduction to the play (Allan, 2001, pp. 35–9).

3   Mendelsohn (2002, p. 64) is correct to say 'the play's conflation of Athens and Marathon thus mirrors the strategy of contemporary civic discourse by which the pre-democratic but still influential ethos of heroic valour, with its emphasis on allegiance to kin (*genos*), had to be subordinated to the democratic imperative . . ', and this imperative appears to include the wartime subordination of civic participation of young men to that of mere fighting units.

4   Stroud (1971)

5   Goldhill (1987)

6   See above, Chapter 2, Note 46.

7   Aeschines, *Against Ctesiphon*, 154.

8   Zuntz (1955), supported by Wilkins (1993, p. xxxiv) and Allan (2001, p. 56). Cropp & Fick argue for a date range between 430–26 (Cropp & Fick, 1985, p. 23).

9   To rephrase a line from a well-known First World War poem. Katherine Tynan, *Flower of Youth*, 1915.

10 Wilkins (1993, pp. 52–3).

11 Whitley (1994).

12 The slightly later *Archanians*, by Aristophanes carries some very similar themes and belongs, in my view, to the same historical context.

13 Although possibly apocryphal, certainly parodic, Plato's *Menexenus* repeats these arguments in terms explicitly linking expectations of young warriors to the heroic events at Marathon, Salamis and Plataea (246d–248d).

14 The chorus then interject a typically Athenian utterance that a just decision cannot be taken until both sides of the argument are heard (180–1). See preceding chapter for discussion of 'deliberation'.

15 Compare Thu. 2.44, on the duty to produce more children to help assist the future security of the city.

16 Thucydides states that around 16,000 were garrisoned for the defence of Athens, a number drawn from the oldest and youngest from the army, and from *metics* who qualified as hoplites (2.13). Allan (2001, p. 154) points out the historic parallel between Athens at the beginning of the Peloponnesian War and the lines at 280–1 when the Herald uses the threat of destruction of the Athenians' crops.

17 For the age range for hoplites, see Christ (2001, p. 404). By modern standards, this inclusion of old men seems extreme, but as recently as World War Two, old and young men would have fought in defence of their besieged city, such as was the case at Berlin in 1945. Christ suggests that those over 50 were most likely exempt from overseas operations but with the latter stages of the war with Persia on Athens' doorstep, it is quite possible that the upper age range of soldiers would have been included in the ranks. Herodotus suggests that 8,000 hoplites (9.28–9) from Athens took part at the battle of Plataea, with many more light infantry and auxiliaries. If Herodotus' estimate of a citizen body of 30,000 is correct (5.97), the vast majority of Athenian hoplites would have been at Plataea.

18 Allan (2001, pp. 183–5) discusses the differing scholarly opinions on whether this scene is humorous, as well as whether there are any comic elements in the play and how this affects the subsequent reception of *Heraclidae*. To me, it is impossible to read this in any way other than comic, particularly when comic speech is made about the physicality of old men elsewhere (120).

19 The term is actually quite uncommon in tragedy. There are limited uses applied in some plays, such as *Persae* (512, 733) *Helen* (12) and *Medea* (1108) but they are far outstripped by terms such as *neos* and various derivatives that appear throughout tragedy, including *Heraclidae* (cf. 120, 469 and see entries on *Prometheus* and *Antigone*). The term's associative field, containing both the paramilitary initiation to adulthood and the mythological character who embodied youth, must be considered of acute significance. In *Persae*, the term is used only when referring to the ranks of the dead young men of the Persians, but in *Helen* and *Medea* it is used in relation to young women about to pass into adulthood. When *hēbēs* is used at line 11 in *Seven against Thebes*, it is specifically in relation to the defence of the city against an invading force of Argives. See McCullogh & Cameron (1980, pp. 1–14).

20 LIMC IV, Vol. I, pp. 458–464. With reference to martial training see p. 461. Hebe also appears as cup-bearer in the presence of Ares, in full combat gear, in a vase painting from the early fifth century, LIMC IV, Vol. II, 1990, p. 276, Hebe I.34, London, British Museum, E.67, plot. Mus. C1 337. Hebe, is widely referenced in ancient textual sources, albeit with conflicting accounts of her place in the

Olympic genealogy (Pindar, *Nemean Ode* 7.1, 8.1; *Homeric Hymn 3 to Pythian Apollo 196*; Hesiod, *Theogony* 17, 950. In *Theogony*, line 922 is especially interesting, placing Hebe as siblings of Ares (god of War) and Eileithyia (goddess of Childbirth), suggestive of a recognizable cohort of divinities associated with generational change and war.

21 Vidal-Naquet (1986) *The Black Hunter*. See also Wilkins (1990, pp. 329–339) who argues for Heracles' close connection with the *ephebia*.

22 Wilkins (1990, p. 334), in an otherwise useful summary of youth and cult in *Heraclidae* fails to avoid the retrojection of Pausanias, for example, into the mythological record of Iolaus: 'The interesting group of Hebe, Iolaos and Alkmene. Whether or not this quartet was recognized in the fifth century is impossible to say but the association is significant'.

23 The iconographic record of Iolaus, which is massive due to his association with Heracles, is too extensive to survey here. There is a huge increase in the popularity of Iolaus on vase painting in the sixth century, when the popularity of Heracles peaked, but he is much less frequently found in the fifth and fourth centuries (LIMC V, vol. I, p. 695).

24 Alcmene at 941; Iolaus at 52.

25 Thu. 1.1.

Chapter 5

1 Thu. 8.1.

2 Hall (2010, pp. 263–85, esp. pp. 269–70) discusses the *hetairiai* in relation to the group dynamic between Electra, Orestes and Pylades in Euripides' *Orestes* and points out how these 'clubs' appear to have been tiered by age groups and placed the greatest value on companionship over familial bonds.

3 The term, Hellenic Youth, '*hellenes neaniskoi*', is somewhat inexplicable but could perhaps refer to Greek but non-Athenian youths.

4 Schein (2013, p. 10–11) speculates on this point and sketches out the potentiality for the audience to draw general historical parallels and ones specifically between the play's characters and contemporary figures.

5 He does appear in reported speech in *Andromache* and overshadows all of the play's action *in absentia*. Indeed, as a character returning from the Trojan Wars with an enslaved Trojan princess and finally killed due to atrocities committed at Troy, Neoptolemus, in this play, is a figure comparable to Agamemnon in Aeschylus' play. He is also referred to in Euripides' *Hecuba* and *Troades*, but only in passing, which

is perhaps surprising given the character's pivotal role in the mythology of the
capture of Troy. However, all these plays are much earlier than *Philoctetes* and
emerged from a historical period quite different from that of Sophocles' play, each
predating the catastrophe of Syracuse of 413, the oligarchic revolution of 411 and
the restoration of democracy in 410. Many fragments of tragedies attributable to
Sophocles have survived since the fifth century. From them we can see that the
playwright had made use of stories associated with Neoptolemus, such as *Hermione*
and *Euryalus*; there are four fragments of a *Philoctetes at Troy*. Others contain
interesting lines on age; fragment 487 of *Peleus* has an unnamed character
proclaim: 'for as a man grows old he becomes a child once again', while *Men of
Scyros* includes: 'For war likes to hunt down men who are young (*andras . . . neous*,
fragment 554) and Neoptolemus is mentioned as a character in fragment 557. Both
these plays may have prominently featured Neoptolemus (Lloyd-Jones, 2003,
pp. 252–3 and 276–7). In *The Women of Phthia*, fragment 694, a character says, 'You
are young; you have much to learn and much to listen to, and need long schooling.'
Here it is very tempting to speculate that this may have been spoken to
Neoptolemus, as has been suggested by others (Lloyd-Jones, 2003, p. 331). An
optimistic review of these fragments would suggest that Sophocles has a particular
interest in the character. However, it must be remembered that Sophocles was
prolific, the *Suda* stating he authored 123 tragedies, and that constructing possible
plotlines, let alone thematic structures, from fragments is extremely problematic.
What can be said of *Philoctetes* is that no other tragedy by Sophocles, complete or
in fragments, so clearly put the young man Neoptolemus as the central figure. He
constitutes a vortex around which all discussion flows.

6   *Discourse* 52 of Dio Chrysostom provides a comparison between Sophocles' play,
the much earlier version by Aeschylus and Euripides' *Philoctetes*, performed some
decades before the 409 production. From Dio Chrysostom, and what fragments
survive, neither of other tragedian's versions appears to feature youth as a theme,
or even younger men as main characters. While Neoptolemus does have a strong
connection with Philoctetes in the various fragments of books in the 'Epic Cycle',
Sophocles is the first to send Achilles' son to Lemnos. See Mandel (1981) for a
comprehensive record of Philoctetes in ancient textual and iconographic sources.

7   Useful bibliographies can be found in Ussher (1990, pp. v–xviii) and Schein (2013,
pp. 347–66). There are a number of sources of particular note in relation to the
investigation of the control of young men, as an ambiguous reflection in the
play of factors in society: an incorporated sophistic analysis of society and
interrogation of Odysseus as sophist in *Philoctetes* (Rose, 1976); for visual aspects
of the play, such as the significance of the young physically supporting the old and
the play's numerous delayed exits, which I believe could be considered as mapping

the frustration of adolescence (Taplin, 1971); on Homeric resonances (Knox, 1964); and the ethical dimensions of character relations (Blundell, 1991).

8 For the clear father and son dimension, see Whitby (1996). Rose (1992, pp. 266–330) argues convincingly that the play's thematic content reflects contemporary friction in Athens between those who would give primacy to education or inherited excellence in shaping the best kind of citizen, and how these competing systems are encoded with political theory supporting oligarchic versus democratic positions.

9 Without risking an attempt at drawing an overly reductivist parallel, Sophocles' appointment as one of the *Probouloi* immediately before the oligarchic revolution of 411, at great old age, is significant in that the playwright would have experienced first-hand the acutely political consequences of the competition between different value systems to the polis, those of the democrats and those of the oligarchs. See Osborne (2012, pp. 270–86). Aristophanes mercilessly mocks the *Probouloi* in *Lysistrata* (387–461), perhaps a reflection of the membership's inefficacy.

10 For *paideia* in general see the dated though encyclopaedic Jaeger (1939). More recently, Carlevale (2000, esp. pp. 28–9) makes useful reference to the role of '*sunousia*' as a backdrop to the play. The fact that young men might act in order to impress their peer group mentors is highly significant. Of course, the practice of *sunousia* was later to have a very significant role in the trial of Socrates in relation to the education of young (aristocratic) men. Havelock (1986, pp. 4–5).

11 *Antigone* (728–9, 734–5). Sophocles relates *neos* as a psychological state to *dianoia* and the inflammation of *thumos* (see chapter 4). In the *Persae*, Xerxes failings are specifically linked to his youth as the Persian defeat is blamed solely on the rash actions of a *neos* (782).

12 Estimations of ancient demographic changes are always highly tentative due to the data sources from which figures can be extracted (Hansen, 1986, pp. 8–25) but it appears likely that the population of Athens during the war years reached its lowest point between 415–411 (Green, 1959, appendix II) and that this problem came not only from battle losses but also a lower birth rate following the plagues of 430–29 and 426–5, further reducing the numbers of young men in the city (Gomme, 1933, pp. 6–7). By Thucydides' estimation the impact of defeat at Syracuse was incomparably great. In 413, 4,000 Athenian hoplites alone set out with the initial expeditionary force (6.31), most likely supported by many more auxiliary troops, and around 5,000 hoplite reinforcements arrived with Demosthenes later in the year (7.42). The force was large, the defeat crushing. Thucydides describes the slaughter of the Athenian army as the greatest of the entire war (7.85) and 7,000 prisoners were taken (7.87).

13 Lines 260, 268, 276 and 284.

14 Particularly Easterling, 1973, pp. 14–34. See also Budelmann (1999).

15 See a most valuable collection of essays in De Jong & Rijksbaron (2006) (eds.), especially Davidson (2006b, pp. 25–38) and De Jong (2006, p. 74).

16 Knox (1964).

17 Patroclus and, as above, Antilochus are both widely represented as young men, cut down in heroic yet futile action. See *Iliad* 23.586–90, 23.756, 15.569–70 in particular for the youthfulness of Antilochus.

18 The famous case of Phrynichus' huge fine, sketched out in Herodotus (6.21), handed down for reminding the Athenians of their own evils is cause to hesitate before suggesting direct parallels, though the literary and historical contexts are quite different, not to mention the time elapsed between Phrynichus' *Capture of Miletus* and Sophocles' play.

19 By contrast in *Antigone* (766) the chorus refer to Haemon as *anēr* whilst levelling age-based criticisms (though this does reflect the confusing view of youth put forward by the old men of the play).

20 Schein (2013, p. 236).

21 Rehm (2006, pp. 95–107). Suggestions that the relationship between Odysseus and Neoptolemus might reflect the older man's relationship with Telemachus, whilst faulty in many ways, does emphasize the multiple ways of connecting the Homeric to the Sophoclean. See Whitby (1996).

22 In all these instances there is a sense of actions that are raging out of control. See Schein (2013, pp. 261–2), for further discussion of the term in other literary contexts. Rehm bases his argument on earlier work by Whitman (1958) published in *Homer and the Heroic Tradition*. Whitman offers a full chapter of discussion on the uses of imagery relating to fire in the *Iliad* (Whitman, 1958, pp. 128–53) and provides many cogent examples of the use of the term fire as synonymous with 'heroic passion and death.' Just one example is the use of 'fire', in place of 'battle', to describe conflict in heroic language. See Whitman (1958, p. 129) and *Iliad* XII 177.

23 Whitman (1958, p. 104).

24 While it is perhaps unwise to link the term *pur* to *neanikos* behaviour directly or exclusively, the term is used to describe psychological states associated with youth such as in *Antigone* (473–9, 964). See also Eur. *Orestes* 621, 697.

25 *Iliad* 15.569–70.

26 Reminiscent of his father's words in the *Iliad* at 1.293.

27 It is not, to my mind, entirely certain that this first line is addressed to Neoptolemus. After all, Odysseus uses the term 'wicked man', *kakist andrōn*, rather than using the terms *teknon, pai* or *neos* after the adjective. It would also make sense that Odysseus has returned to the action having received the report of the

fake merchant and addresses Philoctetes first before quickly establishing the facts of the encounter.

28 Taousiani (2011, pp. 426–44).

29 Ussher (1990, p. 161) interprets Heracles choice of *andros* to describe Neoptolemus to demonstrate the young man's new found maturity.

Chapter 6

1 The character of Orestes and the events depicted in the *Oresteia* have a long and rich history within the ancient Greek literary tradition. While there are interesting passages in Homer (*Od.* 1.29, 298, 3.03), Pindar (*Phythian* 11) and Stesichorus (frgs. 210–19, Davies, 1991, *PMGF*), focus will remain on references within tragedy due to the large number of plays of the fifth century that include *Orestes* (argument for the exceptionality of tragedy in respect of its politically contingent content is made in Chapter 1 when compared against non-tragic sources).

2 While *Orestes* (408) and *Iphigenia in Aulis* (405) are firmly dated, there is no secure evidence for precise dating of the *Electra* plays, nor of *Iphigenia in Tauris*. But structure and style would suggest that these are all plays that are relatively late in tragedy's chronology. See Hall (2010, pp. 232–3, p. 301). *Orestes* was produced just a year after *Philoctetes* and some have noted similarities between the two. West (1987, p. 32) and Falkner (1983, p. 290) see Euripides' modelling of the plotline of *Orestes* on *Philoctetes* as almost parodic in places.

3 Sinclair (1988, pp. 141–2). Plut, *Arist.* 2 paints a very vivid picture of the sort of political entitlement that would later be attributed to members of these 'clubs', having Themistocles say: 'Never may I sit on a tribunal where my friends are to get no more advantage from me than strangers' (2.4).

4 Calhoun (1964, especially pp. 27–9) is still the seminal work on *hetairiai*. Admittedly, much evidence comes from Demosthenes, and thus the following century, but the sketches of the political clubs put forward in these orations are very similar to the account one finds in Thucydides. See 29. 23; 54.14, 39. Gottesman (2014, p. 7) rightly points out the lack of evidence we have for the inner workings of *hetairiai* but marshals well the evidence for links between the 'clubs' and anti-democratic subversive forces (Gottesman, 2014, pp. 48–9, 141–2). See also Murray (1990, pp. 149–61).

5 West (1987, pp. 36–7).

6 Although it appears that such groups also existed outside of Athens. The demagogue, Athenagoras, making his speech to the Syracusans before the

Athenian expeditionary force arrived, warns of the same groups at work in Sicily (Thu. 6.38–9). Thucydides' reported speech suggested such tensions exist in all democracies yet it is only Athens that produced tragedy to express these tensions in dramatic form.

7 Calhoun (1964, pp. 34–6). Aristotle's quotation of an alleged oligarchic oath: 'I will be evilly disposed towards the demos' (1310a9) is one possible formulation, its democratic mirror image found in the oath of Demophantos which was a legislated requirement for members of the *boule* after 410 (Andokides 1.95–8). See also Teegarden (2012).

8 Calhoun (1964, pp. 32–3). See Ashe (2000) for more on the hellfire clubs of England and Ireland in the eighteenth century.

9 Interestingly, modern scholarship on youth gangs also places emphasis on their inhabitancy of public spaces. Indeed, the very latest research claims that a youth 'gang' can only be so categorized if its activities are mainly in public spaces (Medina *et al.*, 2013). The class bias here cannot be more obvious.

10 See Introduction, for modern complexities in defining 'gangs'.

11 Aeschylus, *Choēphoroi*, 900–3

12 Hall (2012a, p. 1).

13 There are many contemporary examples of this type: the British film *Attack the Block*, directed by Joe Cornish in 2011, encourages the audience to side with a thuggish set of young men against alien territorial invasion. Earlier, films such as *Rebel Without a Cause* and *The Wild One* from the 1950s are landmark presentations. And while *Iphigenia in Tauris* has long been considered an influence on the structure of Xenophon's *Anabasis* (Calhoun, 1921), one wonders whether *Orestes* was similarly in the mind of the writer when he created his account of the journey from Asia Minor. That Xenophon, known for Oligarchic views, would have been in his early twenties when the play was performed makes this a real possibility. Walter Hill's *The Warriors*, from 1979, while loosely structured around events in *Anabasis*, shows how group identity is formed and expressed through violence and, to my mind contains characterization that can be traced back to *Orestes*.

14 *Iphigenia in Tauris* is probably to be placed sometime between 416–12, or slightly earlier. See Hall (2012a, Preface, xxx–xxxi).

15 All translation of Euripides' *Orestes* from West (1987).

16 Pylades is mentioned in an interpolation at 33 (West, 1987, p. 183), providing some evidence for the perceived centrality of this character to the action of the play. When he finally arrives on stage he makes no doubt about his allegiance or willingness to participate in group violence.

17 In the 1995 film *La Haine*, by Mathieu Kassovitz, one of the three lead characters, Hubert, remarks: 'It's not the fall that kills you, but the landing.' Throughout the

film the group act in opposition to a variety of Parisian communities. After various adventures in foreign parts of the city, they return to their neighbourhood to a dramatic and violent climax. They fall but we don't see them all land. The viewer becomes the *deus ex machina*, resolving the action in whatever way they choose.

18 *Choēphoroi*, 1053–8.

19 *Philoctetes* 797–801, *Ajax* 815–65. Although finally won round by the arguments of Theseus, Heracles in his name play too seeks suicide, 1146–62. It's true that Ajax and Heracles show clear links between madness and violence – both take aim at specific victims and do not show a propensity for generalized violence, let alone attempted *theomachy*.

20 *Bacchae* 489–518.

21 See Note 28.

22 This accusation would have had interesting contemporary resonances. At 408 Sparta had established a courtship of Persia for logistical support and money. Indeed, the theatre of conflict between Sparta and Athens was largely based around the Ionian coast and Islands, and extending up to the Hellespont. Sparta was in hock to the barbarians (Xen. *Hellenica*, 1.2–1.4).

23 Both speeches also contain, to the modern audience, shockingly sexist attitudes to the role of women in society. The chorus, rather than engage with the arguments, simply say: 'Women always complicate men's affairs in the more disagreeable direction' (605–6). The misogyny of the tragic and mythic material here has a well-established history (Zeitlin, 1978), and Tyndareus subsequently suggests that the burden of guilt should actually fall on Electra (615–21).

24 Cf. Th. 3.82.

25 Menelaus' absence is reported specifically by Orestes at 1058–9. It seems fitting that the outcome, orchestrated by the gerontocratic Tyndareus, is delivered by another old man, albeit one sympathetic to Orestes' plight. In modern terms, this demonstrates that the judiciary and the executive of the local political order are monopolized by old men.

26 The play's hypothesis by Aristophanes the Grammarian (line 5) states that this version of the myth is not found in any other written source.

27 Cf. 734–97. While formally 774–98 is split-line *antilabē*, the length of this section gives a stichomythic effect. Stichomythia is used by Euripides to work out a plan of action in *IT* 1020ff. and *Ion* 970ff. and *Hel.* 813ff (West, 1987, p. 260).

28 Thu. 6.28. The best evidence for these events is still that found in Andokides, *On the Mysteries*, though as forensic oratory this source cannot be used uncritically. See also Furley (1996).

29 Another comedic formulation of words, pointing towards the *deus ex machina* resolution of the play.

30 Hermione seems like an innocent bystander in the play and Electra's kidnapping of her has been considered cruel (Vellacott, 1975, p. 77) or even a 'crowning baseness' (Mullens, 1940, p. 156). And yet, this is the daughter of the woman whom the group consider began the current cycle of violence and whose father is the man who betrayed them. In this light, she could not be more guilty by association. In modern-day girl gangs, the female subsets of male groups often take out revenge on female associates of those whom the males wish to cause harm. Electra's action here fits the pattern of a parallel course of action to the males', attacking the same target group through their women. See Sikes (1997).

31 West (1987, p. 266).

32 A classic modern example of the use of group chanting in literature is found in Golding's *Lord of the Flies*. The lines: 'kill the beast! Cut his throat! Spill his blood!' whilst used before killing a wild boar, also marks the transformation of the group into one that defines itself through the violence it carries out. And it horrifically prefigures the later killing of Simon. It has been argued that Golding drew heavily on Euripides' *Bacchae* when constructing his work (Dick, 1964, pp. 145–6).

33 The two are described by the slave as like 'Bacchants at a mountain cub', perhaps an early indication of Euripides' creative direction: the total societal collapse caused by the maenads in his following play, *Bacchae*, is in many ways the hoped for conclusion by the group in *Orestes*.

34 According to West (1987, p. 288) a 'startling rude way for a young man to accost a senior relative.' Rude, yes, but hardly unexpected, given the build-up to the scene. All Orestes' actions are calculated to give the greatest disrespect to those he believes have betrayed him.

35 This is another allusion to *Medea* and an unwitting prediction of the play's conclusion.

36 In the play's context, this *volte face* demonstrates the weaknesses of Menelaus' character. He is the antithesis of stoic resolve. But to modern readers his capitulation is redemptive, he is willing to lose face in order to protect his daughter.

37 Interestingly, during the events inside the palace, Orestes appears untouched by the Erinyes. It is as if the madness caused by his extreme reaction against society is enough to block out any other form of mental affliction.

38 In the few recent productions of the play, directors do appear to have more sympathy than scholarly commentators on the plight of Orestes and his gang. 'Trapped in a cycle of recriminations and spurred on by his sister and best friend, he is pushed into a state of absolute self-conviction which enables him to rationalize and justify actions well outside the limits of acceptable human behaviour.' Pippa Needs, Director of *Orestes* at the Oxford Playhouse in 2005,

marking the 125th anniversary of the first play to be staged in ancient Greek at Oxford. A decade earlier, The Rapp Arts Center's version of *Orestes* (1996) was subtitled: 'I murdered my mother'. R. Jeffrey Cohen, who directed this version, is one of the very few directors and commentators to give Orestes and his gang some due, saying in the play's programme notes: 'Euripides goes after disaffected youth, vain and political parental leaders, the corruption that ethically bankrupt, but sensationalist and 'smug' choral reporting reveals.... this production has sought to live within the Greek and the contemporary. In terms of disaffected youth, the doublespeak of criminology, and the sensationalized hype of the media, we, as people, have not changed. Today's middle class youth reject parents who reject them'.

Chapter 7

1   It is deeply regrettable that only small fragments of *Alcmaeon in Corinth* are extant. As Hall has pointed out (2004, p. 1; 2010, pp. 367–8) what lines remain from the play do suggest significant thematic similarities between the tragic plays of this tetralogy in relation to the treatment of children by their parents. Furthermore, fragment 75 goes, 'Son of Creon, how true then it has proved, that from noble fathers noble children are born, and from base ones children resembling their father's nature' (Collard & Cropp, 2008, p. 91), and this frames the play's action within an intergenerational framework. As we shall see, in both *Iphigenia in Aulis* and *Bacchae*, there are scenes of generational rupture that could make this line take on an ironic significance. Unfortunately, we shall never know if this was the case unless new papyrus finds transform our knowledge.

2   Evelyn-White (1959) and, more recently, West (2003).

3   Cadmus mentions Pentheus' father, Echion, at 213, but only to state that it is the father's son to whom Cadmus has given authority of rule. When the chorus mention Echion at 265 and 540, it is to unfavourably compare Pentheus' intentions with those his grandfather would make. At 992–6 (and repeated at 1011–16) the chorus make this comparison again, but more strongly reject Pentheus' mortal character against the chthonic origins of Echion. Pentheus' aunts, Ino and Autonoe, and mother, Agave, play major roles in reported speech (especially at 676–774) and Agave does so in a major section at the end of the play, but the play makes no mention of the whereabouts of their husbands. Cadmus' explicit sanctioning of Pentheus' authority, and the absence of all other middle-range male characters suggest, to me, that they are to be understood as being away together.

4　The other major sources being: the pseudo-Aristotelian *Athenian Constitution*; Diodorus Sicilus, *Bibliotheca* and Lysias, *against Demosthenes*.

5　Xen. I.5.16–18.

6　Xen. I.7. 1–35.

7　The final years of Euripides' life are unreliably documented but the biographical tradition places Euripides at Macedon at some point during the final decade of the fifth century. It is more certain that he was dead when the plays were produced by his son (see *Frogs*, Aristophanes, 66–82). Nonetheless, by composition and the production, the plays appear just as tightly responsive to the milieu of Athens as earlier Euripidean works. Geographical distance, if there was any, appears to have little impact in separating the product from the producing culture.

8　Hall (2010, pp. 290–1).

9　There are echoes of Euripides' *Electra* here. In that play, Clytemnestra is lured to her death on the pretence that she was to see her newborn granddaughter. Although the influence of Aeschylus' *Oresteia* means that Clytemnestra is often considered as scheming, she is just as often on the receiving end of murderous plots. Indeed, the actions of Agamemnon in *Iphigenia in Aulis* offer an example of how not to conduct such a plan. Clytemnestra's actions in the earlier *Agamemnon* by Aeschylus are much more polished, perhaps evidence for the earlier misogyny for which Euripides is a useful corrective.

10　This is another potential interpolation. See Michelakis (2006, pp. 105–14).

11　Michelakis (2002, p. 143). The figure of youth, here, is as ultimately powerless as the figure of the old man at the start of the play who is unable to successfully carry out his orders.

12　8.48.3, 8.72.2 and 8.86.5. By contrast, he tends to use the softer term, *homilos*, when referring to the Ekklesia. Hunter (1988) offers perceptive comment on the class bias of this use of language along with the important identification of loss of memory, mental instability and anger as failing components of an individual's psychology that can lead towards submergence in crowd psychology (p. 22). There are numerous other studies of crowds in classical source from which further inspiration can be drawn, including McClelland (1989) and Millar (1998). All subsequent work has been deeply influenced by Canetti (1973) and the corrective of McPhail (1991).

13　The audience, perhaps, would have also recalled the passage in the *Iliad* where Dionysus inflicts madness and death on another King (6.130–40).

14　Dionysus was associated with a whole range of dissolutive qualities in the ancient world, evidenced by the huge variety of literature, sculpture and epigraphy that link him with wine, sex and madness. See Seaford (2006).

15　As Note 7 above, the actual date of production is not entirely secure. An ancient scholion (Schol. Ar. *Frogs*. 67) suggests the play was first produced posthumously.

If Aristophanes' *Frogs*, in which Euripides is brought back from the dead, can be securely dated to 405, then there is a clear *terminus ante quem*. If a specific date of performance cannot be determined, the plot surely belongs to the precipitous period immediately before the defeat of Athens.

16 Zeitlin (1990, p. 113). Moreover, the use of Thebes can be judged to allow the projection of debate on issues critical to Athens on to another scene, where the full tragedy of miscalculation can be safely displayed; pp. 144–5. See also Hall (2011, pp. 51–63).

17 For years the Spartans had courted Persian royalty in the hope of military and financial assistance. Now they had it and it resulted in a string of Spartan successes in the east. After the Athenian failure at Notium in 406, bad news continued to pour in from the theatre of combat (and even the Athenian victory at Arginusae proved to be a Pyrrhic one), now located largely along the coast of Ionia and towards the Bosphorus. Persia, forever a subtle menace, once again became a real threat, and the base of political operations in support of Sparta was Sardis, where Cyrus held the satrapy (Xen. *Hel.* 1.5).

18 The standard fifteen members of the Euripidean model (Calame, 1997, p. 21) would have presented a forbidding sight, the dark mirror image of the chorus that in Euripides often frets, rather than menaces.

19 Seaford (2001, p. 155).

20 *Orestes*, 1100–30. See Chapter 6.

21 For further discussion of the nature of Maenadism see, in particular, Henrichs (1978, 1993, 1995).

22 The staging is conventional (Taplin, 1977) but the speech is jarringly at odds with the tone of the prologue and parodos.

23 I use Seaford's accessible (2001) Aris & Phillips translation throughout.

24 It seems probable that such themes of violence and rejuvenation would have been present in other plays too, such as the fragmentary *Peliades* by Euripides (Collard & Cropp, 2008, pp. 60–71). Fragment 609 of this play also suggests at least part of the action was concerned with group and individual identity and featured a young man as a central character.

25 See Beaumont (2012) on Athenian views on the characteristics of pre-adolescents.

26 Scholarly opinion on the comedic elements of this scene has oscillated wildly over hundreds of years. I share Seidensticker's view (1978, pp. 303–20) that the interaction between the old men is both tragic and comic, intensifying the tragic through an ironic use of the blackest of comedy. See also Foley (1985, pp. 205–58) on the ironic content, widely deployed by Euripides, and deployed for particular effect in *Bacchae* to intensify the sense of the ridiculous *and* the tragic.

27 Evans (2010, pp. 176–8). See also Aris. *Frogs* 344–8 for rejuvenation in Dionysiac ritual.

28 Belfiore (1986, pp. 421–37) has much of interest to say on the role of wine in allowing the non-rational (or youthful) to escape repression by the old, particularly in relation to the concept of *catharsis*. She makes an excellent job of synthesizing a tough Platonic and a softer Aristotelian view of aesthetics relating to ancient poetry.

29 See Richardson (1993, pp. 15–30) for ancient views on the advice-giving abilities of old men.

30 Le Bon (1896) and Kraskovic's (1915). Kraskovic uses various examples from the ancient world to illustrate his points.

31 Freud (2001, pp. 78–9).

32 Freud (2001, p. 308). This *Eros*-opposed, *Thanatos*-associated concept remains a contentious one but seen in an abstract way, supports the proposition that there is a fundamentally destructive and regressive nature of conservative groups.

33 Freud (2001, p. 79).

34 Freud (2001, p. 80).

35 Although it is true that Tiresias warns against *theomachy* (325), a charge levelled at Pentheus by Dionysius in the prologue (45). See Whitmarsh (2016) for a well-balanced treatment of the concept of 'battling the gods'.

36 The moderation brought by older men was considered vitally important at Symposia where wine was abundantly on offer. In a story from Atheneaus (Timaeus 566F 149 in Athen. 37b–d), a group of young symposiasts become so drunk they believe they are aboard a ship upon a stormy sea and begin hurling furniture out into the street. In the ancient world, the absence of older men at Symposia was a well-known risk. Slater (1976) uses this passage to fix Symposia and drunkenness within a maritime metaphorical framework, one greatly influenced by Dionysus.

Bibliography

Allan, W. (2001) Euripides: *The Children of Heracles*, Aris & Phillips, Warminster

Anderson, M. J. (2005) 'Myth' in *A Companion to Greek Tragedy* (ed. Gregory, J.) Blackwell Publishing, Malden, MA

Andrewes, A. (1956) *The Greek Tyrants*, Hutchinson University Library, London

Ashe, G. (2000) *Hell-fire Clubs: A History of Anti-Morality*, Sutton Publishing, Stroud

Audickas, L. (2016) *Social background of MPs 1979–2015* [House of Commons Briefing Paper no. 7483], 25 January 2016

Austin, N. (1969) 'Telemachos Polymechanos' *Californian Studies in Classical Antiquity*, Vol.2, pp. 45–63

Austin, M.M. (1990) 'Greek Tyrants and the Persians, 546–479 BC' *The Classical Quarterly*, Vol.40, no.2, pp. 289–306

Beaumont, L.A. (2012) *Childhood in Ancient Athens: Iconography and Social History*, Routledge, Abingdon

Becker, H.S. (1963) *Outsiders: Studies in the Sociology of Deviance*, Press of Glencoe, New York

Belfiore, E. (1986) 'Wine and *Catharsis* of the Emotions in Plato's *Laws*', *The Classical Quarterly*, Vol.36, pp. 421–437

Belmont, D.E. (1967) 'Telemachus and Nausicaa: A Study of Youth' *The Classical Journal* Vol.63, no.1, pp. 1–9

Bernal, M. (1987) *Black Athena: The Afroasiatic Roots of Classical Civilization*, Rutgers University Press, New Brunswick

Bertman, S. (ed.) (1976) *The Conflict of Generations in Ancient Greece and Rome*, Gruner, Amsterdam

Blok, J. (2002) 'Women in Herodotus' *Histories*' in *Brill's Companion to Herodotus*, pp. 225–242, Brill, Leiden

Blundell, M.W. (1991) *Helping Friends and Harming Enemies: A Study in Sophocles and Greek Ethics*, Cambridge University Press, Cambridge

Bowie, A.M. (1993) *Aristophanes: Myth, Ritual and Comedy*, Cambridge University Press, Cambridge

Brown, A. (ed.) (1987) Sophocles: *Antigone*, Aris & Phillips, Warminster

Brunnsaker, S. (1971) *The Tyrant-Slayers of Kritios and Nestiotes: A Critical Study of the Sources and Restorations*, Svenska Institutet i Athen, Stockholm

Budelmann, F. (1999) *The Language of Sophocles: Communality, Communication, and Involvement,* Cambridge University Press, Cambridge

Bulmer, M. (1984) *The Chicago School of Sociology: Institutionalization, Diversity, and the Rise of Sociological Research,* University of Chicago Press, Chicago

Burkert, W. (1985) *Greek Religion: Archaic and Classical,* Blackwell, Oxford

Butler, J. (2000) *Antigone's Claim,* Columbia University Press, New York

Burian, P. (1977) 'Euripides' *Heraclidae*: An Interpretation' *Classical Philology,* Vol.72, no.1, pp. 1–21

Calame, C. (1997) *Choruses of Young Women in Ancient Greece: Their Morphology, Religious Role and Social Functions* (trans. Collins & Orion), Rowman and Littlefield, London

Calhoun, G.M. (1921) 'Xenophon Tragodos', *Classical Journal* 17, pp. 141–149

Calhoun, G.M. (1964) 'Athenian Clubs in Politics and Litigation' *Studia Historica,* Vol.7, L'erma di Bretschneider, Rome

Canetti, E. (1973) *Crowds and Power,* Penguin, Harmondsworth

Cancik, H. & Schneider, H. (2006) *Brill's New Pauly Online,* http://referenceworks. brillonline.com/entries/brill-s-new-pauly/youth-e529590 (accessed 12 November 2013).

Carey, C. & Reid, R.A. (eds.) (1985) *Demosthenes: Selected Private Speeches,* Cambridge University Press, Cambridge

Carlevale, J. (2000) 'Education, "Phusis", and Freedom in Sophocles' '*Philoctetes*', *Arion. A Journal of Humanities and the Classics,* 8(1), 26–60.

Carter, D.M. (2007) *The Politics of Greek Tragedy,* Bristol Phoenix Press, Exeter

Cartledge, P. (2002) *The Greeks: A Portrait of Self and Others,* Oxford University Press, Oxford

Cartledge, P. (2003) *Spartan Reflections,* University of California Press, Berkeley

Caswell, C.P. (1990) *A Study of Thumos in Early Greek Epic,* Brill, Leiden

Christ, M.R. (2001) 'Conscription of Hoplites in Classical Athens' *The Classical Quarterly,* Vol.51, no.2, pp. 398–422

Cohen, S. (1972) *Folk Devils and Moral Panic,* MacGibbon and Kee, London

Cole, S. (1984). 'The Social Function of Rituals of Maturation: The Koureion and the Arkteia' *Zeitschrift Für Papyrologie Und Epigraphik,* Vol.55, pp. 233–244

Collard, C. & Cropp, M. (eds.) (2008) *Euripides VIII, Fragments: Oedipus – Chrysippus and Other Fragments,* Loeb Classical Library, London

Conacher, D.J. (1980) *Aeschylus' Prometheus Bound: A Literary Commentary,* University of Toronto Press, Toronto

Cropp, M.J. & Fick, G. (1985) Resolution and Chronology in Euripides: The Fragmentary Tragedies, *Bulletin of the Institute of Classical Studies,* Suppl. 43

Dandamaev, M.A. (1989) *A Political History of the Achaemenid Empire*, Brill, Leiden

D'Angour, A. (2011) *The Greeks and the New: Novelty in Ancient Greek Imagination and Experience*, Cambridge University Press, Cambridge

Davidson, J. (2006a) 'Revolutions in Human Time: Age-class in Athens and the Greekness of Greek Revolutions' in Goldhill, S. & Osborne, R. (eds) *Rethinking Revolutions through Ancient Greece*, Cambridge University Press, Cambridge

Davidson, J. (2006b) 'Sophocles and Homer: Some Issues of Vocabulary', in De Jong, I. & Rijksbaron, A. (eds.) *Sophocles and the Greek Language: Aspects of Diction, Syntax and Pragmatics*, pp. 25–38, Brill, Leiden

Davies, J.K. (1971) *Athenian Propertied Families 600–300 BC*, Clarendon Press, Oxford

Davies, J.K. (1978) 'Athenian Citizenship: The Descent Group and the Alternatives' in *The Classical Journal*, Vol.73, no.2 (Dececmber, 1977–January, 1978), pp. 105–121

Davies, M. (1991) *Poetarum Melicorum Graecorum Fragmenta, Vol. I*, Oxford University Press, Oxford

Davies, J.K. (2004) 'Athenian Citizenship: The Descent Group and the Alternatives' in Rhodes, P.J. (ed.) *Athenian Democracy*, Edinburgh University Press, Edinburgh

De Jong, I. (2006) 'Where Narratology Meets Stylistics: The Seven Versions of Ajax' Madness', in De Jong, I. & Rijksbaron, A. (eds.) *Sophocles and the Greek Language: Aspects of Diction, Syntax and Pragmatics*, pp. 73–93, Brill, Leiden

De Jong, I. & Rijksbaron, A. (eds) (2006) *Sophocles and the Greek Language: Aspects of Diction, Syntax and Pragmatics*, Brill, Leiden

De Ste Croix, G.E.M. (2004) *Athenian Democratic Origins*, Oxford University Press, Oxford

Devereux, G. (1970) 'The Psychotherapy Scene in Euripides'*Bacchae*', *Journal of Hellenic Studies*, Vol.90, pp. 35–48

Devereux, G. (1976) *Dreams in Greek Tragedy: An Ethno-Psychoanalytical Study*, University of California Press, Berkeley

Devereux, G. (1985) *The Character of the Euripidean Hippolytos: An Ethno-Psychoanalytical Study*, Scholars Press, Chico, CA

Dick, B. (1964) '*Lord of the Flies* and *The Bacchae*', *The Classical World*, Vol.57, no.4, pp. 145–146

Diels, H. (1951–2), *Die Fragmente der Vorsokratiker*, 3 vols, Kranz, W. (ed.), Weidmann, Zurich

Dover, K.J. (1974) *Greek Popular Morality in the Time of Plato and Aristotle*, Basil Blackwell, Oxford

Easterling, P. (1973) 'Repetition in Sophocles', *Hermes*, Vol.101, no.1, pp. 14–34

Euben, P.J. (1997) *Corrupting Youth: Political Education, Democratic Culture and Political Theory*, Princeton University Press, Princeton

Evans, N. (2010) *Civic Rites: Democracy and Religion in Ancient Athens*, University of California Press, London

Evans Grubb, J. & Parkin, T. (eds.) (2014) *The Oxford Handbook of Childhood and Education in the Classical World*, Oxford University Press, New York

Evelyn-White, H.G. (1959) *Hesiod, The Homeric Hymns and Homerica*, Loeb Classical Library, London

Eyben, E. (1977) *De jonge Romein volgens de literair bronnen der periode ca. 200 v. Chr. tot ca. 500 n. Chr*, Koninklijke Academie voor Wetenschappen, Letteren en Schone Kunsten van België, Brussels

Falkner, M. (1983) 'Coming of Age in Argos: Physis and Paideia in Euripides' '*Orestes*', *The Classical Journal*, Vol.78, No.4 (April–May, 1983), pp. 289–300

Farnell, L.R. (1896–1909) *The Cults of the Greek States Volume 5*, Clarendon Press, Oxford

Felson, N. (1994) *Regarding Penelope: From Character to Poetics*, Princeton University, Princeton, NJ

Finkelberg, M. (ed.) (2011) *The Homer Encyclopedia*, Wiley and Sons, Oxford

Foley, H. (ed.) (1981) *Reflections of Women in Antiquity*, Gordon and Breach Science Publishers, New York

Foley, H. (1985) *Ritual Irony: Poetry and Sacrifice in Euripides*, Cornell University Press, London

Foley, H. (2001) *Female Acts in Greek Tragedy*, Princeton University Press, Princeton

Foley, H. (1989) 'Medea's Divided Self', *Classical Antiquity*, Vol.8, No.1, pp. 61–85.

Forrest, W.G. (1975) 'The Athenian Generation Gap' in 'Studies in the Greek Historians' *Yale Classical Studies*, Vol.24, pp. 37–52

Freud, S. (2001) *The Standard Edition of the Complete Psychological Works of Sigmund Freud: Beyond the Pleasure Principle, Group Psychology and Other Works*, Vol. XVIII (translated from the German by Strachey, J.), Vintage Books, London

Fuchs, J. (1993) 'The Greek Gang at Troy', *The Classical World*, Vol.87 no.1, pp. 62–64

Furley, W. (1996) 'Andokides and the Herms: A Study of Crisis in Fifth-century Athenian Religion', *Bulletin of the Institute of Classical Studies*. Supplement (65), 162

Gagarin, M. (2002) *Antiphon the Athenian: Oratory, Law, and Justice in the Age of the Sophists*, University of Texas Press, Austin

Gambetta, D. & Hertog, S. (2016) *Engineers of Jihad: The Curious Connection between Violent Extremism and Education*, Princeton University Press, Princeton, NJ

Gantz, T.N. (1976) 'The Prophecies of Prometheus', *Ziva Antika*, Vol.26, pp. 31–41

Gardner, J. (1989) 'Aristophanes and Male Anxiety – The Defence of the Oikos', *Greece and Rome*, Vol.36, no.1, pp. 51–62

Garland, R. (1990) *The Greek Way of Life: From Conception to Old Age*, Duckworth, London

Garrison, E.P. (1995) *Groaning Tears: Ethical and Dramatic Aspects of Suicide in Greek Tragedy*, E.J. Brill, Leiden

Gigerenzer, G. & Selten, R. (2001) *Bounded Rationality: the Adaptive Toolbox*. MIT Press, Cambridge, MA

Golden, M. (1990) *Children and Childhood in Ancient Greece*, Johns Hopkins University Press, Baltimore

Goldhill, S. (1987) 'The Great Dionysia and Civic Ideology', *The Journal of Hellenic Studies*, Vol.107, pp. 58–76

Goldhill, S. (2006a) 'The Language of Tragedy: Rhetoric and Communication' in *The Cambridge Companion to Greek Tragedy*, Cambridge University Press, Cambridge

Goldhill, S. (2006b) 'Modern Approaches to Greek Tragedy' in Easterling, E. (ed.) *The Cambridge Companion to Greek Tragedy*, Cambridge University Press, Cambridge

Goldhill, S. (2012) *Sophocles and the Language of Tragedy*, Oxford University Press, New York

Goldhill, S. & Osborne, R. (eds.) (2006) *Rethinking Revolutions through Ancient Greece*, Cambridge University Press, Cambridge

Gomme, A.W. (1933) *The Population of Athens in the Fifth and Fourth Centuries B.C*, Basil Blackwell, Oxford

Gomme, A.W., Andrewes, A. and Dover, K.J. (1978) *A Historical Commentary on Thucydides:* Volume IV, Books IV–V (1–24), Clarendon Press, Oxford

Gomme, A.W., Andrewes, A. and Dover, K.J. (1981) *A Historical Commentary on Thucydides:* Volume V, Book IV–V (1–24), Clarendon Press, Oxford

Gottesman, A. (2008) 'The Pragmatics of Homeric κερτομία', *Classical Quarterly*, NS 58 (1), pp. 1–12

Gottesman, A. (2014) *Politics and the Street in Democratic Athens*, Cambridge University Press, Cambridge

Green, P. (1959) *Armada from Athens*, Hodder and Stoughton, London

Green, A. (1979) *The Tragic Effect: The Oedipus Complex in Tragedy*, Cambridge University Press, London

Griffin, J. (1980) *Homer*, Oxford University Press, Oxford

Griffin, J. (1998) 'The Social Function of Attic Tragedy' *Classical Quarterly*, Vol.48, no.1, pp. 39–61

Griffith, M. (ed.) (1983) *Aeschylus: Prometheus Bound*, Cambridge University Press, Cambridge

Griffith, M. (2003) (ed.) *Sophocles: Antigone*, Cambridge University Press, Cambridge

Hall, E. (1989) *Inventing the Barbarian: Greek Self Definition through Tragedy*, Oxford University Press, Oxford

Hall, E. (2004a) 'Introduction' in Teevan, C. *Alcmaeon in Corinth*, Oberon Modern Plays, London

Hall, E. (2004b) 'Introduction: Why Greek Tragedy in the Late Twentieth Century' in Hall, E. Macintosh, F. & Wrigley, A. (eds.) *Dionysus Since 69: Greek Tragedy at the Dawn of the Third Millennium*, Oxford University Press, Oxford

Hall, E. (2006a) *The Theatrical Cast of Athens: Interactions between Greek Drama and Society*, Oxford University Press, Oxford

Hall, E. (2006b) 'The Sociology of Athenian Tragedy' in Easterling P.E (ed.) *The Cambridge Companion to Greek Theatre*, Cambridge University Press, Cambridge

Hall, E. (2010) *Greek Tragedy: Suffering under the Sun*, Oxford University Press, Oxford

Hall, E. (2011) 'Antigone and the Internationalisation of Theatre in Antiquity' in Mee, E. & Foley, H. (eds.), *Antigone on the Contemporary World Stage*, Oxford University Press, Oxford, pp. 51–63

Hall, E. (2012) *Adventures with Iphigenia in Tauris: A Cultural History of Euripides' Black Sea Tragedy*, Oxford University Press, London

Hall, E. (2012) 'The Necessity and Limits of Deliberation in Sophocles' Theban Plays' in Ormand, K. (ed.) *Blackwell Companion to Sophocles*, Blackwell, Oxford

Hall, E., Macintosh, F. & Wrigley, A. (eds.) (2004) *Dionysus Since 69: Greek Tragedy at the Dawn of the Third Millennium*, Oxford University Press, Oxford

Hall, G.S. (1904) *Adolescence: Its Psychology and its Relations to Physiology, Anthropology, Sociology, Sex, Crime, Religion and Education*, New York, Appleton

Halsey, K. and White, R. (2008) 'Young People, Crime and Public Perceptions: a Review of the Literature' (LGA Research Report F/SR264) [online] NFER, Slough. [Accessed 2 May 2017]

Hansen, M.H. (1986) *Demography and Democracy: The Number of Athenian Citizens in the Fourth Century B.C.*, Forlaget Systime, Vojens

Hansen, H.M. (1999) *The Athenian Democracy in the Age of Demonsthenes: Structure, Principles and Ideology*, Bristol Classical Press, London

Harris, R. (1992) 'The Conflict of Generations in Ancient Mesopotamian Myths', *Comparative Studies in Society and History*, Vol.34, no.4, pp. 621–635

Hartog, F. (1988) *The Mirror of Herodotus: The Representation of the Other in the Writing of History* (trans. Lloyd, J.), University of California Press, Berkeley

Haubold, J. (2013) *Greece and Mesopotamia: Dialogues in Literature*, Cambridge University Press, Cambridge

Havelock, E.A. (trans. and ed.) (1950) *Prometheus: With a Translation of Aeschylus' Prometheus Bound,* University of Washington Press, Seattle

Havelock, E.A. (1986). *The Muse Learns to Write: Reflections on Orality and Literacy from Antiquity to the Present,* Yale University Press, New Haven

Henrichs, A. (1978) 'Greek Maenadism from Olympia to Messalina', *Harvard Studies in Classical Philology,* Vol.82, pp. 121–160

Henrichs, A. (1993) 'He has a God in him: Human and Divine in the Modern Perception of Dionysus' in Carpenter T.H. and Faraone C.A. *Masks of Dionysus,* Cornell University Press, London

Henrichs, A. (1995) 'Why Should I Dance? Choral Referentiality in Greek Tragedy' *Arion,* Vol.3, part 1

Herington, C.J. (1963) 'A Study in the *Prometheia' Phoenix,* Vol.17, pp. 180–197

Hobbs, A. (2000) *Plato and the Hero: Courage, Manliness and the Impersonal God,* Cambridge University Press, Cambridge

Hornblower, S. (2008) *A Commentary on Thucydides:* Volume III, Books 5.25–8.109, Oxford University Press, Oxford

How, W.W. & Wells, J. (1961) *A Commentary on Herodotus* (2 Vols.), Clarendon, Oxford

Hunter, V. (1988) 'Thucydides and the Sociology of the Crowd', *Classical Journal,* Vol.84, no.1, pp. 17–30

Jaeger, W. (1939) *Paideia: The Ideals of Greek Culture Vol I,* Basil Blackwell, Oxford

Kassel, R. & Austin, C. (eds) (1984) *Poetae Comici Graeci, Vol. III,* Walter De Gruyter, Berlin

Katz, J. & Jackson-Jacobs, C. (2004) 'The Criminologist's Gang' in Sumner C. (ed.) *The Blackwell Companion to Criminology,* Blackwell, Oxford

Kehily, M.J. (ed.) (2007) *Understanding Youth: Perspectives, Identities and Practices,* Open University Press, Milton Keynes

Kerenyi, K. & Hillman, J. (1987) *Oedipus Variations: Studies in Literature and Psychoanalysis,* Spring Publications, Dallas

Kleijwegt, M. (1991) *Ancient Youth: The Ambiguity of Youth and Absence of Adolescence in Greco-Roman Society,* J.C. Geiben, Amsterdam

Knausgaard, K.O. (2017) *Autumn,* Harvill Secker, London

Knobloch-Westerwick, S. & Hastall, M. (2010) 'Please Your Self: Social Identity Effects on Selective Exposure to News about In- and Out-Groups' *Journal of Communication,* Vol.60, no.3, pp. 515–535

Knox, B.M.W. (1964) *The Heroic Temper: Studies in Sophoclean Tragedy,* University of California Press, Berkeley

Konstan, D. (1995) *Greek Comedy and Ideology,* Oxford University Press, Oxford

Koziak, B. (2000) *Retrieving Political Emotion: Thumos, Aristotle, and Gender*, Pennsylvania State University Press, University Park, PA.

Kraskovic, L. (1915) *Die Psychologie der Kollektivitaäten*, Vukovar Sriemske Novine, Zagreb

Lape, S. (2004) *Reproducing Athens: Menander's Comedy, Democratic Culture, and the Hellenistic City*, Princeton University Press, Princeton, NJ

Le Bon, G. (1896) *The Crowd: A Study of the Popular Mind*, The Macmillan Company, New York

Lefkowitz, M.R. & Fant, M. (1982) *Women's Life in Greece and Rome*, Duckworth, London

Levi, J. & Schmitt, J.C. (eds.) (1997) *A History of Young People in the West 1: Ancient and Medieval Rites of Passage*, The Belknap Press of Harvard University Press, Cambridge, MA

Lintott, A. (1982) *Violence, Civil Strife and Revolution in the Classical City: 750–330 BC*, Croom Helm, London

Lloyd, G.E.R. (1966) *Polarity and Analogy*, Cambridge University Press, Cambridge

Lloyd, M. (2004) 'The Politeness of Achilles: Off-record Conversation Strategies in Homer and the Meaning of *kertomia*' *Journal of Hellenic Studies*, Vol.124, pp. 75–89

Lloyd-Jones, H. (1971) *The Justice of Zeus*, University of California Press, Berkeley

Lloyd-Jones, H. (2003) 'Zeus, Prometheus, and Greek Ethics' *Harvard Studies in Classical Philology*, Vol.101, pp. 49–72

Loraux, N. (1987) *Tragic Ways of Killing a Woman*, Harvard University Press, Cambridge, MA

MacCary, W.T. (1982) *Childlike Achilles: Ontogeny and Phylogeny in the Iliad*, Columbia University Press, New York

Mandel, O. (1981) *Philoctetes and the Fall of Troy: Plays, Documents, Iconography, Interpretations*. University of Nebraska Press, Lincoln

Mannheim, K. (1952) 'The Problem of Generations' in Mannheim, K. *Essays on the Sociology of Knowledge*, Routledge and Kegan Paul, London

Manning, J.E. (2016) 'Membership of the 114th Congress: A Profile, Congressional Research Service', 7-5700, R43869, www.crs.gov

Markantonatos, A. & Zimmermann, B. (eds.) (2012) *Crisis on Stage: Tragedy and Comedy in Late Fifth-Century Athens*, De Gruyter, Gottingen

Martindale, C. (1993) *Redeeming the Text: Latin Poetry and the Hermeneutics of Reception*, Cambridge University Press, Cambridge

McAuley, R. (2007) *Out of Sight: Crime, Youth and Exclusion in Modern Britain*, Willan, London

McClelland, J.S. (1989) *The Crowd and the Mob: From Plato to Canetti*, Unwin Hyman, London

McCulloch H.Y. & Cameron H.D. (1980) 'Septem 12–13 and the Athenian ephebia' *Illinois Classical Studies*, Vol.5, pp. 1–14

McDonald, K. (2003) 'Marginal Youth, Personal Identity and the Contemporary Gang: Reconstructing the Social World' in Kontos, L. (ed.) *Gangs and Society: Alternative Perspectives,* Columbia University Press, New York

McPhail, C. (1991) *The Myth of the Madding Crowd*, Aldine, New York

Medina, J., Ralphs, R. & Aldridge, J. (2013) 'Gang Transformations, Changes or Demise' in *The Modern Gang Reader*, Maxson, C.L., Egley, A. Jr., Miller, J. and Klein, M.W. (eds), Oxford University Press, Los Angeles

Mendelsohn, D. (2002) *Gender and the City in Euripides' Political Plays*, Oxford University Press, Oxford

Michelakis, P. (2002) *Achilles in Greek Tragedy,* Cambridge University Press, Cambridge

Michelakis, P. (2006) *Euripides: Iphigenia in Aulis*, Duckworth Companions to Greek and Roman Tragedy, London

Millar, F. (1998) *The Crowd in Rome in the Late Republic*, University of Michigan Press, Ann Arbor

Montgomery, H. (2007) 'A Comparative Perspective' in Kehily, M.J. (ed.) *Understanding Youth: Perspectives, Identities and Practices*, Open University Press, Milton Keynes

Mullens, H.G. (1940) 'The Meaning of Euripides' *Orestes'* in *The Classical Quarterly*, Vol.34, nos.3/4, pp. 153–158

Murray, O. (1990) 'The Affair of the Mysteries: Democracy and the Drinking Group' in Murray, O. (ed.) *Sympotica: A Symposium on the Symposion*, Clarendon Press, Oxford

Nash, L. (1978) 'Concepts of Existence: Greek Origins of Generational Thought', *Daedalus*, Vol.107, no.4, pp. 1–21

Nussbaum, M.C. (2001) *The Fragility of Goodness: Luck and Ethics in Greek Tragedy and Philosophy*, Cambridge University Press, Cambridge

Ober, J. (1996) *The Athenian Revolution: Essays on Ancient Greek Democracy and Political Theory*, Princeton University Press, Princeton

Osborne, R. (2010) *Athens and Athenian Democracy*, Cambridge University Press, Cambridge

Osborne, R. (2012) 'Sophocles and Contemporary Politics' in Ormand, K. (ed.) *A Companion to Sophocles,* Blackwell, Chichester

O'Sullivan, P. (2005) 'Of Sophists, Tyrants, and Polyphemus: the Nature of the Beast in Euripides' *Cyclops'* in Harrison, G.W.M. (ed.) *Satyr Drama: Tragedy at Play*, The Classical Press of Wales, Swansea

Pendrick, G.J. (2002) *Antiphon the Sophist: the Fragments*, Cambridge University Press, Cambridge

Pilcher, J. (1994) 'Mannheim's Sociology of Generations: an Undervalued Legacy', *British Journal of Sociology*, Vol.45, no.3, pp. 481–495

Pinker, S. (2002) *The Blank Slate*, Penguin, London

Podlecki, A.J. (1999) *The Political Background of Aeschylean Tragedy*, Bristol Classical Paperbacks, London

Podlecki, A.J. (trans. and ed.) (2005) *Aeschylus: Prometheus Bound*, Aris & Phillips, Chippenham

Pomeroy, S. (1975) *Goddesses, Whores, Wives and Slaves: Women in Classical Antiquity*, Schocken, New York

Rehm. R. (2006) 'Sophocles on Fire – *To Pyr* in Philoctetes', in de Jong, I.J.F. & Rijksbaron, A. (eds.) *Sophocles and the Greek Language: Aspects of Diction, Syntax, and the Greek Language,* Brill, Leiden

Reinhardt, K. (1949) *Aischylos als Regisseur und Theolog*, Francke, Berne

Richardson, B.E. (1993) *Old Age amongst the Ancient Greeks*, Johns Hopkins University Press, Baltimore

Rieu, R.V. (trans.) (2003a) *Homer: The Iliad*, Penguin Classics, Harmondsworth

Rieu, R.V. (trans.) (2003b) *Homer: The Odyssey*, Penguin Classics, Harmondsworth

Robson, J. (2009) *Aristophanes: An Introduction*, Duckworth, London

Robson, J. (2013) *Sex and Sexuality in Classical Athens*, Edinburgh University Press, Edinburgh

Rose, P. (1976) 'Sophocles' Philoctetes and the Teachings of the Sophists', *Harvard Studies in Classical Philology*, Vol.80, pp. 49–105

Rose, P.W. (1992) *Sons of the Gods, Children of the Earth: Ideology and Literary Form in Ancient Greece*, Cornell University Press, Ithaca

Rozier, C. (2015) 'Genealogical History and Character in Homeric Epic', Classics PhD thesis, Durham University, Durham

Ruffell, I. (2012) *Aeschylus: Prometheus Bound*, Bristol Classical Press, Bristol

Schein, S.L. (ed.) (2013) Sophocles: *Philoctetes*, Cambridge University Press, Cambridge

Scullion, S. (2002) 'Tragic Dates', *The Classical Quarterly*, Vol.52, no.1, pp. 81–101.

Seaford, R. (trans.) (2001) *Euripides: Bacchae*, Aris & Phillips, Warminster

Seaford, R. (2006) *Dionysus*, Routledge, London

Searle, J.R. (1971) *The Philosophy of Language*, Oxford University Press, Oxford

Seidensticker, B. (1978) 'Comic Elements in Euripides' Bacchae', *The American Journal of Philology*, Vol.99, no.3, pp. 303–320

Siewert, P. (1977) 'The Ephebic Oath in Fifth-Century Athens', *The Journal of Hellenic Studies*, Vol.97, 102–111

Sikes, G. (1997) *8 Ball Chicks: A Year in the Violent World of Girl Gangs*, Anchor Books, New York

Silk, M.S. (2000) *Aristophanes and the Definition of Comedy*, Oxford University Press, Oxford

Sinclair, R.K. (1988) *Democracy and Participation in Athens*, Cambridge University Press, Cambridge

Slater, W.J. (1976) 'Symposia at Sea', *Harvard Studies in Classical Philology*, Vol.80, pp. 161–170

Sommerstein, A. (2012) 'Problem Kids: Young Males and Society from *Electra* to *Bacchae*' in Markantonatos, A. & Zimmermann, B. (eds.), *Crisis on Stage: Tragedy and Comedy in Late Fifth-Century Athens*, De Gruyter, Gottingen, pp. 343–357

Spentzou, E. (2003) *Readers and Writers in Ovid's Heroides: Transgressions of Genre and Gender*, Oxford University Press, Oxford

Springhall, J. (1998) *Youth, Popular Culture and Moral Panics: Penny Gaffs to Gangsta-Rap, 1830–1996*, Macmillan Press, London

Steiner, G. (1984) *Antigones: How the Antigone Legend has Endured in Western Literature, Art and Thought*, Yale University Press, New Haven, CT

Storey, I.C. (2013) review of 'Ruffell, A. (2011) *Aeschylus: Prometheus Bound. Companions to Greek and Roman Tragedy*, Bristol Classical Press, London' in *Bryn Mawr Classical Review* 2013.04.06

Strauss, B. (1993) *Fathers and Sons in Athens: Ideology and Society in the Era of the Peloponnesian War*, Routledge, London

Strauss, L.C. (2000) *On Tyranny*, University of Chicago Press, Chicago

Stroud, R. (1971) 'Greek Inscriptions Theozotides and the Athenian Orphans', *Hesperia: The Journal of the American School of Classical Studies at Athens*, Vol.40, no.3, pp. 280–301

Struck, P.T. (2016) *Divination and Human Nature: A Cognitive History of Intuition in Classical Antiquity*, Princeton University Press, Princeton

Sutton, D.F. (1993) *Ancient Comedy: The War of the Generations*, Maxwell Macmillan International, New York

Taousiani, A. (2011). 'ΟΥ ΜΗ ΠΙΘΗΤΑΙ: Persuasion Versus Deception in the Prologue of Sophocles' *Philoctetes*', *The Classical Quarterly*, Vol.61, no.2, pp. 426–444

Taplin, O. (1971) 'Significant actions in Sophocles' *Philoctetes*', *Greek, Roman and Byzantine Studies*, Vol.12, pp. 25–44

Taplin, O. (1977) *The Stagecraft of Aeschylus: The Dramatic Use of Exits and Entrances in Greek Tragedy*, Clarendon Press, Oxford

Taylor, J. (1918) 'The Athenian Ephebic Oath', *The Classical Journal*, Vol.13, no.7, pp. 495–501

Teegarden, D.A. (2012) 'The Oath of Demophantos, Revolutionary Mobilization, and the Preservation of Athenian Democracy', *Hesperia: The Journal of the American School of Classical Studies at Athens*, Vol.81, no.3, pp. 433–465

Thomson, G.T. (trans. and ed.) (1932) *Aeschylus: The Prometheus Bound*, Cambridge University Press, London

Thrasher, F. (1927) *The Gang: A Study of 1313 Gangs in Chicago*, Chicago University Press, Chicago

Thury, E.M. (1988) 'A Study of Words Relating to Youth and Old Age in the Plays of Euripides and its Special Implications for Euripides' *Suppliant Women*', *Computers and the Humanities*, Vol.22, no.4, pp. 293–306

Todd, S.C. (1993) *The Shape of Athenian Law*, Clarendon Press, Oxford

Ussher, R.G. (ed.) (1990) *Sophocles: Philoctetes*, Aris & Phillips, Warminster

Van Wees, H. (1999) 'The Mafia of Early Greece: Violent Exploitation in the 7th and Early 6th Centuries BC' in Hopwood, K. (ed.) *Organised Crime in Antiquity*, Duckworth, London

Vasunia, P. (2012) 'Between East and West: Mobility and Ethnography in Herodotus' *Proem*', *History and Anthropology*, Vol.23, no.2, pp. 183–198

Vellacott, P. (1975) *Ironic Drama: A Study of Euripides' Method and Meaning*, Cambridge University Press, London

Vernant, J.-P. (1986) 'Corps obscur, corps éclatant' in Malamoud, C. & Vernant, J.-P. (eds) *Corps des dieux* (*Le temps de la réflexion, 7*), Gallimard, Paris

Vidal-Naquet, P. (1986a) *The Black Hunter: Forms of Thought and Forms of Society in the Greek World*, Johns Hopkins University Press, Baltimore

Vidal-Naquet, P. (1986b) 'The Black Hunter Revisited' in *Proceedings of the Cambridge Philological Society*, 212

Ward, A. (2012) 'The English Riots as Communication: Winnicott, the Antisocial Tendency, and Public Disorder' in Reeves, C. (ed.) *Broken Bounds: Contemporary Reflections on the Anti-Social Tendency*, Karnak Books, London

West, M.L. (trans.) (1987) *Euripides: Orestes*, Aris & Phillips, Warminster

West, M L. (1997) *The East Face of the Helicon: West Asiatic Elements in Greek Poetry and Myth*, Clarendon Press, Oxford

West, M.L (1998) *Aeschylus: Tragoediae*, Teubner, Stuttgart

West, M.L. (ed. & trans.) (2003) *Greek Epic Fragments: from the Seventh to Fifth Centuries BC*, Loeb Classical Library, London

West, M.L. (trans.) (2008a) *Greek Lyric Poetry*, Oxford World's Classics, Oxford

West, M.L (trans.) (2008b) *Hesiod: Theogony and Works and Days*, Oxford World's Classics, Oxford

Whitby, M. (1996) 'Telemachus Transformed? The Origins of Neoptolemus in Sophocles' *Philoctetes*', *Greece & Rome*, Vol.43, no.1, pp. 31–42

White, M. (1955) 'Greek Tyranny', *Phoenix*, Vol.9, no.1, pp. 1–18

Whitehead, D. (1986) *The Demes of Attica 508/7–ca. 250 BC: A Political and Social Study*, Princeton University Press, Princeton

Whitley, J. (1994) 'The Monuments That Stood before Marathon: Tomb Cult and Hero Cult in Archaic Attica', *American Journal of Archaeology*, Vol.98, no.2, pp. 213–230

Whitman, C.H. (1958) *Homer and the Homeric Tradition*, Harvard University Press, Cambridge, MA

Whitmarsh, T. (2016) *Battling the Gods: Atheism in the Ancient World*, Faber and Faber, London

Whyte, W.F. (1943) *Street Corner Society*, University of Chicago Press, Chicago

Wilkins, J. (1990) 'The Young of Athens: Religion and Society in the *Herakleidai* of Euripides', *Classical Quarterly*, Vol.40, pp. 329–339

Wilkins, J. (1993) *Euripides: Heraclidae*, Clarendon Press, Oxford

Williams, R. (1977) *Marxism and Literature*, Oxford University Press, Oxford

Winkler, J.J. & Zeitlin, F.I. (1990) *Nothing to do with Dionysos?: Athenian Drama in its Social Context,* Princeton University Press, Princeton, NJ

Winnicott, D.W. (2000) *Deprivation and Delinquency*, Routledge, London

Zeitlin, F. (1978) 'The Dynamics of Misogyny: Myth and Mythmaking in the *Oresteia* of Aeschylus', *Arethusa*, Vol.11, pp. 149–184

Zeitlin, F. (1990) 'Thebes: Theater of Self and Society in Athenian Drama', in Winkler, J.J. & Zeitlin, F.I. (eds) *Nothing to do with Dionysos?: Athenian Drama in its Social Context*, Princeton University Press, Princeton, NJ

Zeitlin, F. (2004) 'Dionysus in 69' in Hall, E., Macintosh, F. & Wrigley, A. (eds.) *Dionysus since 69: Greek Tragedy at the Dawn of the Third Millennium,* Oxford University Press, Oxford

Zuntz, G. (1947) 'Is the *Heraclidae* Mutilated?' *The Classical Quarterly*, Vol.41, nos.1/2, pp. 46–52.

Zuntz, G. (1955) *The Political Plays of Euripides*, Manchester University Press, Manchester

Index

www.ingramcontent.com/pod-product-compliance
Lightning Source LLC
Chambersburg PA
CBHW071410100726
47908CB00004B/1128